DYING FOR THE JOB

DYING FOR THE JOB

Police Work Exposure and Health

Edited by

JOHN M. VIOLANTI, Ph.D.

Department of Social & Preventive Medicine
School of Public Health & Health Professions
University at Buffalo
The State University of New York
Buffalo, NY

(With 18 Other Contributors)

CHARLES C THOMAS • PUBLISHER, LTD.
Springfield • Illinois • U.S.A.

Published and Distributed Throughout the World by

CHARLES C THOMAS • PUBLISHER, LTD.
2600 South First Street
Springfield, Illinois 62704

© 2014 by CHARLES C THOMAS • PUBLISHER, LTD.

ISBN 978-0-398-08772-2 (paper)
ISBN 978-0-398-08773-9 (ebook)

Library of Congress Catalog Card Number: 2013030943

With THOMAS BOOKS *careful attention is given to all details of manufacturing
and design. It is the Publisher's desire to present books that are satisfactory as to their
physical qualities and artistic possibilities and appropriate for their particular use.*
THOMAS BOOKS *will be true to those laws of quality that assure a good name
and good will.*

Printed in the United States of America
SM-R-3

Library of Congress Cataloging-in-Publication Data

Dying for the job : police work exposure and health / edited by John M. Vi-
olanti, Ph.D., Department of Social & Preventive Medicine, School of Public
Health & Health Professions, University at Buffalo, The State University of
New York Buffalo, New York.
      pages cm
Includes bibliographical references and index.
ISBN 978-0-398-08772-2 (pbk.) -- ISBN 978-0-398-08773-9 (ebook)
  1. Police--Health and hygiene--United States. 2. Police--Job stress--United
States. 3. Police--Mental health services--United States. 4. Stress management--
United States. I. Violanti, John M., editor of compilation.
HV7936.H4D95 2014
363.11'936320973--dc23
                                                                          2013030943

This Book Is Dedicated to Those Who Protect and Serve.
Thank You for What You Do.
Stay Well.

CONTRIBUTORS

Michael E. Andrew, PhD, serves as senior statistician for the Biostatistics and Epidemiology Branch of the Health Effects Laboratory Division of the National Institute for Occupational Safety and Health (NIOSH) at the Centers for Disease Control and Prevention (CDC). His research interests include cardiovascular disease epidemiology with recent focus on associations of workplace stressors with autonomic dysfunction as measured by heart rate variability and protective factors related to workplace stress.

Penelope Baughman, PhD, is an Epidemic Intelligence Service Officer for the CDC and is assigned to the Biostatistics and Epidemiology Branch within the Health Effects Laboratory Division of NIOSH. Her research interests include occupational health, chronic disease epidemiology, and injury prevention.

James B. Burch, MS, PhD, is an Associate Professor in the Department of Epidemiology and Biostatistics, Arnold School of Public Health, University of South Carolina. He also serves as a Health Research Specialist at the Dorn Veterans Affairs Medical Center in Columbia, South Carolina. He also holds appointments in the Cancer Prevention and Control Program and the Center for Colorectal Cancer Research at USC. Dr. Burch received his PhD in Environmental Health with a specialization in Epidemiology from Colorado State University and his MS degree in Pharmaceutical Sciences from the University of Colorado. His long-standing research interests focus on occupational and environmental epidemiology, the use of biological markers to study disease processes in humans, and the role of circadian rhythm disruption in carcinogenesis.

Cecil M. Burchfiel, PhD, **MPH,** is Chief of the Biostatistics and Epidemiology Branch in the Health Effects Laboratory Division of NIOSH at the CDC. His research focuses on cardiovascular disease epidemiology with recent emphasis on associations of workplace stressors with subclinical cardiovascular and metabolic disorders.

Luenda Charles, PhD, is an epidemiologist in the Biostatistics and Epidemiology Branch within the Health Effects Laboratory Division of NIOSH at the CDC. Her research interests include investigating associations of occupational and environmental exposures with sleep disorders, immune dysfunction, and subclinical cardiovascular disease.

Desta Fekedulegn, PhD, is a mathematical statistician in the Health Effects Laboratory Division of NIOSH at the CDC. His research interests include application of statistical methodologies in epidemiological research and associations of occupational stressors and lifestyle factors with adverse health outcomes.

Jack Gu, MSPH, is an statistician in the Biostatistics and Epidemiology Branch within the Health Effects Laboratory Division of NIOSH at the CDC. His research interests include categorical data analysis, experimental design, survival analysis, gene expression analysis, SUDAAN and SAS programming with large data sets, and obesity epidemiology.

Tara A. Hartley, PhD, MPA, MPH, is an epidemiologist in the Biostatistics and Epidemiology Branch in the Health Effects Laboratory Division of NIOSH at the CDC. Her research interests include exploring the association between occupational stress and subclinical cardiovascular disease and metabolic disorders and, more recently, understanding why these associations differ in men and women.

Janie Howsare, LICSW, MPA, is an Assistant Professor at the West Virginia University Department of Behavioral Medicine and Psychiatry. She teaches psychotherapy to child and adolescent fellows, psychiatry residents, and social work and counseling graduate students. She also does clinical teaching and supervision and provides psychotherapy for adolescents and families. Her research interests are risk and protective factors for adolescents who develop substance abuse and the impact of secure and insecure attachment on mental health and effective treatments for posttraumatic stress disorder (PTSD).

Claudia Ma, MPH, is an epidemiologist in the Biostatistics and Epidemiology Branch within the Health Effects Laboratory Division of NIOSH at the CDC. Her research focus is occupational epidemiology. She is currently investigating the role of physical and psychosocial exposures in subclinical cardiovascular disease in working populations.

Erin C. McCanlies, PhD, MPH, MA (Counseling), is an epidemiologist in the Biostatistics and Epidemiology Branch within the Health Effects Laboratory Division at NIOSH at the CDC. Her research interests focus on investigating the etiology and treatment of PTSD, investigating parental occupational exposures alone and in combination with high-risk genes in the risk of autism spectrum disorder, the genetics of metabolic syndrome components, and how sleep and PTSD affects biological measures such as the level of inflammatory markers.

Anna Mnatsakanova, MS, is a statistician in the Biostatistics and Epidemiology Branch within the Health Effects Laboratory Division of NIOSH at the CDC. Her interests include identification of optimal statistical methods, study design and planning, as well as interpretation of observational epidemiological data for studies of occupational stress and subclinical cardiovascular disease.

Kimberley Norris, PhD (Clinical), is a Lecturer in the School of Psychology at the University of Tasmania, where she teaches in both undergraduate and postgraduate clinical psychology units. She also works as a clinical psychologist, where she implements her knowledge of resilience and adaptation to support people dealing with normative and nonnormative life stressors. She has developed and delivered workshops teaching cognitive behavioral therapy skills to psychiatrists and remote area general practitioners. Kimberley completed her PhD in 2010. Her research investigated the reintegration experience of Australian Antarctic expeditioners and their partners following Antarctic employment. This information assisted in developing a more comprehensive understanding of the resilience and vulnerability factors operating within this context at both the individual and the dyadic level. It also highlighted the critical role that family, in addition to the organization, play in shaping the experiences of those exposed to extreme and unusual environments in the course of their employment. Her current research interests can be broadly categorized as resilience and adaption to both normative and nonnormative life events. Specifically, current studies are investigating planning and preparedness for aged care needs and how these influence resilience and adaptation in the transition to aged-care accommodation; adaptation and resilience in first-year university students; resilience following domestic violence; the role of religiosity in resilience; and mental health outcomes in the parents of children with autism. Kimberley is a member of the Australian Mental Health Professionals Network, Australian Psychological Society (APS) and the Tasmanian representative of the APS Teaching and Learning in Psychology Interest Group.

Douglas Paton, PhD, C Psychol, is a Professor in the School of Psychology, University of Tasmania and a Research Fellow at the Joint Centre for Disaster Research in New Zealand. He is a technical advisor on risk communication to the World Health Organization and a member of the Integrated Research for Disaster Reduction (IRDR) committee established as part of the United Nations International Strategy for Disaster Reduction (UN-ISDR) to coordinate research and intervention development for disaster risk communication. He is an expert of international standing (Australian Research Council) and a member of an expert working group of the Australian National Mental Health Disaster Response Taskforce. In 2005, he was the Australian representative on the UNESCO Education for Natural Disaster Preparedness in the Asia-Pacific program established to learn and disseminate lessons from the 2004 Indian Ocean tsunami. His research focuses on developing and testing models of community and organizational preparedness and resilience (adaptive capacity) for disasters. His work adopts an all-hazards, cross-cultural approach with work being undertaken in Australia (bushfire, flooding, tsunami), New Zealand (earthquake, volcanic eruption), Japan (earthquake, volcanic hazards), Indonesia (volcanic hazards), Taiwan (earthquake, typhoon), and Portugal (bushfire).

John E. Vena, PhD, is the Head of the Department of Epidemiology and Biostatistics and University of Georgia Foundation Professor in Public Health at the College of Public Health, University of Georgia. From 2003 to 2008 he served as Professor and Chair of the Department of Epidemiology and Biostatistics at the Arnold School of Public Health at the University of South Carolina. Dr. Vena was Professor of Social and Preventive Medicine at the State University of New York at Buffalo, School of Medicine and Biomedical Sciences, a research fellow at Roswell Park Cancer Institute (1981–2003), and Director of the Environment and Society Institute (1999–2003). Dr. Vena received his BS in Biology from St. Bonaventure University and his MS and PhD degrees in Epidemiology from the State University of New York at Buffalo. Dr. Vena is a Fellow of the American College of Epidemiology and the American Epidemiological Society, a member of the International Society for Environmental Epidemiology, Society for Epidemiologic Research, and the American Public Health Association (APHA). He has published extensively in the field of environmental and occupational epidemiology, and his studies have included descriptive and analytic studies of air and water pollution; bladder cancer and drinking water contaminants; occupational exposures; health of municipal workers, including firefighters and police officers; diet; electromagnetic fields; and persistent environmental toxicants. His current grant activities are funded by the Georgia Cancer Coalition and the National Institutes of Health on the topics of environmental determinants of cancer and systemic lupus erythematosus (SLE); physical activity, stroke, and cognitive function; stress and cardiometabolic disease in police; biomarkers of second-hand smoke (SHS); long-term lung health after exposure to chlorine gas; and health effects of persistent organic pollutants. Since 1981, Dr. Vena has taught courses in epidemiological methods and applications in occupational health and in environmental health and has mentored graduate students, postdoctoral fellows and junior faculty.

John M. Violanti, PhD, is a Full Research Professor in the Department of Social and Preventive Medicine (SPM), School of Public Health and Health Professions, at the university at Buffalo, NY, and has been associated with this department for twenty-five years. Dr. Violanti is a member of the University at Buffalo, NY, Medical School graduate faculty. Prior to his position at Buffalo, he also was a Full Professor at the Rochester Institute of Technology, Department of Criminal Justice. He is a police veteran, serving with the New York State Police for twenty-three years as a trooper, a member of the Bureau of Criminal Investigation, and coordinator for the Psychological Assistance Program for the State Police. Dr. Violanti served in the U.S. Army, 57th Military Police Company from 1963–1966. He has been involved in the design, implementation, and analysis of numerous suicide, stress, and health studies over the past twenty-five years. Dr. Violanti has authored over fifty peer-reviewed articles and sixteen books on suicide, stress, and PTSD. He has lectured nationally and internationally at academic institutions on matters of suicide, stress, and trauma at work.

Michael Wirth, PhD, is currently a Postdoctoral Fellow at the Cancer Prevention and Control Program, Arnold School of Public Health, University of South Carolina. Dr. Wirth received his BS in Biology from Wingate University with a minor in Environmental Biology. During his time as an undergraduate, he had an opportunity to spend a summer at the Wadsworth Center in Albany, NY, as part of a Research Experiences for Undergraduates program working in a microbiology laboratory. Dr. Wirth completed both his MS in Public Health and PhD in Epidemiology at the Arnold School of Public Health, University of South Carolina. Part of his doctoral schooling and work was supported by the Behavioral-Biomedical Interface Program, which is funded in part by training grant T32-5R18CE001240 from the National Institute of General Medical Sciences. In addition, he is currently a member of the APHA. Dr. Wirth's research interest focuses on circadian disruption, especially among shift-work populations, such as police officers. He has either published or is currently working on several manuscripts utilizing police officer populations. One such publication, which was published in *Chronobiology International*, entitled "Shiftwork Duration and the Awakening Cortisol Response Among Police Officers" was awarded honorable mention for the 2012 Alice Hamilton Award from NIOSH, Epidemiology and Surveillance Category. In addition, his focus on circadian disruption extends to cancer outcomes or factors associated with cancer outcomes. In his postdoctoral work, Dr. Wirth is also currently involved in numerous projects focusing on the effect of diet and physical activity on chronic disease outcomes, including cancer. He has a strong interest in incorporating these lifestyle factors with his research on circadian disrupters (e.g. shift work or sleep disruption).

Oliver Wirth, PhD, is a Research Psychologist in the Engineering and Control Technology Branch within the Health Effects Laboratory Division of NIOSH at the CDC. His research interests focus on behavioral factors associated with occupational safety and health. He is currently investigating the role that service animals can play in helping military veterans with PTSD return to civilian life and work.

Franklin H. Zimmerman, MD, FACC, FACP, FAACVPR, is a graduate of Brown University Medical School and trained at Columbia University, St. Luke's Hospital in New York. He is a Senior Attending Cardiologist and Director of Critical Care at Phelps Memorial Hospital in Sleepy Hollow, NY, and Assistant Clinical Professor of Medicine at Columbia University. Dr. Zimmerman is actively involved in clinical medicine with an interest in preventive cardiology and patient education. He has authored numerous research articles and two textbooks of electrocardiography. He has served on the editorial board of the *American Journal of Medicine and Sports* and as a reviewer for leading cardiology journals. Dr. Zimmerman is the founding, Co-Editor-in-Chief of the award-winning national consumer heart-health newsletter, *Heart & Health Reports.* He is a member of the board of directors of Phelps Memorial Hospital Center and the Hypertension Education Foundation and is the founding director of the Heart and Health Education Foundation. Dr. Zimmerman's current research interest is preventing cardiovascular disease in police and fire department personnel.

PREFACE

When one thinks of police work, the immediate danger of this occupation comes to mind. Certainly, law enforcement personnel are subject to the everyday threat of violence, death, and witnessing traumatic events in their work. Less noted, however, is the physical and psychological danger associated with police work, including harmful environmental exposure, stress, and trauma. Based on research, we believe that the adverse health and psychological consequences of this occupation far outweigh the dangers of the street. The primary purpose of this book therefore is to focus on these less-known, less–talked about dangers in policing. The mental well-being, health, and average life span of police officers appear to be affected by these factors.

Hence, the title *Dying for the Job* reflects not so much the danger on the street but more the hidden health dangers associated with policing. Many of the researchers who contributed to this book are epidemiologists and biostatisticians who are part of a NIOSH, CDC, five-year research study on police health titled the *Buffalo Cardio-Metabolic Occupational Police Stress (BCOPS)* study. Still other contributors are experts in cancer, cardiovascular disease, and psychological trauma.

We begin our exposé of police health in Chapter 1 with a discussion of hazardous physical exposures that police officers experience in their daily work. For example, officers are often exposed to chemical hazards in the line of duty. Chemical hazards are classified as solids, liquids, or gases that most commonly enter the body by inhalation, ingestion, or absorption through the skin. Biological hazards include infectious microorganisms, plant or animal toxins, and animals. Microorganisms may (1) cause diseases such as viral hepatitis; (2) cause allergic reactions, such as those associated with molds; (3) deplete oxygen; or (4) produce toxic gases. Animals may attack officers and transmit infections to officers and others at the scene (for example, rabies).

As evidenced by police mortality studies, prevalent diseases associated with chemical exposure include lung disease, cardiovascular abnormalities, skin rashes, and blood-related diseases.

In Chapter 2, Hartley and colleagues discuss health disparities between the police and general U.S. population. Key studies on police officer health, including findings from the five-year BCOPS study conducted for NIOSH, CDC, were compared with results from studies of other U.S. employed adults. Police officers were found to have higher levels of traditional cardiovascular disease risk factors, including more current smokers, and higher levels of obesity, hypertension, and dyslipidemia, than other U.S. employed adults. Officers also had a higher prevalence of the nontraditional risk factors like depression, sleep insufficiency, and shift work.

Zimmerman discusses the association of police work and cardiovascular disease in Chapter 3. According to national data, police officers are at higher risk for death from cardiovascular disease than is the general U.S. population. Doctor Zimmerman outlines the atherosclerotic process, defines risk factors for cardiovascular disease, and compares risk factors between the police and the general population. He suggests that law enforcement agencies promote a culture of wellness, supporting personal health.

In Chapter 4, Wirth, Vena, and Burch conducted a comprehensive review of studies concerning cancer and the police. The majority of these studies suggest that police officers are at higher risk for various types of cancer. Significant increases in mortality among police officers were noted due to all types of cancers combined, digestive organ malignancies; cancer of the esophagus, colon, kidney, bladder, brain, lymphatic and hematopoietic tissues, endocrine glands, and breasts; as well as testicular cancer, melanoma, and Hodgkin's disease. The authors suggest that police work is associated with exposure to a variety of carcinogenic agents, lifestyles, or risk factors, such as shift work, poor diet or a lack of physical activity leading to obesity, alcohol consumption, and air pollution exposure, all of which may increase the risk of cancer.

Baughman and colleagues in Chapter 5 discuss the impact of shift work on police officer health and social well-being. Shift work is a recognized physical and psychological challenge to worker health and performance and is a far-reaching exposure in occupational health. Rearrangement of sleep and work time can have a vast impact not only upon police officers but also upon their families and the people that they seek to protect and serve. The authors suggest that police agencies provide training to improve sleep and diet factors associated with shift work.

Women have been a part of law enforcement for many years, but primarily as support persons. It was not until the 1970s that women participated in police work as equal patrol officers who performed the same work as male officers. In Chapter 6, Hartley and colleagues discuss the additional stressors and some of the health consequences found to be prevalent among policewomen. The authors note that very little research has been conducted on policewomen's health and stress and suggest a national agenda for such research.

Chapter 7 briefly discusses one of the more fatal consequences of stress and trauma in police work – suicide. Violanti outlines various research studies conducted on police suicide, as well as a psychosocial etiology of suicide within the police role. Suggestions are made for prevention efforts.

Within the context of total worker health, Paton and Norris discuss the influence of family and organization on police trauma in Chapter 8. They propose that certain characteristics of family and organization can act as facilitators of resiliency, thus ameliorating the pathogenic impact of traumatic stress in police work. The authors conclude that active factors like peer support, supervisor support, organizational culture, trust, empowerment and family dynamics are amenable to change and offer the potential for their being managed as part of a proactive organizational traumatic stress risk-management strategy.

In Chapter 9, Andrew and colleagues discuss the protective effect of resiliency on police psychological trauma. The authors discuss resiliency in terms of hardiness, psychological flexibility, and attachment. Social support is seen as a key factor in the social context of increased resiliency. Organizational implementation of resiliency training is discussed.

Police officers are repeatedly exposed to traumatic situations, including motor vehicle accidents, armed conflicts, and witnessing violent death, across their working lives. Such exposure leaves them highly susceptible to posttraumatic stress. In Chapter 10, McCanlies and colleagues provide a comprehensive overview and treatment of PTSD as it may be applied to police work. Additionally, they discuss the probable physical outcomes that may be associated with PTSD.

Treatment for groups at increased risk for PTSD is the subject of Chapter 11. McCanlies and colleagues discuss the various treatment approaches that are generally utilized in high-risk groups and how they may be applied to police work.

We sincerely hope that this book will add to the reader's understanding of some of the "hidden dangers" in police work. At a recent Law Enforcement Executives Summit that the editor of this book attended (Dr. Violanti), United States Attorney General Eric Holder Jr. stated that officer safety and wellness is a high priority. Among his concerns were the health consequences and traumatic stress on police personnel. Additionally, recent events such as 9/11, Hurricane Katrina, the Sandy Hook school tragedy, and the Boston Marathon bombings emphasize the need to have a vibrant, healthy police force. The police performed admirably during these national tragedies, and it is necessary to maintain this high level of reliability by initiating health and stress prevention efforts. The brave men and women who serve this vital societal service deserve no less.

J.M.V.

CONTENTS

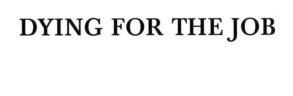

DYING FOR THE JOB

Chapter 1

POLICE WORK MAY BE HAZARDOUS TO YOUR HEALTH: AN EXAMINATION OF HARMFUL PHYSICAL WORK EXPOSURES

JOHN M. VIOLANTI

There is an immediate need to study the exposure risk of law enforcement practitioners, focusing on the causal relationship between occupational exposure of practitioners and increased incidence of health problems and disease. As an occupational group, law enforcement officers have greater morbidity and mortality rates than the general public has, principally due to cancer and cardiovascular disease (Violanti, Vena & Petralia, 1998). Various law enforcement agencies have calculated the cost of inservice-related disease to be between $400,000 and $750,000. Surveys suggest work-related disease accounts for 20 to 50 percent of early retirements. For the law enforcement agency, good health represents a sound investment. Studies of law enforcement officers indicate that healthy officers have 40 to 70 percent less *absenteeism* than officers with health problems (Commission on Accreditation for Law Enforcement Agencies [CALEA], 2002). The costs associated with *disability* are high:

- Partial disability means a loss of flexibility in assignments
- Total disability results in a loss of valued personnel
- There is the expense of disability payments
- There is the expense of rehiring and retraining

One study estimated the cost of early disability at 165 percent of an officer's salary. Healthy officers miss fewer days of work, and they are less likely to suffer diseases, thereby spending a smaller share of the agency's health care dollars. Finally, wellness increases loyalty, reduces turnover, and generally improves morale. Prevention of disease from hazardous law enforcement exposures depends on four fundamental tasks (Levy, Wagner, Rest & Weeks, 2005):

- Anticipation – of the potential for disease or injury
- Recognition – of occupational disease and injury. Ongoing gathering, analysis, and dissemination of data on the occurrence of disease and injury in law enforcement. Recognition can rely on existing data sources, such as death causes, workers' compensation, or health records.
- Evaluation – for helping to determine if a causal relationship exists. Basic parameters of relevance when measuring exposure to chemical and physical hazards are concentration or intensity of exposure; duration, frequency, and latency; and determinants of exposure. Additionally, it is necessary to look at health outcomes associated with hazards.
- Control – The precautionary principle of the public health is to prevent illness and injury even in the absence of thoroughly documented hazards.

HAZARDOUS EXPOSURES IN LAW ENFORCEMENT

Law enforcement officers are often exposed to chemical hazards in the line of duty. Chemical hazards are classified as solids, liquids, or gases that most commonly enter the body by inhalation, ingestion, or absorption through the skin. Harmful effects depend on the nature of substances, the magnitude of exposure and dose, and the duration of exposure. As seen in Chapter 4 by Wirth, Vena, and Burch (this book), the predominant increased disease risk for officers routinely exposed to hazardous chemicals is cancer. This is evidenced by several police mortality studies (Feur & Rosenman, 1986; Finklestein, 1998; Pyorala, Miettinen, Laakso & Pyorala, 2000; Violanti et al., 1998). Other prevalent diseases associated with chemical exposure include lung disease, cardiovascular abnormalities, skin rashes, and blood-related diseases. Inhalation is the most common route of entry for chemical hazards, although chemicals may be ingested if they contaminate food, drink, or smoking materials or are coughed up and swallowed. Evaluating the potential health effects of airborne particles (dusts, mists, and fumes) in law enforcement requires knowledge of their identity. Particle diameter determines the site of their deposition in the lung, which, in turn, determines the site of injury and whether the particle is absorbed systemically. Some explosive and flammable gases and vapors; organic particles, such as coal, grain, and sugar; and some metal aerosols, such as magnesium and aluminum, may also create risk of fire or explosion.

Biological hazards include infectious microorganisms, plant or animal toxins, and animals. Microorganisms may: (1) cause diseases such as viral hepatitis; (2) cause allergic reactions, such as those associated with molds; (3) deplete oxygen; or (4) produce toxic gases. Plants may produce toxins. Animals may attack and transmit infections to officers and others at the scene (for example, rabies).

Clandestine Methamphetamine Labs

Hazards imposed by clandestine methamphetamine laboratories are a concern for law enforcement. In 2004 alone, there were 17,033 methamphetamine lab-related seizures by U.S. law enforcement agencies as reported by the Department of Justice (Mitka, 2005). Law enforcement personnel have been the most-studied population to date. Police officers exposed to active labs have a seven to fifteen-fold greater risk of becoming ill during response activities as compared to exposures to setup, in-transit, and former labs. They are also likely to be exposed to physical hazards such as spills, fires, explosions, and uncontrolled reactions. The poor handling and disposal of these chemicals, as well as the mixing of incompatible compounds, can create hazards. Common household chemicals used in meth labs include flammable and volatile solvents such as methanol, ether, benzene, methylene chloride, trichloroethane, and toluene (Table 1-1).

Other common chemicals include muriatic acid, sodium hydroxide, table salt, and ammonia. Meth-related chemicals not commonly found in large amounts in homes include anhydrous ammonia, red phosphorous, iodine, and reactive metals. Other hazardous chemicals can be formed during the "cooking" process. Many chemicals may contaminate a property after cooking meth. Carpeting, wallboard, ceiling tile, or fabric may absorb spilled or vaporized chemicals. Furniture or draperies may become contaminated. Outdoor disposal sites may also

Table 1-1. Common Chemicals Used in Clandestine Labs

Acetaldehyde	Acetic acid	Acetic anhydride	Acetone	Allyl chloride
Allylbenzene	Aluminum	Ammonia	Ammonium acetate	Ammonium formate
Ammonium hydroxide	Benzaldehyde	Benzene	Benzyl chloride	Chloroform
Ephedrine	Ethyl ether	Formamide	Freon	Hexane
Hydriodic acid	Hydrochloric acid	Iodine	Isopropanol	Lead acetate
Lithium aluminum hydride	Magnesium	Mercuric chloride	Methanol	Methylamine
Monomethylamine	N-Methylformamide	Nitroethane	Norpseudo-ephedrine	Palladium
Phenyl-2-propanone	Phenylacetic acid	Phenyl-propanolamine	Phosphoric acid	Propiophenone
Raney nickel	Red phosphorus	Sodium	Sodium carbonate	Sodium cyanide
Sodium hydroxide	Thionyl chloride	Toluene		

Source: Wisconsin Division of Public Health, "web page no longer available."

require evaluation and cleanup (Thrasher, Von Derau & Burgess, 2009).

Research has found that there are health hazards associated with breathing in trichloroethylene found in meth labs. Occupational exposure may cause signs and symptoms of central nervous system (CNS) depression such as headaches, dizziness, altered mood, loss of memory, and inability to concentrate or sleep. These effects have also been related to long-term occupational exposure to other organic solvents and are sometimes generally referred to as "organic solvent syndrome." In general, symptoms of CNS depression are commonly reported in employees exposed to average trichloroethylene levels of 100 parts per million (ppm) and above. One limited study reported symptoms such as dizziness, headache, insomnia, and altered mood in a small number of employees exposed to up to 40 ppm. There is some evidence that exposure to trichloroethylene may cause liver and kidney injury in some people following long-term occupational exposure. The International Agency for Research on Cancer (IARC) has concluded that there is some evidence for the carcinogenicity of trichloroethylene in humans. The overall IARC evaluation is that trichloroethylene is probably carcinogenic to humans. Three well-designed studies of people with occupational exposure to trichloroethylene showed higher levels of liver and biliary tract cancers and non-Hodgkins lymphoma (*see* Canadian Occupational Safety and Health web site at http://www.ccohs.ca/ccohs.html).

Lead Exposure From Firearm Use

Shooting with lead-containing ammunition in firing ranges is a well-known source of lead exposure in adults, and police officers may be at risk of lead intoxication. More stringent national lead regulations stimulated a survey of blood lead (PbB) in Swedish police officers with regular shooting habits. Löfstedt, Seldén, Stréus, and Bodin (1999) found that the mean PbB in male officers was 0.24 mmol/L (5.0 mg/dL); a positive correlation of PbB with the number of bullets annually fired both on and off duty was observed. This finding remained in a multiple regression analysis including age, smoking habits, and latency from last shooting exercise. Occupational and recreational lead exposure from firing ranges still seems to be a source of lead exposure in police officers.

Lead From Firing Ranges

Shooting with lead-containing ammunition in firing ranges is a well-known source of lead exposure in adults, and police officers may be at risk of lead intoxication (Löfstedt, Seldén, Storéus, & Bodin, 1999). Lead exposure at indoor firing ranges occurs primarily through the inhalation of lead particles suspended in the range air. The main sources of airborne lead result from ignition of the primer material containing lead syphnate and the shearing of lead particulates off the bullet as it passes through the weapon (Valway, Martyny, Miller, Cook & Mangione, 1989). Fragmentation when the bullet strikes the target or backstop may also contribute to the airborne lead concentration. Although occupational studies have suggested that exposure to lead from indoor firing ranges may be a health risk for frequent users, the extent of the risk has not be determined (Capellaro, Scagliola, Pira, Botta & Scansetti, 1990; Valway et al., 1989).

Fingerprint Powders

Fingerprint powders vary in their constituents, and some have been known to contain toxic components (Van Netten, Souter & Teschke, 1990). Lead and mercury appear to be common ingredients currently used in fingerprint powders, and additional subsequent analyses of fingerprint powders have identified the presence of polycyclic aromatic hydrocarbons (PAHs). Many of these chemicals are known cancer-causing agents, and therefore the use of such powders has been discontinued. Individuals who use this powder are typically unaware of the harmful constituents because material safety sheets supplied by the manufacturer are lacking the necessary detail (Van Netten et al., 1990). Schilling (2008) initiated a study including twenty-two individuals from the Upper Darby, Pennsylvania, police force. Results of the study showed cancer of the large intestine was apparent in police detectives. In another study that involved the Baltimore County Police Department Crime Laboratory and studied ninety-one death certificates, results confirmed statistically significant excess of large intestinal cancer and also an association between respiratory tract cancers and individuals who had worked in the crime laboratory (Schilling, 2000).

Dead Bodies

Law enforcement officers are often exposed to dead bodies at crime scenes or during investigative autopsies. All dead bodies are potentially infectious, and standard precautions should be implemented for every case. Although most organisms in the dead body are unlikely to infect healthy persons, some infectious agents may be transmitted where workers are in close contact with blood, body fluids, and tissues of a dead body that died with infectious diseases. To minimize the risks of transmission of known and also unsuspected infectious diseases, dead bodies should be handled in such a way that workers' exposure to blood, body fluids, and tissues is reduced. A rational approach should include staff training and education, safe working environment, appropriate work practices, the use of recommended safety devices, and vaccination against hepatitis B. In case of penetrating injury or mucocutaneous exposure to blood or body fluids of the dead body, the injured or exposed areas should be washed with copious amount of running water. Minor penetrating injuries should be encouraged to bleed. All incidents of exposure to blood or body fluids from the dead body, either parenteral or mucous membrane exposures, should be reported to the supervisor. The injured person should immediately seek medical advice for proper wound care and postexposure management (U.S. Department of Health, 1994).

Blood-Borne Pathogens

Guang and Jenkins (2007) conducted an analysis involving police officers that were exposed to blood-borne pathogens. Needlestick or sharps injuries were the primary source of exposure in hospitals and nonhospital health-care settings. Skin and mucous membranes were the primary route of exposure. Human bites accounted for a significant portion of the exposures in law enforcement and other non–health-care settings (for example, HIV transmission).

Air Pollution

Benzene is an organic air pollutant. The Department of Human and Health Services classifies benzene as a human carcinogen. Benzene is often emitted into urban air supplies from motorized vehicles. It is hypothesized that policemen working outdoors are highly exposed to traffic pollutants, and this exposure could result in higher cancer rate among policemen. Occupational exposure to engine exhaust among police officers may be of etiological importance for both renal cancer and non-Hodgkin's lymphoma (Forastiere et al., 1994). Blair and associates (1993) and Delancey and colleagues (2009) confirmed evidence that benzene exposure may be associated with non-Hodgkin's lymphoma.

Traffic police officers often spend several hours per day directing traffic in congested traffic areas. This activity may lead to a large exposure to air pollution caused by motor vehicles. Of particular concern are persistent organic pollutants (POP). POPs are pollutants that are resistant to breakdown by chemical, biological, and photolytic processes (Ritter, Solomon & Forget, 2007). AHs and other POPs are commonly found in urban air pollution. These substances persist in the environment and form bioaccumulation in exposed humans. Excessive or prolonged exposure could have a possible carcinogenic affect.

AHs have also been correlated with smoking. Szaniszlo and Ungvary (2001) measured urine concentration of 1-OH-P, an indicator of total PAH absorbed, in police officers in Budapest. Their measurements of police officers on street duty indicated no significant exposure; however, those police officers that smoked had a 1-OH-P concentration six times that of nonsmoking police officers. A study by Carere and associates (2002) measured benzene exposure in traffic policemen and monitored sister chromatid exchanges in lymphocytes, as well as DNA damage by alkaline comet assay in mononuclear blood cells. This study also found no significant difference in DNA damage or chromatid exchanges in traffic policemen compared to office workers despite finding much higher benzene exposure in traffic policemen.

AHs were also studied by Burgaz, Demircigil, Karahalil, and Karakaya (2002). In this study the 1-hydroxyprene (1-OHP) levels were assessed, as well as, chromosomal aberration frequencies in lymphocytes in order to measure the effects of urban air pollutants. Burgaz and colleagues (2002) found that 1-OHP levels were significantly higher in nonsmoking policemen than in a nonsmoking control group and a group of smoking traffic policemen. The study also found that policemen had a significant amount of cytogenetic damage in lymphocytes.

Traffic Particles

Tonne and coworkers (2009) modeled exposure to traffic particles using a latent variable approach and investigated whether long-term exposure to traffic particles was associated with an increase in the occurrence of acute myocardial infarction (AMI) using data from a population-based coronary disease registry. Cases of individually validated AMI were identified between 1995 and 2003 as part of the Worcester Heart Attack Study. Modeled exposure to traffic particles was highest near the city. Cases of AMI occurred in those more exposed to traffic and traffic particles than in controls. An interquartile-range increase in modeled traffic particles was associated with a 10 percent (95%, confidence interval [CI] 4% to 16%) increase in the odds of AMI. These results provide some support for an association between long-term exposure to traffic particles and risk of AMI.

Potential physiological effects of in-vehicle, roadside, and ambient $PM_{2.5}$ particles were investigated in young, healthy, nonsmoking, male North Carolina Highway Patrol troopers (Riediker et al., 2004). Nine troopers (age 23 to 30) were monitored on four successive days while working the 3 PM to midnight shift. Each patrol car was equipped with air-quality monitors. Blood was drawn 14 hours after each shift, and ambulatory monitors recorded the electrocardiogram throughout the shift and until the next morning. In-vehicle $PM_{2.5}$ (average of 24 $\mu g/m^3$) was associated with decreased lymphocytes (−11% per 10 $\mu g/m^3$) and increased red blood cell indices (6%), C-reactive protein (32%), von

Willebrand factor (12%), next-morning heart beat cycle length (6%), next-morning heart rate variability parameters, and ectopic beats throughout the recording (20%). The observations in these healthy young men suggest that in-vehicle exposure to $PM_{2.5}$ may cause physiological changes that involve inflammation, coagulation, and cardiac rhythm.

Radar

Traffic radar devices have been manufactured to emit one of three nonionizing microwave frequencies: 10.525 GHz in early radar devices, 24.15 GHz in devices made after 1975, 33.4 to 36.0 GHz in those devices introduced in the 1990s. This range of frequencies is considered to be "high frequency." Experimental studies show that the exposure to high-frequency fields has no carcinogenic effect in the sense of initiating a tumor cell, but exposure to high-frequency fields may indirectly promote tumor growth or facilitate the absorption of carcinogenic substances into the cell (Baird, Lewis, Kremer & Kilgore 1981; Fisher, 1991; Garland et al., 1990). Theoretical approaches to biochemical mechanisms of tumor induction initiated by high-frequency fields assume that proteins changed by heat shock may work as tumor promoters (Hardin, 1992; Jauchem & Merritt, 1990). There is a series of experimental studies giving evidence that some of the effects just indicated may be initiated by continuous high-frequency fields, such as elevated permeability of the blood-brain barrier, changes in the immune system, or infertility (Occupational Safety & Health Administration [OSHA], 2002). Although there is currently little knowledge on the potential association between police radar use and cancer and no mechanism has been established to explain how microwaves, which are nonionizing, could lead to the development of cancer, it has been implicated as a potential trigger. NIOSH reported that exposure to emissions from police radar might increase the risk of leukemia and testicular, brain, eye, and skin cancers (Lotz, Rinski & Edwards, 1995). In 1992, the FDA issued a warning that police officers should not place the front surface of a radar unit within 6 inches of any body part while transmitting (Volkers, 1991). It was not uncommon practice previously, however, for police to rest the radar gun against their lap, chest, or other body parts while the gun was not in use. Therefore, an individual using radar during an 8-to-12-hour shift for many years could experience significant accumulated exposures (Van Netten et al., 1990).

Noise

Approximately 30 million people are exposed to hazardous levels of noise at their work sites (National Institute of Occupational Safety and Health [NIOSH], 1998). NIOSH recommends that the limit for occupational noise exposures is 85 decibels (dB) as an 8-hour time-weighted average. Exposures at or above this level are considered hazardous (NIOSH, 1998). Police officers are exposed daily in their work to a variety of noises that may exceed the NIOSH-recommended decibel level. Noise from traffic, radio transmissions, sirens, crowds, and gunfire are examples.

Several studies have been conducted by NIOSH on police noise exposure:

- Evaluated exposures to noise of firing range instructors at an outdoor firing range in California using personal noise dosimetry measurements over 2 days during live fire training. Noise monitoring results indicated that all participants' noise exposures exceeded the NIOSH standard and some exceeded the OSHA standard. Sound level meter measurements revealed that peak noise levels during gunfire were greater than 160 dB (NIOSH, 1993a).
- Conducted a health hazard evaluation (HHE) at the Saint Bernard Police Department located in Saint Bernard, Ohio, to assess potential occupational exposures to hazardous noise levels generated at the facility during the handgun firing exercises. Peak sound pressure levels measured within the firing range were as high as 160 dB,which exceeded the OSHA peak exposure criteria of 140 dB (NIOSH, 2011).
- Evaluated noise levels at call and dispatch centers: (1) Acoustic trauma from a sudden spike in noise levels (e.g., from feedback into the headsets or a sudden change in volume), (2) background noise from the incoming call, and (3) background noise and other stressors in the workplace. Background noise in the workplace (radios played by other workers, conversations, noise from heating and air conditioning systems) or from the callers' locations may cause workers to turn up the headset volume, resulting in sudden increase in noise levels transmitted into their ears. Some communication systems may experience feedback or interference

that could cause spikes or squeals from the headset. Some workers complain of fluctuations in noise levels in the headset or having little control over headset volume (NIOSH, 2007).

• Conducted hearing tests before and after firing their weapon on indoor and outdoor ranges in the Ft. Collins, Colorado, police department. Noise from all pistols, shotguns, and rifles used by the department were measured. Weapon noise was found to be between 159 and169 dB peak, which is greater than a 140 dB peak exposure guideline from NIOSH (NIOSH, 2003).

• Evaluated potential hearing loss experienced by police officers in the Cincinnati Police Canine Unit. Between April and September, 2006, noise exposure assessments and hearing tests were conducted on nine police officers assigned to the canine unit. Three officers showed hearing loss. Preemployment hearing test results showed inconsistencies in tests and poor quality control. Noise levels exceeded the NIOSH criterion six times and approached the OSHA limit once (NIOSH, 2006).

While noise-induced hearing loss is irreversible. It is preventable and its risk can be reduced with the application of noise controls and occupational hearing loss prevention programs. Some prevention strategies suggested by NIOSH were as follows:

• The police department should research new hearing protection devices that incorporate radio communications into the device and are still compatible with other protection devices such as helmets and glasses.

• The police department should begin a hearing conservation program with annual hearing tests.

• Officers should wear hearing protection whenever they are at the firing ranges.

• Officers should not be exposed to noise impulses above 140 dB for any amount of time.

Hazardous Materials

The potential for law enforcement exposure to hazardous materials in the United States is significant. Officers are often called upon to investigate traffic accidents involving hazardous materials or to handle disaster situations where chemical are released in the air. More than

60,000 chemicals are produced annually in the United States, approximately 2000 of which the U.S. Department of Transportation (DOT) considers hazardous. More than 4 billion tons of chemicals are transported yearly by surface, air, or water routes. These shipments are initiated from more than 100,000 different locations, with more than 1 million people directly involved in the transportation process. More than 500,000 shipments of hazardous materials are made every day, totaling approximately 1.5 billion tons per year. In an attempt to better define the magnitude of this problem, the Agency for Toxic Substances Disease Registry developed the Hazardous Substances Emergency Events Surveillance (HSEES) system. Fifteen state health departments participate in the reporting system. In these states, the system has shown the following findings:

- About 9000 releases of hazardous substances occur annually, with 75 percent occurring at chemical facilities and 25 percent occurring during transportation.
- Most transportation-related incidents occurred during ground transport (85%) and 26 percent occurred in residential areas.
- Human error and equipment failure account for most releases.
- The most common substances involved were inorganic substances (24%) followed by volatile organic compounds (20%).
- More than 2000 people are victims of hazardous materials releases in these states each year. Approximately 50 percent of these are transported to hospitals. Respiratory and eye irritation are the most common types of injury. Over a 4-year period, 132 hazardous material–related deaths occurred.
- More than 7500 people required decontamination during hazmat events over a 4-year period in these states. Of these, 2,643 were decontaminated at medical facilities (Cox & Darling, 2013).

PREVENTION

As evidenced by research, law enforcement work can be hazardous. Most hazards, however, can be anticipated. Knowledge about hazards and the methods to control them exist in many places: the scientific literature, regulatory agencies, workers' compensation organizations, the collective experience of workers and their employers, insurance companies, industry and trade organizations, labor unions, health and safety professionals, and elsewhere. These are sources that we propose to search for information on law enforcement exposures, consequences, and prevention strategies.

At times, this knowledge is acquired and applied only after injuries, illnesses, or even catastrophes have occurred. It is better, however, to prevent rather than to treat. Although the officer's health should be a first concern of the police agency, it is also important to consider the "bottom line" in these economic times of scarce funding. As we have previously mentioned, various law enforcement agencies have calculated the *cost of in-service-related disease to be between $400,000 and $750,000* (CALEA, 2002). Education and training of the occupational safety and health workforce must extend from traditional occupational health and safety professionals – nurses, physicians, industrial hygienists, and safety specialists – to include first responder occupations such as law enforcement. Indeed, occupational safety and health education must extend to the general public, with basic concepts of prevention of occupational diseases and injuries introduced as elements of primary and secondary education. New educational materials designed for this extended occupational health and safety workforce are therefore needed.

Biological monitoring may be necessary at particularly hazardous sites such as meth labs. Biological surveillance is a form of surveillance to estimate exposure based on biological assays of material, such as urine, blood, and exhaled air, collected from workers. Data from such examinations may be an important complement to industrial hygiene and can provide data for formal epidemiological investigations. Biological monitoring should never be a substitute for effective environmental monitoring of toxic exposures, however, and because the difference between a biomarker of exposure and a sign of injury may not be clear, of the potential ethical implications. Monitoring can be used for analysis of future police operations.

A systematic analysis of the law enforcement environment will help determine if intervention to control hazards is needed and will help inform the intervention effort. Several disciplines and tools can be critical aids in analyzing and evaluating data and other information obtained through surveillance and screening efforts. There are as many examples as there are work processes. Examples include substituting water for organic solvents, employing closed systems when using volatile chemicals, and isolating and controlling access to high-hazard police operations. When chemical or biological hazards are released into the environment, workers may absorb them by any of several routes.

Engineering controls and personal protective equipment prevent absorption by blocking these routes. Airborne chemical hazards – gases, vapors, particulate matter, and microorganisms – are common. Inhalation is a frequent route of absorption, and ventilation is a frequent engineering control. Ventilation can control not only toxic substances but also oxygen deficiency, air temperature, and humidity. In general, there are two types of ventilation for hazard control: local exhaust and dilution. Local exhaust ventilation removes contaminated air from as close to its source as possible, removing it from the worker's breathing zone, cleaning it by means appropriate to the hazard (for example, dust particles may be removed by a filter and organic vapors with an absorbent material), and releasing it outside the workplace. In designing local exhaust ventilation systems, it is common practice to design controls that would enclose the source of the hazard completely and provide access as necessary for work and maintenance. This allows fewer opportunities for hazards to escape into the officer's breathing zone and reduces the need to remove and treat large quantities of air.

Workplaces and the people who work in specific workplaces change over time. The law enforcement workplace is dynamic. Therefore, an effective and comprehensive program for prevention of occupational disease and injury requires ongoing monitoring of hazards and health in order to ensure the adequacy of controls in place and prevention strategies in use and to assist in the recognition of new problems before they become widespread. The intensity of the monitoring should be proportionate to the level of risk and the stability of the work process. Workplace hazard surveillance and worker health surveillance, along with periodic updating of a comprehensive hazard inventory, are useful approaches for ongoing monitoring.

IMPLICATIONS FOR POLICE PRACTICE

Physical health, well-being, and safety and efficiency at work are important factors for any police agency to consider. When one considers the monetary and human costs of health-impaired officers, it is essential to promote awareness and plausible prevention strategies.

The results of this study will provide policymakers with objective evidence based on rigorous scientific standards to determine the impact of hazardous exposure on law enforcement officers, their health, safety, and performance. With such evidence in hand, police agencies can better plan specific and detailed prevention strategies. The present chapter takes into account the reality that police forces will be increasingly asked to provide coverage for extended durations of time. Events such as 9/11 and the deployment of working officers into active armed forces combat will ultimately lead to increased work hours for agencies already facing financial and personnel cutbacks. With the advent of increased work hours there will be a greater risk of aversive health exposures and performance decrements, and yet it is during these times that the highest level of vigilance is required. As we have stated throughout this chapter, the impact of harmful exposures by law enforcement officers is yet to be adequately explored.

REFERENCES

Achutan, C., & Tubbs, R. L. (2007). Cincinnati police canine unit noise evaluation. *National Institute for Occupational Safety and Health* (2006). NIOSH HETA 2006-0223-3029.

Baird, R. C., Lewis, R. L., Kremer, D. P., & Kilgore, S. B. (1981). *Field Strength Measurements of Speed Measuring Radar Units,* NBSIR 81-2225. Washington, DC: National Bureau of Standards.

Blair, A., Linos, A., Stewart, P. A., Burmeister, L. F., Gibson, R., Everett, G., Schuman, L., & Cantor, K. P. (1993). Evaluation of risks for non-Hodgkin's lymphoma by occupation and industry exposures from a case-control study. *American Journal of Industrial Medicine, 23,* 301–312.

Burgaz, S., Demircigil, G. C., Karahalil, B., & Karakaya, A. E. (2002). Chromosomal damage in peripheral blood lymphocytes of traffic policemen and taxi drivers exposed to urban air pollution. *Chemosphere, 47,* 57–64.

Canadian Centre for Occupational Health and Safety. (2013). CHEMINFO: Trichloroethylene. Retrieved from http://www.ccohs.ca/ccohs.

Capellaro, E., Scagliola, D., Pira, E., Botta, G. C., & Scansetti G. (1990). Lead exposure in underground pistol firing ranges. *Giornale italiano di medicina del lavoro ed ergonomia, 12,* 157–161.

Carere, A., Andreoli, C., Galati, R., Leopardi, P., Marcon, F., Rosati, M. V., . . . Crebelli, R. (2002). Biomonitoring of exposure to urban air pollutants: analysis of sister chromatid exchanges and DNA lesions in peripheral lymphocytes of traffic policemen. *Mutation Research – Genetic Toxicology and Environmental Mutagenesis, 518,* 215–224.

Commission on Accreditation for Law Enforcement Agencies (CALEA). Smith, J. E., & Tooker, G. C. (2002). Health and fitness in law enforcement. Retrieved from http://www.calea.org/Online/newsletter/No87/healthfitness.htm#_ftnref7.

Cook, C. K., Tubbs, R. L., & Klien, M. K. (1993b). Police officers' exposures to noise generated by gun firing exercises. Saint Bernard Police, Saint Bernard, Ontario. *National Institute for Occupational Safety and Health* (1993). HHE 92-0034-2356.

Cox, R. D., & Darling, R. G. (2013). Hazmat. Retrieved from http://emedicine.medscape.com/article/764812.

Delancey, J. O., Alavanja, M. C., Coble, J., Blair, A., Hoppin, J. A., Austin, H. D., & Beane-Freeman, L. E. (2009). Occupational exposure to metribuzin and the incidence of cancer in the Agricultural Health Study. *Annals of Epidemiology, 19,* 388–395.

Feuer, E., & Rosenman, K. (1986) Mortality in police and firefighters in New Jersey. *American Journal of Industrial Medicine, 9,* 517–529

Finkelstein, M. M. (1998). Cancer incidence among Ontario police officers. *American Journal of Industrial Medicine, 34,* 157–162.

Fisher, P. D. (1993). Microwave Exposure Levels Encountered by Police Traffic Radar Operators. *IEEE Transactions on Electromagnetic Compatibility, 35,* 36–45.

Forastiere, F., Perucci, C. A., DiPietro, A., Miceli, M., Rapiti, E., Bargagli, A., & Borgia, P. (1994). Mortality among policemen in Rome. *American Journal of Industrial Medicine, 26,* 785–798.

Garland, F. C., Shaw, E., Gorham, E. D., Garland, C. F., White, M. R., & Sinsheimer, P. J. (1990). Incidence of leukemia in occupations with potential electromagnetic field exposure in United States Navy personnel. *American Journal of Epidemiology, 132,* 293–303.

Guang, X., & Jenkins, E. L. (2007). Potential work related exposures to blood borne pathogen by industry and occupation in the United States. *American Journal of Industrial Medicine, 50,* 285–292. doi: 10.1002/ajim.20441

Hardin, B. D. (1992). Testimony. In: *The Effects of Traffic Radar Guns on Law Enforcement Officers.* Hearing before the Ad Hoc Subcommittee on Consumer and Environmental Issues of the Committee on Governmental Affairs, United States Senate, August 10, 1992.

Jauchem, J. R., & Merritt, J. H. (1991). The epidemiology of exposure to electromagnetic fields: An overview of recent literature. *Journal of Clinical Epidemiology, 44,* 895–906.

Levy, B. S., Wagner, G. R., Rest, K. M., & Weeks, J. L. (Eds.). (2005). *Preventing Occupational Disease and Injury* (2nd ed.). Washington, DC: American Public Health Association.

Löfstedt, H., Seldén, A., Storéus, L., & Bodin, L. (1999). Blood lead in Swedish police officers. *American Journal of Industrial Medicine, 35,* 519–522.

Lotz, W. G., Rinsky, R. A., & Edwards, R. D. (1995). Occupational exposure of police officers to microwave radiation from traffic radar devices. National Technical Information Service Publication PB95-261350. Cincinnati, OH: NIOSH.

Mitka, M. (2005). Meth lab fires put heat on burn centers. *Journal of the American Medical Association, 16,* 2009–2010.

National Institute for Occupational Safety and Health (NIOSH). (1998). Occupational Noise Exposure: Revised criteria 1998. Report 99-106. Retrieved from http://www.cdc.gov/niosh/hhe/reports/pdfs/2007-0235-3064.pdf. Accessed November 26, 2012.

National Institute for Occupational Safety and Health (NIOSH). (1993a). Exposures to Noise of Police Firing Range Instructors. Retrieved from http://www.cdc.gov/niosh/hhe/reports. Accessed November 26, 2012.

OSHA. (2002). Occupational exposure of police officers to microwave radiation from traffic radar devices. https://www.osha.gov/SLTC/radiofrequencyradiation/fn-radpub.html.

Pyorala, M., Miettinen, H., Laakso, M., & Pyorala, K. (2000). Plasma insulin and all cause, cardiovascular and noncardiovascular mortality: The 22 year follow-up results of Helsinki policemen study. *Diabetes Care, 23,* 1097–1109.

Riediker, M., Cascio, W. E., Griggs, T. R., Herbst, M. C., Bromberg, P. A., Neas, L., Williams, R. W., & Delvin, R. B. (2004). Particulate matter exposure in cars is associated with cardiovascular effects in healthy young men. *American Journal of Respiratory Critical Care Medicine, 169,* 934–940.

Ritter, L., Solomon, K. R., & Forget, J. (2007). Persistent Organic Pollutants. An assessment report on: DDT, Aldrin, Dieldrin, Endrin, Chlordane, Heptachlor, Hexachlorobenzene, Mirex, Toxaphene, Polychlorinated Biphenyls, Dioxins, and Furans. Prepared for The International Programme on Chemical Safety (IPCS), December, 1995.

Shilling, (2008). Fingerprint powders in police work. *Journal of Occupational and Environmental Medicine, 66,* 797–804.

Szaniszlo, J., & Ungvary, G. (2001). Polycyclic aromatic hydrocarbon exposure and burden of outdoor workers in Budapest. *Journal of Toxicology and Environmental Health, 62,* 297–306.

Thrasher, D. L., Von Derau, K., & Burgess, J. (2009). Health effects from reported exposure to methamphetamine labs: A poison center-based study. *Journal of Medical Toxicology, 5,* 200–204.

Tonne, C., Yanosky, J., Gryparis, A., Melly, S., Mittleman, M., Goldberg, R., von Klot, S., & Schwartz, J. (2009). Traffic particles and occurrence of acute myocardial infarction: A case-control analysis. *Occupational and Environmental Medicine, 66,* 797–804. doi:10.1136/oem.2008.045047

Tubbs, R. L., Achutan, C., Kardous, C., Driscoll, R., & Frank, J. (2007). Reducing noise hazards for call and dispatch center operators. *National Institute for Occupational Safety and Health* (2007). Disease Control and Prevention, NIOSH HETA 2007–0235–3064.

Tubbs, R. L., & Murphy, W. J. (2003). Ft. Collins, CO police firing range hearing evaluation. *National Institute for Occupational Safety and Health* (2003). NIOSH HETA 2002-013102898.

U.S. Department of Health (1994). *Precautions for Handling and Disposal of Dead Bodies.*

Valway, S. E., Martyny, J. W., Miller, J. R., Cook, M., & Mangione, E. J. (1989). Lead absorption in indoor firing range users. *American Journal of Public Health, 79,* 1029–1032.

Van Netten, C., Souter, F., & Teschke, K. E. (1990). Occupational exposure to elemental constituents in fingerprint powders. *Archives of Environmental Health, 45,* 123–127.

Violanti, J. M., Vena, J. E., & Petralia, S. (1998). Mortality of a police cohort: 1950–1990. *American Journal of Industrial Medicine, 33,* 366–373.

Volkers, N. (1991). Traffic radar and cancer: Smoking gun? *Journal of the National Cancer Institute, 83,* 1290.

Wisconsin Division of Public Health. *Meth labs.* "Web page no longer available."

Chapter 2

HEALTH DISPARITIES
AMONG POLICE OFFICERS

TARA A. HARTLEY, DESTA FEKEDULEGN, CECIL M. BURCHFIEL,
ANNA MNATSAKANOVA, MICHAEL E. ANDREW, AND JOHN M. VIOLANTI

Some may say they are addicted to the adrenaline and excitement, the challenges of wearing a uniform. I am addicted to the service I am able to provide to the community. I see this as a noble thing and an honorable cause. Some would say there is no job worth sacrificing your life for. But we in this profession strap that notion on every day we come to work and know that the next shift could be the last.

Anonymous officer, NIOSH Science Blog
(Centers for Disease Control, 2008)

SOURCES OF STRESS IN POLICE WORK

In their report *Stress in America,* the American Psychological Association found that nearly two thirds of Americans cite their job as a top source of stress (American Psychological Association [APA], 2012). Nearly 70 percent of Americans experience physical (i.e., fatigue, changes in sleep) and nonphysical (i.e., feeling overwhelmed) symptoms attributed to stress, yet only one third report doing a good job managing their stress (APA, 2012). Numerous scientific studies have found associations between work stress and poor health outcomes, including psychological disorders such as depression and anxiety (D'-Souza, Strazdins, Lim, Broom & Rodgers, 2003; Griffin, Greiner, Stansfeld & Marmot, 2007), and physical disorders such as poor sleep quality (Knudsen, Ducharme & Roman, 2007) and cardiovascular disease (CVD) (Chandola et al., 2008).

Policing has long been considered to be one of the most stressful occupations in the United States (Gershon, Lin & Li, 2002; Marmar et al., 2006). Like other occupations, the day-to-day duties may be planned and at times mundane: reporting to their supervisor, completing paperwork, balancing deadlines, and struggling with insufficient manpower and pay. Add to this the surges of physical and psychological pressure that come with responding to a fatal traffic accident, speeding through a neighborhood in search of a criminal, or witnessing a fellow officer being gunned down and the not so "day-to-day" duties like working a night shift and then staying over to sit in the courthouse waiting to testify.

Inherent police stressors, in other words, activities that involve threats to the officer's physical or psychological well-being, have the highest potential for psychological trauma, including PTSD (Marmar et al., 2006; Violanti & Aron, 1993). These events bring about unpredictable and stressful bursts of intense and strenuous physical activity, placing high demand on the cardiovascular system (Kales, Tsismenakis, Zhang & Soteriades, 2009). Inherent stressors can also affect sleep quality and overall physical health, thus increasing the likelihood of physical injury to the officer, other officers, or the public. Organizational stressors involve duties that affect most workers: lack of supervisor and coworker support, job insecurity, and insufficient pay (Violanti & Aron, 1993). In prior research, officers have rated these organizational characteristics as more stressful than inherent events (Taylor & Bennell, 2006). Officers must also contend with shift work, extended work hours, and off-duty court time. Shift work, in other words, working a nonday shift or rotating shifts, requires a constant rearrangement of the officer's sleep and awake times leading to poorer sleep quality, fatigue, and CVD risk factors (Puttonen, Härmä & Hublin, 2010). These types of work schedules also result in lost opportunities to be with family and friends at night and on the weekends.

Police officers acknowledge the potential health risks associated with this occupation. Over one-third (38%) of police officers believe employment as a police officer, particularly the stress associated with being a police officer, increased their risk of CVD (Franke, Collins & Hinz, 1998). In a separate study, female officers felt that being either a police officer (68%) or a *female* police officer (42%) contributed to their chronic disease risk (Yoo & Franke, 2011).

In a science blog (CDC, 2008), police officers were asked to identify the key stressors in policing. Responses to the NIOSH Science Blog (CDC, 2008) included:

The cumulative effect of career stress:

> I am now over 45 years old and am seeing some of the symptomatic results of the stress involved in this job in myself. It's an accumulation. Doesn't go away or subside. It just is.

Examples of stressors experienced during their career:

> As the years have progressed, I have seen co-workers quit, get fired for doing stupid things, get arrested for doing criminal things, kill themselves, kill the ones they supposedly love, and get killed in the line of duty. I have seen officers killed in accidents and I have seen officers murdered while performing their jobs.

The physical and psychological effects of the job:

> As for me atfer [sic] 20+ years of civil service I have high blood pressure/ hypertension, (controlled with meds), unk(nown) [sic] stress disorder (controlled by will power, diet, exercise and rest), cervical disc herniation (neck) and numeruos [sic] failed relationships.

And the daily struggle with stress:

> I manage stress throughout the day well and can respond to the needs of the job when on duty. But, it catches up to me later when I am off. Stress manifests in me as poor sleep, night terrors (nightmares), and what I think is a combination of PTSD symptoms and depression.

INDICATORS OF POLICE HEALTH

Prior scientific research seems to support these testimonies. Vena, Violanti, Marshall, and Fiedler (1986) found that white male police officers died on average seven years earlier than the general U.S. white male population (Arias, 2010). Subsequent studies have identified specific risk factors and conditions for the, at the time, unexpected finding. Many of these risk factors are associated with CVD. Police officers have some of the poorest CVD health profiles of any occupation, including higher overall CVD risk factor levels (Franke, Ramey & Shelley, 2002; Hartley, Burchfiel, Fekedulegn, Andrew & Violanti, 2011; Ramey, Downing & Franke, 2009; Ramey, Perkhounkova, Downing & Culp, 2011; Wright, Barbosa-Leiker & Hoekstra, 2011) and overt CVD (Franke et al., 2002; Ramey et al., 2009). CVD accounts for 22 percent of on-duty events for police officers (Kales et al., 2009).

Improvements in health and specifically traditional CVD risk factors are a large component of the U.S. Healthy People 2020 initiative. In the 2020 recommendations, nine of the twelve leading health indicators can be tied directly to CVD, including improvements in smoking cessation; oral health; nutrition, physical activity, and obesity; clinical preventive services; decreased substance abuse; environmental quality; mental health; access to health care; and social determinants including the workplace (U.S. Department of Health and Human Services [HHS], 2012).

A key focus of Healthy People 2020 is on health disparities. A health disparity is defined as a "particular type of health difference that is closely linked to social, economic, and/or environmental disadvantage" (HHS, 2010). Health disparities are generally thought of as existing in differing groups, such as racial or ethnic groups, between men and women, or within social classes or mental health status. However, health disparities may also exist between occupational groups. In policing, the combination of shift work, the potential to be placed in life and death situations and organizational pressures may contribute to disparities in health.

In a recent article, demographic, lifestyle, and cardiovascular risk factor characteristics were compared between police officers from a large epidemiological study with U.S. employed adult participants in other large epidemiological population-based studies (Hartley, Burchfiel, Fekedulegn, Andrew & Violanti, 2011). The goal was to determine whether police officers have a more adverse cardiovascular profile than other employed adults. Several differences were found and will be discussed. The comparisons are in Table 2-1. Data for the police officers came from the BCOPS study. BCOPS is a cross-sectional study exploring the association between work-related stress and subclinical CVD. Between 2004 and 2009, 464 police officers from the Buffalo, New York, Police Department participated in the study, which included a series of questionnaires, collection of salivary cortisol and blood samples, and ultrasounds of the carotid and brachial arteries.

**Table 2-1. Health Disparities of BCOPS Study Participants Compared
With the General U.S. Employed Population***

Characteristics	BCOPS			General Employed Population Estimate		
	Characteristic	*Study Population*		*Characteristic*	*Study Population*	
	% or Mean	*Mean Age*	*% Women*	*% or Mean*	*Mean Age*	*% Women*
Demographics and Workplace						
Men	73.8[a]	41.5	–	57.6[b]	43.1	–
Women	26.2[a]	41.5	–	42.4[b]	43.1	–
White	76.7[a]	41.5	26.2	81.4[b]	43.1	42.4
Black	20.3[a]	41.5	26.2	11.2[b]	43.1	42.4
Hispanic**	1.8[a]	41.5	26.2	14.3[b]	43.1	42.4
Day Shift	53.1[c]	41.2	28.6	84.0[d]	40.5	48.2
Afternoon Shift	26.3[c]	41.2	28.6	5.6[d]	40.5	48.2
Night Shift	20.6[c]	41.2	28.6	3.1[d]	40.5	48.2
Military Veteran	26.0[e]			7.5[f]		
Lifestyle Behaviors						
Current Smokers	16.7[a]	41.5	26.2	13.6[g]	56.4	46.9
Sleep < 6 hours/24-hour period	32.0[h]	40.7	27.4	8.0[i]	41.5	50.1
Psychosocial						
Depression	12.0[h]	40.7	27.4	6.8[j]	48.3	50.6
Cardio-Metabolic Risk Factors						
Overweight (BMI 25–29.9 kg/m^2)	41.5[a]	41.5	26.2	40.0[g]	56.4	46.9
Obese (BMI ≥ 30 kg/m^2)	40.5[a]	41.5	26.2	32.1[g]	56.4	46.9
Total Cholesterol, mg/dL	200.8[k]	41.1	25.9	193.2[g]	56.4	46.9
Systolic Blood Pressure, mm Hg	120.9[k]	41.1	25.9	121.6[g]	56.4	46.9
Metabolic Syndrome	26.7[a]	41.5	26.2	20.6[l]	41.0	46.5
Abdominal Obesity	33.3[a]	41.5	26.2	49.0[m]	39.5	47.6
Reduced HDL-Cholesterol	42.6[a]	41.5	26.2	22.3[m]	39.5	47.6
Elevated Triglycerides	31.5[a]	41.5	26.2	29.4[m]	39.5	47.6
Hypertension	39.5[a]	41.5	26.2	30.1[m]	39.5	47.6
Glucose Intolerance	23.6[a]	41.5	26.2	32.4[m]	39.5	47.6

Data Sources: [a] Hartley, Burchfiel, Fekedulegn, Andrew, Knox, et al., 2011; [b] U.S. Bureau of Labor Statistics, 2008; [c] Ma et al., 2011; [d] McMenamin, 2007; [e] Hartley, Burchfiel, et al., 2012; [f] U.S. Bureau of Labor Statistics, 2012; [g] Fujishiro et al., 2011; [h] Slaven et al., 2011; [i] Luckhaupt, Tak & Calvert, 2010; [j] Reeves et al., 2011; [k] Hartley, Shankar, et al., 2011; [l] Davila et al., 2010; [m] Ervin, 2009

* The study populations for depression and the individual metabolic syndrome components were not restricted to employed status.
** Hispanic race or ethnicity. In BCOPS, Hispanic was collected as "Race." In BLS, Hispanic was collected as "Ethnicity." A person could then list "Race" as "White" and also list "Ethnicity" as "Hispanic." As a result, the BLS percentages will not sum to 100 like those for BCOPS.

Modified from Hartley, T. A., Burchfiel, C. M., Fekedulegn, D., Andrew, M. E., & Violanti, J. M. (2011). Health disparities in police officers: Comparisons to the general population. *International Journal of Emergency Mental Health, 13*(4), 211–220.

COMPARISONS OF POLICE WITH
OTHER EMPLOYED GROUPS

Shift Work, Second Jobs, and Overtime

Policing is a 24-hour occupation; shift work and overtime are necessities to ensure public safety. Using payroll records to calculate shift type over the past 15 years of their career, Ma and colleagues (2011) found that only 53 percent of the police officers in the BCOPS study worked a day shift. The remaining officers were split between afternoon shift (26.2%) and night shift (20.6%). By comparison, 84 percent of the U.S. workforce worked day shift, with only 5.6 percent working evening and 3.1 percent working night shift (McMenamin, 2007). Night shift work can have considerable consequences on health and safety. Shift work has been associated with obesity, metabolic syndrome (Met-Syn), diabetes, CVD, and mood and anxiety disorders, most likely as a result of circadian rhythm disruption (Hartenbaum & Zee, 2011).

Some officers may prefer to work the afternoon or night shift because it allows them to work a second job or spend time with family. About 36 percent of the officers in the BCOPS study reported working a second job and averaged about 7.5 hours per week at that second job (Ma et al., 2011). Nearly all state and local police agencies (93%) allow officers to have outside employment, yet the majority (75%) of those agencies set limits on the number of hours and types of establishments where the officer can work (Reaves, 2012a).

Policing requires officers to be flexible in their work schedule and often results in mandated overtime. According to the Bureau of Justice Statistics (BJS), nearly all police agencies (95%) allow officers to work overtime and more than 75 percent do not set limits on the number of overtime hours (Reaves, 2012b). In the BCOPS study, police officers averaged over 3 hours of overtime per week (Ma et al., 2011). Reasons for overtime include starting the shift early, staying late or working an extra shift to ensure adequate manpower, court time, public events that require additional police presence, and completing paperwork. The combination of night shift work, overtime, and the requirements of a second job could potentially increase the health effects found for shift work alone.

Hours of Sleep

The National Sleep Foundation recommends that adults sleep between 7 and 9 hours each night (National Sleep Foundation, 2011). Short sleep duration has been associated with CVD risk factors, including hypertension, glucose intolerance and MetSyn, and increased risk for CVD and diabetes (Mullington, Haack, Toth, Serrador & Meier-Ewert, 2009). It may not be surprising that police officers, who are exposed to irregular working hours, required overtime, and traumatic events, on average do not get adequate sleep. In the BCOPS study, 32 percent of officers reported sleeping less than 6 hours in a 24-hour period (Slaven et al., 2011). This is four times higher than for employed workers completing the National Health Interview Survey (Luckhaupt, Tak & Calvert, 2010). Among police officers, sleep loss has been associated with higher levels of perceived stress in men and among those with higher ranks and greater workloads (Charles et al., 2011). Sleep loss can also be a consequence of shift work. Chronic sleep loss can lead to excessive fatigue and impaired alertness. Arnedt and colleagues (2005) suggested that such sleepiness creates impairment comparable to that of 0.04 to 0.05 percent blood alcohol content. These outcomes can have immediate consequences for police officers because the nature of their job requires them to function in a hypervigilant state.

Cigarette Smoking

Cigarette smoking is a well-known modifiable risk factor for CVD, cancer, and respiratory disease (Arnett et al., 1998). The percentage of police officers who currently smoke cigarettes was 16.7 percent in the BCOPS study (Hartley, Burchfiel, Fekedulegn, Andrew, Knox, et al., 2011). This is slightly higher than for employed participants of the Multi-Ethnic Study of Atherosclerosis (MESA) (13.6%) (Fujishiro et al., 2011). The prevalence is much lower, however, than that for all employed workers (30%) and protective service workers (36.6%) who participated in a national study of health (Bang & Kim, 2001) and than that reported for Milwaukee police officers (32.1%) (Ramey, Downing & Knoblauch, 2008).

There are sex differences associated with smoking and health outcomes. Current daily smoking is a stronger risk factor in women than in men, and these sex differences are greater in women under the age of 45 (Njølstad, Arnesen & Lund-Larsen, 1996). One theory behind the difference is that smoking produces an antiestrogenic effect that results in women losing their "natural" protection against CVD (Bolego, Poli & Paoletti, 2002). Estrogen production in premenopausal women is considered to be protective against CVD. In the BCOPS study, women officers were twice as likely to be current smokers as men were (27.3% vs. 13.2%) (Hartley, Burchfiel, Fekedulegn, Andrew, Knox, et al., 2011). Women officers were also more likely to be former smokers than men were (30.3% vs. 20.1%) (Hartley, Burchfiel, Fekedulegn, Andrew, Knox, et al., 2011).

Depressive Symptoms

As discussed earlier, policing in general is considered to be highly stressful (Gershon et al., 2002). Job strain, low decision authority and low social support at work have been significantly associated with major depressive disorder (Blackmore et al., 2007). Prior studies have found an association between depressive symptoms and MetSyn (Pyykkönen et al., 2011). MetSyn is a clustering of risk factors associated with CVD and type 2 diabetes and will be discussed in more detail later.

In the BCOPS study, the prevalence of depression was found to be around 12 percent (Hartley, Knox, et al., 2012; Slaven et al., 2011). This prevalence was nearly twice as high compared to the general population (6.8%; Reeves et al., 2011). This somewhat surprising finding may be attributed to a few key differences. First, age is a significant risk factor for depression. According to the National Institute of Mental Health, adults 30 to 44 years of age are 120 percent more likely and adults 45 to 59 are 100 percent more likely to experience depression during their lifetime than those over the age of 60 (NIMH, 2013). More than 90 percent of the BCOPS study participants fall into these working age categories (Hartley, Knox, et al., 2012). Workers in this age category may experience caregiver stress due to providing child care and/or elder care in addition to their responsibilities as a police officer. Younger officers with fewer years of service are more likely to work a nonday shift, which may add additional stress (Ma et al., 2011).

Second, the comparison study sample was not restricted to employed adults (BCOPS study included only police officers), included a higher percentage of women (50.6% vs. 27.4%), and possibly included a higher percentage of persons who have chronic medical conditions and those who are unemployed. Depression is known to be higher among women, those with chronic medical conditions, and those who are unemployed (Marcotte, Wilcox-Gök & Redmon, 1999; Egede, 2007). In the BCOPS study, 10 percent of male and 16 percent of female officers had depression (Hartley, Knox, et al., 2012). In the comparison study, the prevalence of depression was 5 percent for men and 8 percent for women (Reeves et al., 2011). Given that the percentage of women in the comparison study group was double that of the BCOPS study, this contrast is noteworthy.

Finally, the self-reported questionnaires used in each study were different. The BCOPS study used the Center for Epidemiologic Studies-Depression Scale (Hartley, Knox, et al., 2012) and the National Health and Nutrition Examination Survey used the Patient Health Questionnaire-9 (Reeves et al., 2011). Both are widely used in epidemiological research, but comparisons between the two should be made with caution.

Metabolic Syndrome

MetSyn is a clustering of risk factors that increase the risk of developing CVD and diabetes (Grundy et al., 2005). These five risk factors are abdominal obesity, hypertension, elevated triglycerides, low levels of high-density lipoprotein cholesterol (HDL-C), and glucose intolerance. A person is considered to have MetSyn if they have three or more of these risk factors. Davila and associates (2010) reported that the prevalence of MetSyn was 20.6 percent among U.S. workers and 26.1 percent among protective service workers (including police officers). In the BCOPS study, the prevalence of MetSyn was 26.7 percent and was nearly four-fold higher for male officers compared to women officers (33.0% for men, 8.8% for women) (Hartley, Burchfiel, Fekedulegn, Andrew, Knox, et al., 2011). The next sections describe differences in the individual MetSyn components.

Overweight and Obesity

Obesity is associated with other CVD risk factors, such as hypertension, glucose intolerance, and dyslipidemia, and obesity has been associated with CVD independent of other risk factors (Poirier et al., 2006).

Overweight is defined as a body mass index (BMI) between 25 and
29.9 kg/m²; obesity is defined as BMI of 30 kg/m² or higher (Poirier et
al., 2006). Over 80 percent of the police officers in the BCOPS study
are considered overweight or obese (Hartley, Burchfiel, Fekedulegn,
Andrew, Knox, et al., 2011). The percentage of officers who were overweight (41.5%) was similar to that of the general employed population
(40%; Fujishiro et al., 2011) but levels of obesity were higher for police
officers (40.5%) than for the employed group (32.1%) (Fujishiro et al.,
2011). Ramey, Downing, and Knoblauch (2008) reported that 47 percent of Milwaukee police officers self-reported being overweight and
25 percent self-reported being obese.

The obesity component of MetSyn uses abdominal obesity, as measured by waist circumference, instead of BMI. Waist circumference has
been found to be a better predictor of CVD and metabolic risk factors,
including glucose and low-density lipoprotein cholesterol (LDL-C) levels and blood pressure, than BMI is (Zhu et al., 2002). In the BCOPS
study, the prevalence of abdominal obesity (waist circumference of ≥
102 cm or 40 inches in men, ≥ 88 cm or 34.5 inches in women) was
33.3 percent, with men having a much higher prevalence than women:
38.9 percent versus 17.7 percent (Hartley, Burchfiel, Fekedulegn, Andrew, Knox, et al., 2011). Using data from Ervin's study of U.S. adults
(2009), the prevalence of abdominal obesity, defined in the same manner as the BCOPS study, was 49 percent overall and much higher for
women than for men: 57.3 percent versus 41.5 percent. Despite the lower prevalence for police officers and specifically for women officers, the
odds of having abdominal obesity significantly increased with increased police stress in female officers only (Hartley, Burchfiel, Fekedulegn, Andrew, Knox, et al., 2011). This means that the more police
stress the officer reported, the more likely she was to have elevated
waist circumference levels.

Blood Lipid Levels

The risk of CVD increases with increasing levels of total serum cholesterol, LDL-C, and triglycerides, and with decreasing levels of HDL-
C (American Heart Association, 2012a). Diet, physical activity and cigarette smoking have all been shown to affect lipid levels (American
Heart Association, 2012b). Total cholesterol levels above 240 mg/dL
more than double an individual's risk of coronary heart disease (Amer-

ican Heart Association, 2013a). High cholesterol in combination with high blood pressure or diabetes further increases that risk (American Heart Association, 2012c).

In the BCOPS study, the mean serum total cholesterol levels were 200.8 mg/dL (Hartley, Shankar, et al., 2011) in line with the American Heart Association guidelines (≤ 200 mg/dL), and 7 points above the mean for the employed MESA participants (Fujishiro et al., 2011). Using self-reported high blood cholesterol (i.e., hypercholesterolemia), Ramey and colleagues (2008) found a similar prevalence of high cholesterol between Milwaukee police officers and the general Wisconsin population (28.5% for police, 28.1% for general population). The percentage of BCOPS study officers with low levels of HDL-C (< 40 mg/dL men, < 50 mg/dL women, or taking fibrate or nicotinic acid medication) was 42.6 percent and nearly double that of the National Health and Nutrition Examination Survey (NHANES) participants (22.3%), whereas the percentage of officers with elevated triglycerides (≥ 150 mg/dL or taking fibrate or nicotinic acid medication) was slightly higher than the NHANES participants (31.5% vs. 29.4%) (Ervin, 2009; Hartley, Burchfiel, Fekedulegn, Andrew, Knox, et al., 2011).

As reported earlier, the prevalence of MetSyn and the individual components were lower for women officers compared to men. The prevalence of elevated triglycerides was four fold higher, and the prevalence of reduced HDL-C was nearly twice as high for men than for women: elevated triglycerides, 39.6% versus 8.8%; reduced HDL-C, 48.3% versus 26.5% (Hartley, Burchfiel, Fekedulegn, Andrew, Knox, et al., 2011). Among female officers, however, as their reported police stress levels increased, so did the odds of having high triglycerides and low HDL-C; no associations were found for male officers (Hartley, Burchfiel, Fekedulegn, Andrew, Knox, et al., 2011).

Hypertension (High Blood Pressure)

Nearly one third of U.S. adults have hypertension (systolic blood pressure ≥ 140 mmHg or diastolic blood pressure ≥ 90 mmHg), and less than half of those have their hypertension under control (Gillespie, Kuklina, Briss, Blair & Hong, 2011). The higher the blood pressure, the higher the risk of having a heart attack, stroke, heart failure or kidney disease (HHS, 2004). The risk of coronary heart disease in those with hypertension increases by 5 to 10% with every additional CVD risk factor (i.e. dyslipidemia, cigarette smoking, diabetes) (HHS, 2004).

Several characteristics of policing are also known risk factors for hypertension: irregular physical exertion, poor diet, shift work, noise exposure, PTSD, and high job demand/low job control (Kales et al., 2009). More than one quarter (27.4%) of Milwaukee police officers reported being told by their physician that they have hypertension, compared to only 17.6 percent of Wisconsin residents (Ramey et al., 2008). Using a combination of objective (i.e., standardized blood pressure measurements of ≥130 mmHg systolic or ≥85 mmHg diastolic) and subjective (i.e., self-reported physician-diagnosed hypertension, self-reported antihypertensive medication use) measures, 39.5 percent of the BCOPS study officers had hypertension compared to 30.1 percent of U.S. adults (Ervin, 2009). This definition of hypertension follows the guidelines for the hypertension component of MetSyn (discussed earlier) and may include those who are prehypertensive (HHS, 2004). Individuals with prehypertension are at even greater risk for developing hypertension than are normotensives and can be good candidates for lifestyle modifications.

Glucose Intolerance

The last component of MetSyn is glucose intolerance. Glucose intolerance includes individuals who have a fasting glucose level of ≥ 100 mg/dL and those who are taking hypoglycemic (glucose-lowering) medications. Up to 70 percent of individuals with elevated fasting glucose levels will go on to develop diabetes (Nathan et al., 2007). Levitzky and colleagues (2008) found that the odds of having incident coronary heart disease was 70 percent higher for women with fasting glucose levels between 100 and 125 mg/dL compared to those women with values below 100. According to the American Heart Association, adults with diabetes are between two and four times more likely to have CVD or a stroke than are those without diabetes (American Heart Association, 2013a).

In the BCOPS study, less than one quarter of officers (23.6%) had glucose intolerance (Hartley, Burchfiel, Fekedulegn, Andrew, Knox, et al., 2011) compared to 32.4 percent of U.S. adults (Ervin, 2009). The lower prevalence of glucose intolerance is similar to the lower reported prevalence of diabetes previously published for police officers: 2.1 percent in the BCOPS study (Hartley, Burchfiel, Fekedulegn, Andrew,

Knox, et al., 2011), 3.1 percent among the Milwaukee, Wisconsin, Police Department (Ramey et al., 2008), and 1.5 percent among officers from nine Midwestern states (Franke et al., 2002).

POLICE SUBGROUPS AT GREATER RISK

State and local law enforcement agencies target specific demographic groups during recruitment. In 2008, more than 50 percent of officers reported that their agencies had special recruitment efforts. Of these, 56 percent targeted women, 59 percent racial or ethnic minorities, and 51 percent military veterans (Reaves, 2012b). Interestingly, these groups are often considered health disparate groups. Throughout this chapter, levels of CVD risk factors for police officers in general have been discussed. Within policing, however,these groups of officers may be at greater risk for adverse physical and psychological health than other police officers are.

Gender

In 2007, women accounted for less than 15 percent of all police officers in the United States, with variation by type and size of police agency (Langton, 2010). Approximately 15 percent of officers in the larger local police departments were women, compared to 13 percent in large sheriffs' offices, 6 percent in small local police departments and state police agencies, and 4 percent in small sheriffs' offices (Langton, 2010). By comparison, in the United States about 46 percent of workers age 20 and older are female (United States Bureau of Labor Statistics, 2008). It has been shown that female police officers experience additional sources of stress beyond the traditional stressors associated with policing, some of which have been attributed to working in a male-dominated occupation. These include sexual harassment and discrimination, breaking from traditional domestic roles, and balancing work and family responsibilities (see Chapter 6).

Ethnicity

Increased racial/ethnic representation in policing has also been a target for recruitment. Approximately 34 percent of officers in federal agencies, 25 percent in local police departments, and 19 percent of sheriffs' offices in the United States were not white (Burch, 2012; Reaves, 2010; Reaves, 2012b). Blacks composed the largest minority representation in local police departments (12%) and sheriffs' offices (9%); Hispanics are the largest minority in federal agencies (20%) (Burch, 2012; Reaves, 2010; Reaves, 2012). The police agency representing the BCOPS study is a large urban force, which may provide opportunity for more diverse representation. More than three quarters (77%) of the study population were white, 20 percent were black, and 2 percent were Hispanic (Hartley, Burchfiel, Fekedulegn, Andrew, Knox, et al., 2011). Data from the U.S. BLS is comparable. Blacks represent 11 percent of the U.S. workforce; however, the U.S. BLS asks about Hispanic/Latino ethnicity separately from race (2008). Fourteen percent of the U.S. workforce regardless of race was of Hispanic or Latino ethnicity (U.S. BLS, 2008).

Military Experience

In 2011, 10.4 million veterans or 7.5 percent of U.S. civilian employed adults were military veterans (U.S. BLS, 2012). Veterans of World War II (December 1941–December 1946), the Korean War (July 1950–January 1955), and the Vietnam War (August 1964–April 1975) represent the largest percentage of veterans (31.6%), followed by Gulf War I veterans (August 1990–August 2001; 22.1%), and Gulf War II veterans (September 2001–present; 16.4%). Nearly one third of veterans are from other service periods (29.9%) (U.S. BLS, 2012). Women account for less than 10 percent of these 10.4 million veterans (U.S. BLS, 2012). Data on the percentage of police officers who are military veterans are difficult to find. In 2011, 14.5 percent of veterans worked in service-related occupations, including policing, and 21.7 percent worked in government industry, which would also include policing (U.S. BLS, 2012). In the BCOPS study, approximately 26 percent of participants had prior military experience; most served in the Gulf War I or II eras (Hartley, Burchfiel, et al., 2012).

CONCLUSIONS

In this chapter, key studies on police officer health, including findings from the Buffalo Cardio-metabolic Occupational Police Stress (BCOPS) Study, were compared with results from studies of other U.S. employed adults. Police officers have higher levels of traditional CVD risk factors, including more current smokers, higher levels of obesity, hypertension, and dyslipidemia, than other U.S. employed adults. Officers also have higher prevalence of the nontraditional risk factors like depression, sleep insufficiency, and shift work. Specific groups of officers who may be more adversely affected by these stressors, including women and ethnic minorities who are underrepresented in policing and military veterans who may be at greater risk for psychological disorders including PTSD and depression, were also discussed.

Both the scientific literature and accounts from police officers describe the stressors associated with being an officer. These include the routine organizational stressors common to other workers, along with unique stressors like shift work and exposure to dangerous and potentially life-threatening situations. Officers recognize the potential health effects associated with these stressors. Prior research has demonstrated associations between these stressors and poor health outcomes using cross-sectional studies, which limit the ability to determine if the exposure led to the outcome. Future studies of police officers should use a prospective study design so that the association and the potential biological mechanisms responsible for these health disparities can be better understood.

Disclaimer: The findings and conclusions in this report are those of the authors and do not necessarily represent the views of the National Institute for Occupational Safety and Health.

REFERENCES

American Heart Association. (2012a). *About cholesterol.* Retrieved on March 25, 2013, from http://www.heart.org/HEARTORG/Conditions/Cholesterol/AboutCholesterol/About-Cholesterol_UCM_001220_Article.jsp

American Heart Association. (2012b). *Prevention and treatment of high cholesterol.* Retrieved on March 25, 2013, from http://www.heart.org/HEARTORG/Conditions/Cholesterol/PreventionTreatmentofHighCholesterol/Prevention-and-Treatment-of-High-Cholesterol_UCM_001215_Article.jsp

American Heart Association. (2012c). *Why cholesterol matters.* Retrieved on March 25, 2013, from http://www.heart.org/HEARTORG/Conditions/Cholesterol/Why CholesterolMatters/Why-Cholesterol-Matters_UCM_001212_Article.jsp

American Heart Association. (2013a). *Cardiovascular disease & diabetes.* Retrieved on March 25, 2013, from http://www.heart.org/HEARTORG/Conditions/Diabetes/WhyDiabetesMatters/Cardiovascular-Disease-Diabetes_UCM_313865_Article.jsp

American Heart Association. (2013b). *What your cholesterol levels mean.* Retrieved on March 25, 2013, from http://www.heart.org/HEARTORG/Conditions/Cholesterol/AboutCholesterol/What-Your-Cholesterol-Levels-Mean_UCM_305562_Article.jsp

American Psychological Association. (2012). *Missing the mark on stress management.* Retrieved on March 25, 2013, from http://www.stressinamerica.org

Arias, E. (2010). Department of Health and Human Service, CDC. United States life tables, 2006. *National Vital Statistics Reports, 58*(21), 1–40.

Arnedt, J. T., Owens, J., Crouch, M., Stahl, J., & Carskadon, M. A. (2005). Neurobehavioral performance of residents after heavy night call vs after alcohol ingestion. *Journal of the American Medical Association, 294*(9), 1025–1033.

Arnett, D. K., Sprafka, J. M., McGovern, P. G., Jacobs, D. R. Jr., Shahar, E., McCarty, M., & Luepker, R. V. (1998). Trends in cigarette smoking: the Minnesota Heart Survey, 1980 through 1992. *American Journal of Public Health, 88*(8), 1230–1233.

Bang, K. M., & Kim, J. H. (2001). Prevalence of cigarette smoking by occupation and industry in the United States. *American Journal of Industrial Medicine, 40*(3), 233–239.

Blackmore, E. R., Stansfeld, S. A., Weller, I., Munce, S., Zagorski, B. M., & Stewart, D. E. (2007). Major depressive episodes and work stress: Results from a national population survey. *Journal of Management Education, 97*(11), 2088–2093.

Bolego, C., Poli, A., & Paoletti, R. (2002). Smoking and gender. *Cardiovascular Research, 53*(3), 568–576.

Burch, A. M. (2012). *Sheriffs' offices, 2007-Statistical tables.* U.S. Department of Justice. Office of Justice Programs, Bureau of Justice Statistics. NCJ 238558. Retrieved on March 25, 2013, from www.bjs.gov/content/pub/pdf/so07st.pdf

Centers for Disease Control and Prevention (CDC). (2008). *Police and stress.* NIOSH Science Blog. Retrieved on March 25, 2013, from http://blogs.cdc.gov/niosh-science-blog/2008/06/police/

Chandola, T., Britton, A., Brunner, E., Hemingway, H., Malik, M., Kumari, M., . . . Marmot, M. (2008). Work stress and coronary heart disease: What are the mechanisms? *European Heart Journal, 29*(5), 640–648.

Charles, L. E., Slaven, J. E., Mnatsakanova, A., Ma, C., Violanti, J. M., Fekedulegn, D., . . . Burchfiel, C. M. (2011). Association of perceived stress with sleep duration and sleep quality in police officers. *International Journal of Emergency Mental Health, 13*(4), 229–241.

Davila, E. P., Florez, H., Fleming, L. E., Lee, D. J., Goodman, E., LeBlanc, W. G., . . . Clarke, T. (2010). Prevalence of the metabolic syndrome among U.S. workers. *Diabetes Care, 33*(11), 2390–2395.

D'Souza, R. M., Strazdins, L., Lim, L. L., Broom, D. H., & Rodgers, B. (2003). Work and health in a contemporary society: Demands, control, and insecurity. *Journal of Epidemiology and Community Health, 57*(11), 849–854.

Egede, L. E. (2007). Major depression in individuals with chronic medical disorders: Prevalence, correlates and association with health resource utilization, lost productivity and functional disability. *General Hospital Psychiatry, 29*(5), 409–416.

Ervin, R. B. (2009). Prevalence of metabolic syndrome among adults 20 years of age and over, by sex, age, race and ethnicity, and body mass index: United States. *National Health Statistics Reports, 13*, 1–8.

Franke, W. D., Collins, S. A., & Hinz, P. N. (1998). Cardiovascular disease morbidity in an Iowa law enforcement cohort, compared with the general Iowa population. *Journal of Occupational and Environmental Medicine, 40*(5), 441–444.

Franke, W. D., Ramey, S. L., & Shelley, M. C. (2002). Relationship between cardiovascular disease morbidity, risk factors, and stress in a law enforcement cohort. *Journal of Occupational and Environmental Medicine, 44*(12), 1182–1189.

Fujishiro, K., Roux, A. V. D., Landsbergis, P., Baron, S., Barr, R. G., Kaufman, J. D., . . . Stukovsky, K. H. (2011). Associations of occupation, job control and job demands with intima-media thickness: The Multi-Ethnic Study of Atherosclerosis (MESA). *Occupational and Environmental Medicine, 68*(5), 319–326.

Gershon, R. R., Lin, S., & Li, X. (2002). Work stress in aging police officers. *Journal of Occupational and Environmental Medicine, 44*(2), 160–167.

Gillespie, C., Kuklina, E. V., Briss, P. A., Blair, N. A., & Hong, Y. (2011). Vital signs: Prevalence, treatment, and control of hypertension – United States, 1999–2002 and 2005–2008. *Morbidity and Mortality Weekly Report, 60*(04), 103–108.

Griffin, J. M., Greiner, B. A., Stansfeld, S. A., & Marmot, M. (2007). The effect of self-reported and observed job conditions on depression and anxiety symptoms: A comparison of theoretical models. *Journal of Occupational Health Psychology, 12*(4), 334.

Grundy, S. M., Cleeman, J. I., Daniels, S. R., Donato, K. A., Eckel, R. H., Franklin, B. A., . . . Costa, F. (2005). Diagnosis and management of the metabolic syndrome. An American Heart Association/National Heart, Lung, and Blood Institute Scientific Statement. *Circulation, 112*, 2735–2752.

Hartenbaum, N. P., & Zee, P. C. (2011). Shift work and sleep optimizing health, safety, and performance. *Journal of Occupational and Environmental Medicine, 53*, S1–S10.

Hartley, T. A., Burchfiel, C. M., Fekedulegn, D., Andrew, M. E., Knox, S. S., & Violanti, J. M. (2011). Association between police officer stress and the metabolic syndrome. *International Journal of Emergency Mental Health, 13*(4), 243–256.

Hartley, T. A., Burchfiel, C. M., Fekedulegn, D., Andrew, M. E., & Violanti, J. M. (2011). Health disparities in police officers: Comparisons to the U.S. general population. *International Journal of Emergency Mental Health, 13*(4), 211–220.

Hartley, T. A., Knox, S. S., Fekedulegn, D., Barbosa-Leiker, C., Violanti, J. M., Andrew, M. E., & Burchfiel, C. M. (2012). Association between depressive symptoms and metabolic syndrome in police officers: Results from two cross-sectional studies. *Journal of Environmental and Public Health, 2012*, 861219. Retrieved March 25, 2013, from http://www.hindawi.com/journals/jeph/2012/861219/

Hartley, T. A., Shankar, A., Fekedulegn, D., Violanti, J. M., Andrew, M. E., Knox, S. S., & Burchfiel, C. M. (2011). Metabolic syndrome and carotid intima media thickness in urban police officers. *Journal of Occupational and Environmental Medicine, 53*(5), 553–561.

Kales, S. N., Tsismenakis, A. J., Zhang, C., & Soteriades, E. S. (2009). Blood pressure in firefighters, police officers, and other emergency responders. *American Journal of Hypertension, 22*(1), 11–20.

Knudsen, H. K., Ducharme, L. J., & Roman, P. M. (2007). Job stress and poor sleep quality: Data from an American sample of full-time workers. *Social Science & Medicine, 64*(10), 1997–2007.

Langton, L. (2010). *Women in Law Enforcement, 1987–2008.* U.S. Department of Justice, Office of Justice Programs, Bureau of Justice Statistics. NCJ 230521. Retrieved on March 25, 2013, from http://bjs.gov/content/pub/pdf/wle8708.pdf

Levitzky, Y. S., Pencina, M. J., D'Agostino, R. B., Meigs, J. B., Murabito, J. M., Vasan, R. S., & Fox, C. S. (2008). Impact of impaired fasting glucose on cardiovascular disease: The Framingham Heart Study. *Journal of the American College of Cardiology, 51*(3), 264–270.

Luckhaupt, S. E., Tak, S., & Calvert, G. M. (2010). The prevalence of short sleep duration by industry and occupation in the National Health Interview Survey. *Sleep, 33*(2), 149–159.

Ma, C. C., Burchfiel, C. M., Fekedulegn, D., Andrew, M. E., Charles, L. E., Gu, J. K., . . . Violanti, J. M. (2011). Association of shift work with physical activity among police officers: The Buffalo cardio-metabolic occupational police stress study. *Journal of Occupational and Environmental Medicine, 53*(9), 1030–1036.

Marcotte, D. E., Wilcox Gök, V., & Redmon, P. D. (1999). Prevalence and patterns of major depressive disorder in the United States labor force. *The Journal of Mental Health Policy and Economics, 2*(3), 123–131.

Marmar, C. R., McCaslin, S. E., Metzler, T. J., Best, S., Weiss, D. S., Fagan, J., . . . Neylan, T. (2006). Predictors of posttraumatic stress in police and other first responders. *Annals of the New York Academy of Sciences, 1071*(1), 1–18.

McMenamin, T. M. (2007). A time to work: Recent trends in shift work and flexible schedules. *Monthly Labor Review, 130,* 3–15.

Mullington, J. M., Haack, M., Toth, M., Serrador, J., & Meier-Ewert, H. (2009). Cardiovascular, inflammatory and metabolic consequences of sleep deprivation. *Progress in Cardiovascular Diseases, 51*(4), 294–302.

Nathan, D. M., Davidson, M. B., DeFronzo, R. A., Heine, R. J., Henry, R. R., Pratley, R., . . . American Diabetes Association. (2007). Impaired fasting glucose and impaired glucose tolerance: Implications for care. *Diabetes Care, 30*(3), 753–759.

National Institute of Mental Health (NIMH). (2013). *Major depressive disorder among adults.* Retrieved on March 25, 2013, from http://www.nimh.nih.gov/statistics/1MDD_ADULT.shtml

National Sleep Foundation. (2011). *How much sleep do we really need?* Retrieved on March 25, 2013, from http://www.sleepfoundation.org/article/how-sleep-works/how-much-sleep-do-we-really-need.

Njølstad, I., Arnesen, E., & Lund-Larsen, P. G. (1996). Smoking, serum lipids, blood pressure, and sex differences in myocardial infarction: A 12-year follow-up of the Finnmark Study. *Circulation, 93*(3), 450–456.

Poirier, P., Giles, T. D., Bray, G. A., Hong, Y., Stern, J. S., Pi-Sunyer, F. X., & Eckel, R. H. (2006). Obesity and cardiovascular disease: Pathophysiology, evaluation, and effect of weight loss. *Circulation, 113*(6), 898–918.

Puttonen, S., Härmä, M., & Hublin, C. (2010). Shift work and cardiovascular disease: pathways from circadian stress to morbidity. *Scandinavian Journal of Work, Environment & Health, 36*(2), 96–108.

Pyykkönen, A. J., Räikkönen, K., Tuomi, T., Eriksson, J. G., Groop, L., & Isomaa, B. (2012). Association between depressive symptoms and metabolic syndrome is not explained by antidepressant medication: Results from the PPP-Botnia Study. *Annals of Medicine, 44*(3), 279–288.

Ramey, S. L., Downing, N. R., & Knoblauch, A. (2008). Developing strategic interventions to reduce cardiovascular disease risk among law enforcement officers: The art and science of data triangulation. *American Association of Occupational Health Nursing Journal, 56*(2), 54–62.

Ramey, S. L., Downing, N. R., & Franke, W. D. (2009). Milwaukee police department retirees: Cardiovascular disease risk and morbidity among aging law enforcement officers. *American Association of Occupational Health Nursing Journal, 57*(11), 448–453.

Ramey, S. L., Perkhounkova, Y., Downing, N. R., & Culp, K. R. (2011). Relationship of cardiovascular disease to stress and vital exhaustion in an urban, midwestern police department. *American Association of Occupational Health Nursing Journal, 59*(5), 221–227.

Reaves, B. A. (2010). *Local police department, 2007.* U.S. Department of Justice, Office of Justice Programs, Bureau of Justice Statistics. NCJ 231174. Retrieved on March 25, 2013, http://www.bjs.gov/content/pub/pdf/lpd07.pdf

Reaves, B. A. (2012a). *Federal law enforcement officers, 2008.* U.S. Department of Justice, Office of Justice Programs, Bureau of Justice Statistics. NCJ 238250. Retrieved on March 25, 2013, from http://bjs.gov/content/pub/pdf/fleo08.pdf

Reaves, B. A. (2012b). *Hiring and retention of state and local law enforcement officers, 2008 – statistical tables.* U.S. Department of Justice, Office of Justice Programs, Bureau of Justice Statistics. NCJ 238251. Retrieved on March 25, 2013, from http://www.bjs.gov/content/pub/pdf/hrslleo08st.pdf

Reeves, W. C., Strine, T. W., Pratt, L. A., Thompson, W., Ahluwalia, I., Dhingra, S. S., . . . CDC. (2011). Mental illness surveillance among adults in the United States. *MMWR Surveillance Summary, 60*(suppl 3), 1–29.

Slaven, J. E., Mnatsakanova, A., Burchfiel, C. M., Smith, L. M., Charles, L. E., Andrew, M. E., Ma, C., Fekeduelgn, D., & Violanti, J. M. (2011). Association of sleep quality with depression in police officers. *International Journal of Emergency Mental Health, 13*(4), 267–277.

Taylor, A., & Bennell, C. (2006). Operational and organizational police stress in an Ontario police department: A descriptive study. *The Canadian Journal of Police and Security Services, 4*, 223–234.

U.S. Department of Health and Human Services (HHS). Healthy People. (2012). *Leading health indicators.* Retrieved on March 25, 2013, from http://www.healthy-people.gov/2020/LHI/default.aspx

U.S. Department of Health and Human Services (HHS). Healthy People. (2010). *Disparities.* Retrieved on March 25, 2013, from http://www.healthypeople.gov/2020/about/DisparitiesAbout.aspx

U.S. Department of Health and Human Services (HHS). NIH. (2004). *The seventh report of the Joint National Committee on prevention, detection, evaluation, and treatment of high blood pressure.* Retrieved on March 25, 2013, from http://www.nhlbi.nih.gov/guidelines/hypertension/jnc7full.pdf

U.S. Bureau of Labor Statistics (U.S. BLS). (2008). *Labor force characteristics by race and ethnicity, 2007.* Retrieved on March 25, 2013, from www.bls.gov/cps/cpsrace2007.pdf

U.S. Bureau of Labor Statistics (U.S. BLS). (2012). *Employment situation of veterans – 2011.* Retrieved on March 25, 2013, from http://www.bls.gov/news.release/vet.nr0.htm

Vena, J. E., Violanti, J. M., Marshall, J., & Fiedler, R. C. (1986). Mortality of a municipal worker cohort: III. Police officers. *American Journal of Industrial Medicine, 10*(4), 383–397.

Violanti, J. M., & Aron, F. (1993). Sources of police stressors, job attitudes, and psychological distress. *Psychological Reports, 72*(3), 899–904.

Wright, B. R., Barbosa-Leiker, C., & Hoekstra, T. (2011). Law enforcement officer versus non–law enforcement officer status as a longitudinal predictor of traditional and emerging cardiovascular risk factors. *Journal of Occupational and Environmental Medicine, 53*(7), 730–734.

Yoo, H., & Franke, W. D. (2011). Stress and cardiovascular disease risk in female law enforcement officers. *International Archives of Occupational and Environmental Health, 84*(3), 279–286.

Zhu, S., Wang, Z., Heshka, S., Heo, M., Faith, M. S., & Heymsfield, S. B. (2002). Waist circumference and obesity-associated risk factors among whites in the third National Health and Nutrition Examination Survey: Clinical action thresholds. *The American Journal of Clinical Nutrition, 76*(4), 743–743.

Chapter 3

CARDIOVASCULAR RISK
IN LAW ENFORCEMENT

Franklin H. Zimmerman

EPIDEMIOLOGY

The motto of law enforcement is to protect and serve. In order to accomplish this task, police officers acknowledge and recognize an inherent risk to personal safety (LaTourrette, 2011). Overall, the occupational fatality rate of law enforcement personnel is three to five times greater than the national average (Houser, Jackson, Bartis & Peterson, 2010). An analysis of all-cause occupational fatalities per 100,000 individuals from the years 1992 to 1997 found a much higher rate in police personnel (14.2) compared with the general population (5.0) (Maguire, Hunting, Smith & Levick, 2002). In the 11-year period of 1992 to 2002, researchers found a law enforcement fatality rate of 11.8 per 100,000 individuals (Tiesman, Hendricks, Bell & Amandus, 2010). A more recent report from 2010 suggests an increasing occupational risk, with a mortality rate per 100,000 of 18.0, compared with the national average of 3.5 (U.S. Bureau of Labor Statistics, 2011). The greatest occupational risk to police officers is trauma, which may result from homicide (40–50%), transportation-related incidents (35–40%), or suicide (5%) (Tiesman et al., 2010).

Cardiovascular disease represents a significant cause of occupation-related morbidity and mortality. According to data compiled by the National Law Enforcement Officers Memorial Fund from the 10-year period of 2000 to 2010 (2001 excluded because of the September 11th attacks), 7 percent of occupational deaths in law enforcement personnel were related to fatal heart attack (National Law Enforcement Officers Memorial Fund, 2011). In recognition of this risk, in 2003 Congress enacted the "Hometown Heroes Act," which created a statutory presumption that public safety officers who die of stroke or heart attack while performing strenuous activities in the line of duty are eligible for death benefits.

THE ATHEROSCLEROTIC PROCESS

The leading cause of cardiovascular morbidity and mortality in both law enforcement personnel and civilians is due to atherosclerosis (Roger et al., 2011). This process is characterized by the gradual formation of plaque within the walls of the coronary arteries and other large- and medium-sized blood vessels. Plaque formation is a complex process that involves the accumulation of lipid-rich, inflammatory, and prothrombotic cells. Over time, plaque compromises the normal flow of blood to the heart muscle, creating a mismatch of supply and demand that may cause symptoms of angina (chest discomfort, shortness of breath, or exercise intolerance). Alternatively, a partially obstructive plaque may suddenly rupture and acutely occlude a coronary artery with thrombus. This may precipitate an acute coronary syndrome, myocardial infarction, or sudden cardiac death.

Atherosclerosis begins at an early age. Accordingly, even the newest police recruit is not immune. Compelling data demonstrating significant coronary atherosclerosis in young, otherwise healthy, individuals have been reported in military personnel dying of combat wounds. A study of Korean War soldiers killed in combat showed that 77 percent had visible coronary atherosclerosis, with 3 percent having a complete obstruction of an artery (Enos, Holmes & Beyer, 1953). A similar analysis of combat casualties from the Vietnam War described atherosclerosis in 45 percent, with 5 percent having severe coronary obstruction (McNamara, Molot, Stremple & Cutting, 1971). The Bogalusa Heart Study found autopsy evidence of coronary plaque in 8 percent of individuals as young as age 2 to 15 years (Berenson et al., 1998). In the same study, the prevalence of coronary plaque increased to 69 percent in individuals age 26 to 39 years. More recent analysis using intravascular ultrasound in recipients of heart transplants found coronary atherosclerosis in 17 percent of donor hearts age 13 to 19 years and in 37 percent of donors age 20 to 29 (Tuzcu et al., 2001).

Research to determine whether active law enforcement personnel are more prone to atherosclerosis than the general public is has been inconclusive. A study using carotid intima-media thickness to detect early atherosclerosis found police officers with comparatively increased values (Joseph, Violanti, Donahue, Andrew, Trevisan, Burchfiel, et al., 2009). Another using brachial artery reactivity as a surrogate for vascular disease found active duty officers with more endothelial dysfunction than a comparison civilian group had (Joseph et al., 2010). In contrast, a study of active New York City police using coronary artery calcium scoring via electron beam computed tomography found no evidence of premature vascular disease (Wanahita et al., 2010).

RISK FACTORS FOR CARDIOVASCULAR DISEASE

The likelihood of developing cardiovascular disease is related to a variety of risk factors. Traditional risk factors include age, male gender, a family history of cardiovascular disease, hypertension, dyslipidemia, obesity, diabetes, cigarette smoking, and a sedentary lifestyle. Similar to the general U.S. population, law enforcement personnel have a high prevalence of conventional cardiovascular risk factors (Zimmerman, 2012) (Table 3-1).

Risk factors can be further categorized into those that are nonmodifiable (age, gender, family history), medically treatable (hypertension, dyslipidemia, diabetes), and modifiable by lifestyle (obesity, smoking, lack of physical activity). Risk factors may also cluster together to compose the metabolic syndrome, which is characterized by abdominal (visceral) obesity, atherogenic dyslipidemia, elevated blood pressure, and insulin resistance (Grundy, Brewer, Cleeman, Smith & Lenfant, 2004). Metabolic syndrome may be considered present in an individual who has any three of the following five components: (1) abdominal obesity, with a waist circumference in inches of > 40 in men or > 35 in women; (2) elevated triglycerides of ≥ 150 mg/dL or drug treatment for elevated triglycerides; (3) reduced HDL-C of < 40 mg/dL in men or < 50 mg/dL in women or drug treatment for low HDL-C; (4) elevated blood pressure of ≥ 130 mmHg systolic, ≥ 85 mmHg diastolic, or drug treatment for hypertension; and (5) impaired fasting glucose of ≥ 100

mg/dL, or drug treatment for diabetes (Grundy et al., 2004).

Individuals involved in public safety are also subject to occupation-specific conditions that may increase cardiovascular risk. These include sudden physical stress, chronic psychological stress, and shift work.

TRADITIONAL RISK FACTORS IN LAW ENFORCEMENT PERSONNEL

Table 3-1. Prevalence of Cardiovascular Risk Factors in Active Law Enforcement Personnel

Risk Factor	Prevalence (%)
Hypertension	15.3–38.5
Dyslipidemia	25–76
Overweight or obese	71.6–89
Diabetes	1.5–3.3
Smoking	6–44
Metabolic syndrome	16–26.1

Source: Zimmerman, F. H. (2012).

Hypertension

Nearly one in three adult Americans has hypertension (Centers for Disease Control, 2011c). In comparison, the prevalence of hypertension in active law enforcement personnel ranges from 15 to 38.5 percent (Zimmerman, 2012). An analysis of 672 active Milwaukee police officers found that 27.4 percent had hypertension, which was significantly greater than in the general population (Ramey, Downing & Knoblauch, 2008). A study of active law enforcement personnel in nine states reported that 21.5 percent had hypertension, compared with 19.7 percent in a civilian group, a difference of borderline significance (Franke, Ramey & Shelley, 2002; Ramey, 2003). Analyses from the Buffalo Cardio-Metabolic Occupational Police Stress study have reported rates of hypertension varying from 22.5 percent to 24.4 percent (Joseph et al., 2009, 2010). Other studies of law enforcement personnel from Nebraska and California report a prevalence of hypertension of 16 percent and 17 percent, respectively (Williams, Petratis, Baechle, Ryschon, Campain & Sketch, 1987; Wood, Kreitner, Friedman, Edwards & Sova, 1982).

Dyslipidemia

Elevated levels of cholesterol and triglycerides are a major health issue in the United States. The 1999 to 2006 NHANES estimated that between 53.2 percent and 56.1 percent of Americans have dyslipidemia (Ford, Li, Pearson, Zhao & Mokdad, 2010). Studies in law enforcement personnel demonstrate a prevalence of dyslipidemia over a wide range, between 25 percent and 76 percent. The Buffalo active police study reported a prevalence of elevated cholesterol of 57.4 to 62.1 percent (Joseph et al., 2009, 2010). An analysis of 2818 active law enforcement officers in nine states found dyslipidemia in 33.2 percent, which was significantly greater than in the civilian group (Franke et al., 2002; Ramey, 2003). A California study of highway patrol officers demonstrated markedly elevated total cholesterol levels of > 300 mg/dL in 10 percent of individuals (Wood et al., 1982).

Obesity

Two thirds of the U.S. population is either overweight (BMI ≥ 25) or obese (BMI ≥ 30) (Flegal, Carroll, Ogden & Curtin, 2010). Abdominal obesity is believed to confer specific cardiovascular risk and is present in more than one half of Americans (Jacobs et al., 2010; Li, Ford, McGuire & Mokdad, 2007). The prevalence of active police officers who are either overweight or obese may be even higher than it is in the general population, reported in 71 to 89 percent of individuals (Zimmerman, 2012). Frank obesity has been reported in 25 to 39 percent of active police officers (Zimmerman, 2012; Hartley et al., 2011; Nabeel, Baker, McGrail & Flottemesch, 2007; Rajaratnam et al., 2001). After graduation from the academy, weight increases with years of service (Boyce, Jones, Lloyd & Boone, 2008; Morioka & Brown, 1970). Abdominal obesity is also common, present in 31 to 32 percent of personnel in one municipality (Hartley et al., 2011; Violanti et al., 2009).

Diabetes

More than 11 percent of the population has diabetes, estimated at 25.6 million Americans (Centers for Disease Control and Prevention, 2011a). Of these, between 90 percent and 95 percent have type 2 diabetes (Engelgau et al., 2004). Compared with civilians, active law enforcement personnel have a lower prevalence of diabetes, reported in 1.5 to 3.1 percent of officers (Zimmerman, 2012).

Cigarette Smoking

According to 2010 data, an estimated 19.3 percent of Americans are current cigarette smokers (Centers for Disease Control and Prevention, 2011b). In law enforcement personnel, tobacco use varies widely. In an analysis of police personnel in nine states, 36 percent were current smokers (Franke et al., 2002; Ramey, 2003). Tobacco use was reported in 22 percent of Omaha police (Willams et al., 1987), 32.1 percent of Milwaukee officers (Ramey et al., 2008), and in 36.9 percent from an Alabama department (Colligon, Green & Pinkard, 1995). A 1982 study of California highway patrol officers reported current smoking in 44 percent (Wood et al., 1982). More recent data suggest a lower prevalence of tobacco use, reported in 6 percent of Iowa police (Yoo, Eisenmann & Franke, 2009) and 13.6 to 19 percent of Buffalo officers (Charles et al., 2008; Hartley et al., 2011; Joseph et al., 2009, 2010).

Metabolic Syndrome

Metabolic syndrome appears to confer an increased risk of cardiovascular disease and all-cause mortality (Mottillo et al., 2010). The 2003 to 2006 NHANES found that more than one third of Americans met the criteria for metabolic syndrome (Ervin, 2009). There are limited data regarding metabolic syndrome in police officers. In the Buffalo cohort, metabolic syndrome was found in 26.1 percent (Hartley et al., 2011). Another analysis found metabolic syndrome in 23.1 percent of 421 active law enforcement personnel (Yoo et al., 2009).

Sedentary Lifestyle

A sedentary lifestyle is a risk factor for cardiovascular disease (Grundy, Barlow, Farrell, Vega & Haskell, 2012; Reddigan, Ardern, Riddell & Kuk, 2011; Shiroma & Lee, 2010). Accordingly, recommendations call for all adults to engage in at least 30 minutes of moderate physical activity on most (preferably all) days of the week (Haskell et al., 2007). Nevertheless, more than half of all American adults fail to meet these goals (King, Mainous, Carnemolla & Everett, 2009). Law enforcement personnel are no exception and may even lag behind the general population in physical fitness (Hoffman & Collingwood, 2005). An analysis of cardiovascular fitness among American workers found that two thirds of individuals employed in public safety were of low or moderate physical fitness (Lewis et al., 2011). Studies from three separate municipalities found that officers were below average in fitness compared with age-matched civilians (Klinzing, 1980; Pollock, Gettman & Meyer, 1978; Rose, Robertson & Royer, 1973). A Canadian study reported that of ninety-eight active police officers tested, only 55 percent could complete all of the job-related fitness tasks (Rhodes & Farenholtz, 1992).

Why is law enforcement physical fitness lacking? One key reason is the sedentary nature of modern policing. Whereas in prior eras police officers routinely derived considerable exercise from patrol, law enforcement today is highly technology driven and largely deskbound. Candidates who graduate from the police academy are required to meet the vigorous physical standards required of recruits. Fitness in police officers typically declines over time, however (Boyce, Hiatt & Jones, 1992; Church & Robertson, 1999; Copay & Charles, 1998; Garner, 1997a, b; Hoffman & Collingwood, 2005). A comparison of senior officers versus new recruits concluded that the routine physical demands of policing were not vigorous enough to maintain fitness (Stamford, Weltman, Moffatt & Fulco, 1978).

Conceivably, sedentary police officers could maintain adequate fitness levels with an exercise program. Unfortunately, there is ample evidence that police officers routinely fail to engage in regular exercise (Franke et al., 2002; Franke & Andeson, 1994; Ramey, 2003; Ramey et al., 2008; Richmond, Wodak, Kehoe & Heather, 1998; Wood et al., 1982). Departmental health, exercise and wellness programs are customarily lacking, making it more difficult for the officer to maintain adequate fitness (Church & Robertson, 1999; Copay & Charles, 1998; Garner, 1997a, b).

OCCUPATION-SPECIFIC RISK FACTORS

Sudden Physical Stress

In the course of a largely sedentary workday, a police officer may suddenly be called upon to perform demanding physical activity. Critical job tasks may include engaging in prolonged foot pursuit, running up inclines or stairs, heavy lifting and carrying, extraction of victims, applying restraints, or applying physical force for apprehension or in self-defense. Adding to the physical requirements of these activities is the nearly 20-pound weight of the officer's duty belt, which typically includes a weapon, handcuffs, flashlight, and baton. Body armor may add an additional 7 to 8 pounds of weight, markedly increasing metabolic workload. All of these produce a major physiological demand on the cardiovascular system.

Once on duty, the officer's cardiovascular system is fully engaged. Studies in first responders demonstrate that heart rate (HR) and blood pressure rise at the onset of hearing an alarm (Barnard & Duncan, 1975; Kuorinka & Horhonen, 1981). A British Columbia study analyzed the HR response of seventy-six randomly selected officers during a typical shift (Anderson, Litzenberger & Plecas, 2002). The researchers found that mean HR during patrol increased by twenty-three beats per minute over resting values. HR was noted to rise with anticipatory psychological stress, such as the officer placing a hand on a holstered gun or interviewing a suspect. In addition, officers who experienced an on-duty critical event maintained an elevated HR for the remainder of their shifts. If physical force was used during the shift, maximum HR increased by 88 to 112 beats per minute, with 72 to 85 percent utilization of HR reserve (HR reserve = maximum age predicted HR minus resting HR).

A sudden physical encounter may have particular cardiovascular implications for the police officer. Over a lifetime, routine physical activity lowers the risk of cardiovascular disease and improves longevity compared with sedentary individuals (Leitzmann et al., 2007; Shiroma & Lee, 2010). However, a single episode of vigorous exertion transiently increases the risk of an acute coronary event by a factor of two to ten over resting values (Dahabreh & Paulus, 2011). Episodic physical activity may also trigger lethal cardiac arrhythmias and sudden cardiac death (Dahabreh & Paulus, 2011).

A first responder such as a police officer may be at particular cardiovascular risk. Unlike an athlete who prepares in advance for the physical and emotional tasks of competition, the police officer must respond to an emergency instantly. In experimental models of sudden physical exertion, a warm-up period delayed the occurrence of coronary ischemia, ventricular arrhythmias, and transient left ventricular dysfunction (Barnard, Gardner, Diaco, MacAlpin & Kattus, 1973; Barnard, MacAlpin, Kattus & Buckberg, 1973; Foster et al., 1981; Foster, Dymond, Carpenter & Schmidt, 1982). Delaying responsiveness to warm up is not likely to be feasible for police officers responding to an emergency call.

Psychological Stress

Work-related emotional stress is a risk factor for cardiovascular disease (Möller, Theorell, de Faire, Ahlborn & Hallqvist, 2005; Tennant, 2000). Police officers are routinely exposed to acute and chronic psychological stress (Carlier, Lamberts & Gersons, 1997; Collins & Gibbs, 2003; Liberman, Fagan, Weiss & Marmar, 2002; Violanti & Aron, 1994, 1995). Law enforcement personnel must deal with a potential threat to personal safety as well as remorse after the use of deadly force (Violanti & Aron, 1994, 1995). Chronic organizational stress contributes to officer burnout, because individuals are placed in situations of high responsibility with low control (Kirkcaldy, Cooper & Ruffalo, 1993; Liberman et al., 2002; Schaufeli & Peeters, 2000; Violanti & Aron, 1994, 1995). Additional stressors include the potential for internal institutional review, as well as scrutiny and criticism by the public or media.

Psychological stress ultimately has physiological consequences. Experimental studies performed in police officers exposed to simulated stressful situations demonstrate a rise in serum catecholamines and cortisol levels (Piercecchi-Marti et al., 1999). Police officers suffering from PTSD are more likely to have metabolic syndrome (Violanti et al., 2006). Nonphysical, emotional, and environmental stressors are known to be potential triggers for acute myocardial infarction (Kloner, 2006).

Shift Work

The nature of public safety demands continuous service. Accordingly, shift work is utilized to provide for a 24-hour workday without interruption. This may have adverse effects on the sleep hygiene and overall health and wellness of police officers. A recent meta-analysis of thirty-four studies reported that shift work was associated with myocardial infarction and stroke (Vyas et al., 2012). Shift work and associated sleep disorders are associated with generalized atherosclerosis (Haupt et al., 2008) and associated cardiac risk factors, including metabolic syndrome (Karlsson, Knutsson & Lindahl, 2001; Violanti et al., 2009), obesity (Antunes, Levandovski, Dantas & Hidalgo, 2010), and hypertension (Pickering, 2006). Dietary patterns are altered by shift work and promote excessive consumption of calories from snacks (Nedeltcheva et al., 2009; Ramey et al., 2008; Ramey, Shelley, Welk & Franke, 2003; Violanti et al., 1995).

Health Promotion and Conclusions

The previous discussion illustrates that police officers are at risk for cardiovascular risk factors and their complications. Accordingly, health promotion and prevention is a public safety imperative. Treatment of modifiable risk factors is essential, utilizing both pharmacological treatment and lifestyle modification. Tobacco use should be prohibited in every department. Encouraging physical fitness is critical, because individuals who exercise regularly markedly lower their risk of an acute cardiac event that might be triggered by vigorous exertion (Mittleman & Mostofsky, 2011; Tofler & Muller, 2006).

Municipalities should partner with law enforcement agencies to promote a culture of wellness, supporting nutrition and fitness programs. Despite budgetary obstacles such an approach is fiscally sound, because officers who are more fit have less absenteeism (Rivera, 2008; Steinhardt, Greenhow & Stewart, 1991). Departments that have initiated wellness programs for their personnel have improved cardiovascular risk factors and reduced the rate of complications in their officers (Anshel & Kang, 2008; Briley, Montgomery & Blewett, 1992; Panos, 2006). Each individual officer also needs to embrace recommendations to promote personal health, regardless of departmental mandates. Ultimately, a preventative approach is the preferred method to protect and serve our vital public safety workforce.

REFERENCES

Anderson, G. S., Litzenberger, R., & Plecas, D. (2002). Physical evidence of police officer stress. *Policing, 25*, 399–420.

Anshel, M. H. & Kang, M. (2008). Effectiveness of motivational interviewing on changes in fitness, blood lipids, and exercise adherence of police officers: An outcome-based action study. *Journal of Correct Health Care, 14*, 48–62.

Antunes, L. C., Levandovski, R., Dantas, G., & Hidalgo, M. P. (2010). Obesity and shift work: Chronobiological aspects. *Nutrition Research Review, 23*, 155–168.

Barnard, R. J., & Duncan, H. W. (1975). Heart rate and ECG responses of fire fighters. *Journal of Occupational Medicine, 17*, 247–250.

Barnard, R. J., Gardner, G. W., Diaco, N. V., MacAlpin, R. X., & Kattus, A. A. (1973). Cardiovascular responses to sudden strenuous exercise – heart rate, blood pressure, and ECG. *Journal of Applied Physiology, 34*, 833–837.

Barnard, R. J., MacAlpin, R., & Kattus, A. A., & Buckberg, B. (1973). Ischemic response to sudden strenuous exercise in healthy men. *Circulation, 48*, 936–942.

Berenson, G. S., Srinivasan, S. R., Bao, W., Newman, W. P., III, Tracy, R. E., & Wattigney, W. A. (1998). Association between multiple cardiovascular risk factors and atherosclerosis in children and young adults. *New England Journal of Medicine, 338*, 1650–1656.

Boyce, R. W., Hiatt, A. R., & Jones, G. R. (1992). Physical fitness of police officers as they progress from supervised recruits to unsupervised sworn officer fitness programs. *Wellness Perspectives, 8*, 31–37.

Boyce, R. W., Jones, G. R., Lloyd, C. L., & Boone, E. L. (2008). A longitudinal observation of police: Body composition changes over 12 years with gender and race comparisons. *Journal of Exercise Physiology Online, 11*, 1–13.

Briley, M. E. Montgomery, D. H., & Blewett, J. (1992). Worksite nutrition education can lower total cholesterol levels and promote weight loss among police department employees. *Journal of the American Dietetic Association, 92*, 1382–1384.

Carlier, I. V., Lamberts, R. D., & Gersons, B. P. (1997). Risk factors for posttraumatic stress symptomology in police officers: A prospective analysis. *Journal of Nervous and Mental Disorders, 185*, 498–506.

Centers for Disease Control and Prevention. (2011a). National Diabetes Fact Sheet: National Estimates and General Information on Diabetes and Pre-diabetes in the United States. Atlanta, GA: U.S. Department of Health and Human Services, Centers for Disease Control and Prevention.

Centers for Disease Control and Prevention. (2011b). Vital signs: Current cigarette smoking among adults aged ≥ 18 years, United States, 2005–2010. *Morbidity and Mortality Weekly Report, 60*, 1207–1212.

Centers for Disease Control and Prevention. (2011c). Vital signs: Prevalence, treatment, and control of hypertension – United States, 1999–2002 and 2005–2008. *Morbidity and Mortality Weekly Report, 60*, 103–108.

Charles, L. E., Burchfiel, C. M., Violanti, J. M., Fekedulegn, D., Slaven, J. E., Browne R. W., . . . Andrew, M. E. (2008). Adiposity measures and oxidative stress among police officers. *Obesity, 16*, 2489–2497.

Church, R. L., & Robertson, N. (1999). How state police agencies are addressing the issue of wellness. *Policing, 22*, 304–312.

Colligon, J., Green, M., & Pinkard, W. (1995). Assessing officers' lifestyles: The importance of health risk appraisals. *Police Chief, 62*, 48–52.

Collins, P. A., & Gibbs, A. C. C. (2003). Stress in police officers: A study of the origins, prevalence and severity of stress-related symptoms within a county police force. *Occupational Medicine (London), 53*, 256–264.

Copay, A. G., & Charles, M. T. (1998). Police academy fitness training at the police training institute, University of Illinois. *Policing, 21*, 416–431.

Dahabreh, I. J., & Paulus, J. K. (2001). Association of episodic physical and sexual activity with triggering of acute cardiac events. *Journal of the American Medical Association, 30*, 1225–1233.

Engelgau, M. M., Geiss, L. S., Saaddine, J. B., Boyle, J. P., Benjamin, S. M., Gregg, E. W., . . . Narayan, K. M. (2004). The evolving diabetes burden in the United States. *Annals of Internal Medicine, 140*, 945–950.

Enos, W. F., Holmes, R. H., & Beyer, J. (1953). Coronary disease among United States soldiers killed in action in Korea. *Journal of the American Medical Association, 152*, 1091–1093.

Ervin, R. B. (2009). Prevalence of metabolic syndrome among adults 20 years of age and over, by sex, age, race and ethnicity, and body mass index: United States, 2003–2006. *National Health Statistics Reports, May 5* (13), 1–7.

Flegal, K. M., Carroll, M. D., Ogden, C. L., & Curtin, L. R. (2010). Prevalence and trends in obesity among US adults, 1999–2008. *Journal of the American Medical Association, 303*, 235–241.

Ford, E. S., Li, C., Pearson, W. S., Zhao, G., & Mokdad, A. H. (2010). Trends in hypercholesterolemia, treatment and control among United States adults. *International Journal of Cardiology, 140*, 226–235.

Foster, C., Anholm, J. D., Hellman, C. K., Carpenter, J., Pollock, M. L., & Schmidt, D. H. (1981). Left ventricular function during sudden strenuous exercise. *Circulation, 63*, 592–596.

Foster, C., Dymond, D. S., Carpenter, J., & Schmidt, D. H. (1982). Effect of warm-up on left ventricular response to sudden strenuous exercise. *Journal of Applied Physiology, 53*, 380–383.

Franke, W. D., & Anderson, D. F. (1994). Relationship between physical activity and risk factors for cardiovascular disease among law enforcement officers. *Journal of Occupational Medicine, 36*, 1127–1132.

Franke, W. D., Ramey, S. L., & Shelley, M. C. (2002). Relationship between cardiovascular disease morbidity, risk factors, and stress in a law enforcement cohort. *Journal of Occupational and Environmental Medicine, 44*, 1182–1189.

Garner, R. (1997a). Post-academy fitness programs: Part I. *TELEMASP Bulletin, 4*, 1–8.

Garner, R. (1997b). Post-academy fitness programs: Part II. *TELEMASP Bulletin, 4*, 9–17.

Grundy, S. M., Barlow, C. E., Farrell, S. W., Vega, G. L., & Haskell, W. L. (2012). Cardiorespiratory fitness and metabolic risk. *American Journal of Cardiology, 109*, 988–993.

Grundy, S. M., Brewer, B. Jr, Cleeman, J. I., Smith, S. C. Jr, & Lenfant, C. (2004). Definition of metabolic syndrome: Report of the National Heart, Lung, and Blood Institute/American Heart Association conference of scientific issues related to definition. *Circulation, 109*, 433–438.

Hartley, T. A., Shankar, A., Fekedulegn, D., Violanti, J. M., Andrew, M. E., Knox, S. S., & Burchfiel, C. M. (2011). Metabolic syndrome and carotid intima media thickness in urban police officers. *Journal of Occupational and Environmental Medicine, 3*, 553–561.

Haskell, W. L., Lee, I. M., Pate, R. R., Powell, K. E., Blair, S. N., Franklin, B. A., . . . Bauman, A. (2007). Physical activity and public health: Updated recommendations for adults from the American College of Sports Medicine and the American Heart Association. *Medical Science and Sports Exercise, 39*, 1423–1434.

Haupt, C. M., Alte, D., Dörr, M., Robinson, D. M., Felix, S. B., John, U., & Völzhe, H. (2008). The relation of exposure to shift work with atherosclerosis and myocardial infarction in a general population. *Atherosclerosis, 201*, 205–211.

Hoffman, R., & Collingwood, T. R. (2005). *Fit For Duty* (2nd ed.). Champaign, IL: Human Kinetics.

Houser, A. N., Jackson, B. A., Bartis, J. T., & Peterson, D. J. (2010). Emergency responder injuries and fatalities: An analysis of surveillance data. Santa Monica, CA: RAND Publishing. Available at: http://www.rand.org.

Jacobs, E. J., Newton, C. C., Wang, Y., Patel, A. V., McCullough, M. L., Campbell, P., . . . Gpstur, S. M. (2010). Waist circumference and all-cause mortality in a large US cohort. *Archives of Internal Medicine, 170*, 1293–1301.

Joseph, P. N., Violanti, J. M., Donahue, R., Andrew, M. E., Trevisan, M., Burchfiel, C. M., & Dom, J. (2009). Police work and subclinical atherosclerosis. *Journal of Occupational and Environmental Medicine, 51*, 700–707.

Joseph, P. N., Violanti, J. M., Donahue, R., Andrew, M. E., Trevisan, M., Burchfiel, C. M., & Dom, J. (2010). Endothelial function, a biomarker of subclinical cardiovascular disease, in urban police officers. *Journal of Occupational and Environmental Medicine, 52*, 1004–1008.

Karlsson, B., Knutsson, A., & Lindahl, B. (2001). Is there an association between shift work and having a metabolic syndrome? *Journal of Occupational and Environmental Medicine, 58*, 747–752.

King, D. E., Mainous, A. G., Carnemolla, M., & Everett, C. J. (2009). Adherence to healthy lifestyle habits in US adults, 1988–2006. *American Journal of Medicine, 122*, 528–534.

Kirkcaldy, B., Cooper C. L., & Ruffalo, P. (1993). Work stress and health in a sample of U.S. police. *Psychological Reports, 76*, 700–702.

Klinzing, J. E. (1980). The physical fitness status of police officers. *Journal of Sports Medicine, 20*, 291–296.

Kloner, R. A. (2006). Natural and unnatural triggers of myocardial infarction. *Problems in Cardiovascular Disease, 48*, 285–300.

Kuorinka, I., & Horhonen, O. (1981). Firefighters' reaction to alarm, an ECG and heart rate study. *Journal of Occupational Medicine, 23*, 762–766.

LaTourrette, T. (2011). Safety and health protection efforts in the police service. *Police Chief, 77*, 74–78.

Leitzmann, M. F., Park, Y., Blair, A., Ballard-Barbash, R., Mouw, T., Hollenbeck, A. R., & Schatzkin, A. (2007). Physical activity recommendations and decreased mortality. *Archives of Internal Medicine, 167*, 2453–2460.

Lewis, J. E., Clark, J. D., III, LeBlanc, W. G., Fleming, L. E., Caban-Martinez, A. J., Arheart, K. L., . . . Lee, D. J. (2011). Cardiovascular fitness levels among American workers. *Journal of Occupational and Environmental Medicine, 53*, 1115–1121.

Li, C., Ford, E. S., McGuire, B. J., & Mokdad, A. H. (2007). Increasing trends in waist circumference and abdominal obesity among U.S. adults. *Obesity, 15*, 216–224.

Liberman, A. M., Fagan, J. A., Weiss, D. S., & Marmar, C. R. (2002). Routine occupational stress and psychological distress in police. *Policing, 25*, 421–439.

Maguire, B. J., Hunting, K. L., Smith, G. S., & Levick, N. R. (2002). Occupational fatalities in emergency medical services: A hidden crisis. *Annals of Emergency Medicine, 40*, 625–632.

McNamara, J. J., Molot, M. A., Stremple, J. F., & Cutting, R. T. (1971). Coronary artery disease in combat casualties in Vietnam. *Journal of the American Medical Association, 216*, 1185–1187.

Mittleman, M. A., & Mostofsky, E. (2011). Physical, psychological and chemical triggers of acute cardiovascular events. *Circulation, 124*, 346–354.

Moller, J., Theorell, T., de Faire, U., Ahlbom, A., & Hallqvist, J. (2005). Work related stressful life events and the risk of myocardial infarction. Case-control and case-crossover analyses within the Stockholm heart epidemiology programme (SHEEP). *Journal of Epidemiology Community Health, 59*, 23–30.

Morioka, H. M., & Brown, M. L. (1970). Incidence of obesity and overweight among Honolulu police and firemen. *Public Health Reports, 5*, 433–440.

Mottillo, S., Filion, K. B., Genest, J., Joseph, L., Pilote, L., Poirier, P., . . . Eisenberg, M. J. (2010). The metabolic syndrome and cardiovascular risk: A systematic review and meta-analysis. *Journal of the American College of Cardiology, 56*, 1113–1132.

Nabeel, I., Baker, B. A., McGrail, M. P., Jr, & Flottemesch, T. J. (2007). Correlation between physical activity, fitness, and musculoskeletal injuries in police officers. *Minnesota Medicine, 90*, 40–43.

National Law Enforcement Officers Memorial Fund. (2011). Available at http://www.nleomf.org. Accessed July 26, 2011.

Nedeltcheva, A. V., Kilkus, J. M., Imperial, J., Kasza, K,. Schoeller, D. A., & Penev, P. D. (2009). Sleep curtailment is accompanied by increased intake of calories from snacks. *American Journal of Clinical Nutrition, 89*, 126–133.

Panos, M. (2006). Making a fitness program successful. *Law and Order, 58*, 62–66.

Pickering, T. G. (2006). Could hypertension be a consequence of the 24/7 society? *Journal of Clinical Hypertension, 8*, 819–822.

Piercecchi-Marti, M. D., Leonetti, G., Pelissier, A. L., Conrath, J., Cianfarani, F., & Valli, M. (1999). Evaluation of biological stress markers in police officers. *Medicine Law, 18*, 125–144.

Pollock, M. L., Gettman, L. R., & Meyer, B. U. (1978). Analysis of physical fitness and coronary heart disease risk of Dallas area police officers. *Journal of Occupational Medicine, 20*, 393–398.

Rajaratnam, S. M. W., Barger, L. K., Lockley, S. W., Shea, S. A., Wang, W., Landrigan, C. P., . . . Harvard Work Hours, Health and Safety Group. (2011). Sleep disorders, health, and safety in police officers. *Journal of the American Medical Association, 306*, 2567–2578.

Ramey, S. L. (2003). Cardiovascular disease risk factors and the perception of general health among male law enforcement officers. *American Association of Occupational Health Nurses, 51*, 219–226.

Ramey, S. L., Downing, N. R., & Knoblauch, A. (2008). Developing strategic interventions to reduce cardiovascular disease risk among law enforcement officers. *American Association of Occupational Health Nurses, 56*, 54–62.

Ramey, S. L., Shelley, M. C., Welk, G. J., & Franke, W. D. (2003). Cardiovascular disease risk reduction efforts among law enforcement officers: An application of the PRECEDE-PROCEED planning model. *Evidence Based Preventive Medicine, 1*, 43–52.

Reddigan, J. I., Ardern, C. I., Riddell, M. C., & Kuk, J. L. (2011). Relation of physical activity to cardiovascular disease mortality and the influence of cardiometabolic risk factors. *American Journal of Cardiology, 108*, 1426–1431.

Rhodes, E. C., & Farenholtz, D. W. (1992). Police officer's physical abilities test compared to measures of physical fitness. *Canadian Journal of Sport Science, 17*, 228–233.

Richmond, R. L., Wodak, A., Kehoe, L., & Heather, N. (1998). How healthy are the police? A survey of life-style factors. *Addiction, 93*, 1729–1737.

Rivera, C. (2001). Physical fitness for officers at all levels. *Law and Order, 49*, 80–84.

Roger, V. L., Go, A. S., Lloyd-Jones, D. M., Adams, R. J., Berry, J. D., Brown, T. M., . . . American Heart Association Statistics Committee and Stroke Statistics Subcommittee. (2011). Heart disease and stroke statistics – 2011 update: A report from the American Heart Association. *Circulation, 123*, e18–e209.

Rose, K. D., Robertson, R. J., & Royer, F. M. (1973). Physical fitness status in an urban police force. *Nebraska Academy of Science, 2*, 163–175.

Schaufeli, W. M., & Peeters, M. C. W. (2000). Job stress and burnout among correctional officers: A literature review. *International Journal of Stress Management, 7*, 19–48.

Shiroma, E. J., & Lee, I. M. (2010). Physical activity and cardiovascular health. *Circulation, 122*, 743–752.

Stamford, B. A., Weltman, A., Moffatt, R. J., & Fulco, C. (1978). Status of police officers with regard to selected cardio-respiratory and body compositional fitness variables. *Medical Science Sports, 10*, 294–297.

Steinhardt, M., Greenhow, L., & Stewart, J. (1991). The relationship of physical activity and cardiovascular fitness to absenteeism and medical care claims among law enforcement officers. *American Journal of Health Promotion, 5*, 455–460.

Tennant, C. (2000). Work stress and coronary heart disease. *Journal of Cardiovascular Risk, 7*, 273–276.

Tiesman, H. M., Hendricks, S. A., Bell, J. L., & Amandus, H. A. (2010). Eleven years of occupational mortality in law enforcement: The census of fatal occupational injuries, 1992–2002. *American Journal of Industrial Medicine, 53*, 940–949.

Tofler, G. H., & Muller, J. E. (2006). Triggering of acute cardiovascular disease and preventive strategies. *Circulation, 114*, 1863–1872.

Tuzcu, E. M., Kapadia, S. R., Tutar, E., Ziada, K. M., Hobbs, R. I., McCarthy, P. M., . . . Nissen, S. E. (2001). High prevalence of coronary atherosclerosis in asymptomatic teenagers and young adults: Evidence from intravascular ultrasound. *Circulation, 103*, 2705–2710.

U.S. Bureau of Labor Statistics. (2011). Available at: http://www.bls.gov. Accessed October 10, 2011.

Violanti, J. M., & Aron, F. (1994). Ranking police stressors. *Psychological Reports, 75*, 824–826.

Violanti, J. M., & Aron, F. (1995). Police stressors: Variations in perception among police personnel. *Journal of Criminal Justice, 23*, 287–294.

Violanti, J. M., Burchfiel, C. M., Hartley, T. A., Mnatsakanova, A., Fekedulegn, D., Andrew, M. E., & Villa, B. J. (2009). Atypical work hours and metabolic syndrome among police officers. *Archives of Environmental and Occupational Health, 64*, 194–201.

Violanti, J. M., Fekedulegn, D., Hartley, T. A., Andrew, M. E., Charles, L. E., Mnatsakanova, A., & Burchfiel, C. M. (2006). Police trauma and cardiovascular disease: Association between PTSD symptoms and metabolic syndrome. *International Journal of Emergency Mental Health, 8*, 227–237.

Vyas, M. V., Garg, A. X., Iansavichus, A. V., Costella, J., Donner, A., Laugsand, L. E., . . . Hackam, D. G. (2012). Shift work and vascular events: Systemic review and meta-analysis. *British Medical Journal, 345*, e4800.

Wanahita, N., See, J. L., Giedd, K. N., Friedmann, P., Somekh, N. N., & Bergmann, S. R. (2010). No evidence of increased prevalence of premature coronary artery disease in New York City police officers as predicted by coronary artery calcium scoring. *Journal of Occupational Environmental Medicine, 52*, 661–665.

Williams, M. A., Petratis, M. M., Baechle, T. R., Ryschon, K. L., Campain, J. J., & Sketch, M. H. (1987). Frequency of physical activity, exercise capacity, and atherosclerotic heart disease risk factors in male police officers. *Journal of Occupational Medicine, 29*, 596–600.

Wood, S. D., Kreitner, R., Friedman, G. M., Edwards, M., & Sova, M. A. (1982). Cost-effective wellness screening: A case study of 4,524 law enforcement officers. *Journal of Police Science and Administration, 10*, 273–278.

Yoo, H. L., Eisenmann, J. C., & Franke, W. D. (2009). Independent and combined influence of physical activity and perceived stress on the metabolic syndrome in male law enforcement officers. *Journal of Occupational and Environmental Medicine, 51*, 46–53.

Zimmerman, F. H. (2012). Cardiovascular disease and risk factors in law enforcement personnel: A comprehensive review. *Cardiology Review, 20*, 159–166.

Chapter 4

RISK OF CANCER INCIDENCE AND CANCER MORTALITY AMONG POLICE OFFICERS

Michael Wirth, John E. Vena, and James Burch

Police officers serve a vital role in maintaining safety and order in the United States and throughout the world. Law enforcement officers, however, suffer disproportionately from numerous health problems, including chronic heart disease, diabetes, metabolic disorders, psychological stress, depression, suicide, sleep disorders, and cancer (Franke, Cox, Schultz & Anderson, 1997; Violanti, Vena & Petralia, 1998). Although a majority of this workforce is exposed to various known or suspected carcinogens, there have been only a limited number of studies to assess cancer risks and document the spectrum and duration of exposure to risk factors for cancer in this occupation. The number, variety, and depth of epidemiological investigations have been limited compared to the large number of cancer studies that have been performed among other occupations with similar occupational characteristics, stressors, and demands, such as doctors, nurses, firefighters, and military personnel.

Police officers face stressful and sometimes life-threatening work and often work irregular hours, including nights or rotating shifts, which have been associated with disruption of circadian rhythms, as well as immune and endocrine dysregulation (Gordon, Cleary, Parker & Czeisler, 1986; Violanti et al., 2007; Wirth et al., 2011). Circadian rhythms help maintain homeostasis in a variety of physiological processes, such as the immune, endocrine, cardiovascular, and autonomic nervous systems, and when disrupted may increase susceptibility to disease, including cancer. In 2007, the International Agency for Research on Cancer (IARC) concluded that shift work is a (Group 2A) probable human carcinogen (IARC, 2010). Circadian desynchronization may alter the expression of clock genes that control cellular processes considered hallmarks of carcinogenesis, including the DNA damage response, cell proliferation, and apoptosis in most tissues (Burch, Wirth & Yang, 2013; Greene, 2012).

Besides disruption of circadian rhythms, police officers experience a greater prevalence or exposure to other suspected or known cancer risk factors. Among police officers, compared to general U.S. or other populations, that have been associated with increased cancer risk, there is an elevated prevalence of several behavioral or lifestyle factors including alcohol use (Violanti et al., 2009), obesity (Ramey, Downing & Franke, 2009), and reductions in physical activity (Richmond, Wodak, Kehoe & Heather, 1998) or sleep quality (Charles et al., 2007).

Police officers are also exposed to known or suspected carcinogens, including traffic-related airborne particulate matter (Riediker et al., 2004) or other air pollutants (Hu et al., 2007), radar and other forms of nonionizing radiation (Breckenkamp, Berg & Blettner, 2003; van Netten, Brands, Hoption Cann, Spinelli & Sheps, 2003), and hazardous or toxic materials at crime scenes, for example agents associated with methamphetamine manufacture (Mitka, 2005; Thrasher, Von Derau & Burgess, 2009). Figure 4-1 displays the relationship between various police-related exposures and their influence on bodily and cellular processes that can potentially lead to cancer development or progression through chronic inflammation, changes in cell cycle control, DNA damage, or immune and hormone dysregulation, among others (Arendt, 2005; Carere et al., 2002; Chida, Hamer, Wardle, & Steptoe, 2008; Friedenreich & Orenstein, 2002; Hastings, O'Neill, & Maywood, 2007; Mukamal & Rimm, 2008; Ozlu & Bulbul, 2005; Roberts, Dive, & Renehan, 2010; Seitz & Poschl, 1997; Youngstedt & Kripke, 2004).

According to the Federal Bureau of Investigation (FBI), there were 1,017,954 law enforcement employees, including 699,850 police officers in the United States as of 2007 (FBI, 2008). Cancer is the second leading cause of death in the United States, and because police officers are exposed to numerous carcinogens, there is potential for increased cancer burden in this occupation. This chapter provides a comprehensive summary of studies focusing on cancer risk and mortality among police officers.

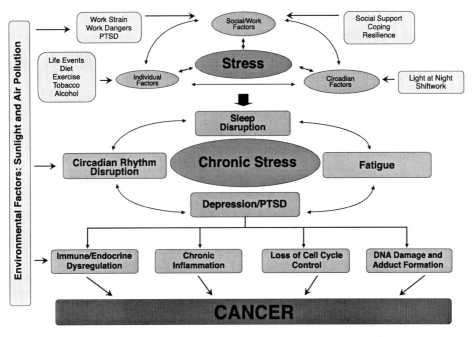

Figure 4-1. Conceptual model of potential police exposures leading to chronic stress and then changes in cellular and bodily processes which promote cancer development or progression.

MORTALITY STUDIES

Vena, Violanti, Marshall, and Fiedler (1986) examined mortality among 2,376 white male police officers in a study of municipal workers from Buffalo, New York, on active duty between 1950 and 1979 with a minimum work duration of 5 years. Overall, standardized mortality ratios (SMRs) among police officers were comparable to the U.S. white male population (SMR = 1.06; 95% CI = 0.98–1.14), indicating the lack of a strong healthy worker effect that was suspected, given the highly selective nature of police employment. Mortality from all malignant neoplasms (SMR = 1.27; 95% CI = 1.08–1.49), cancers of the digestive organs and peritoneum (SMR = 1.57; 95% CI = 1.18–2.04), esophagus (SMR = 2.86; 95% CI = 1.23–5.64), and colon (SMR = 1.80; 95% CI = 1.10–2.79) were statistically significantly elevated. Vena and associates also examined the impact of duration of employment as a police officer on cancer mortality. After 10 to 19 years of employment, statistically significant increases in SMRs for digestive (10–19 years: SMR =

2.86, p < 0.01) and lymphatic or hematopoietic tissues (SMR = 4.0, p < 0.01) were observed. Elevated SMRs for digestive (SMR = 1.96, p < 0.01) and lymphatic or hematopoietic tissues (SMR = 2.86, p < 0.01) were also observed with 40 or more years of police work. In addition, those working more than 40 years also had a four-fold increase in bladder cancer mortality (SMR = 3.75, p < 0.05), and brain cancer mortality was elevated among officers employed 20 to 29 years (SMR = 3.64, p < 0.05) (Vena et al., 1986). This retrospective cohort mortality study was one of the only studies to look at cancer mortality by years worked and latency. Internal cohort analyses were also conducted to account for the healthy worker effect by comparing mortality rates among police officers to all other municipal workers, most of whom were firefighters. Compared to firefighters, police officers had elevated rate ratios for all malignant neoplasms; all digestive neoplasms, including the esophagus and colon; and cancer of the respiratory system (Vena et al., 1986). However, a study by Feuer and Rosenman (1986) found no differences in mortality for cancers of the colon or respiratory system when firefighters were compared to police officers.

In 1998, Violanti, Vena, and Petralia (1998) updated the Buffalo Police cohort and extended follow-up through December 31, 1990. The cancer mortality patterns remained, with elevated mortality rates from all malignant neoplasms (SMR = 1.25; 95% CI = 1.09–1.41), and for cancers of the digestive organs and peritoneum (SMR = 1.51; 95% CI = 1.20–1.87), esophagus (SMR = 2.13; 95% CI = 1.01–3.91), and colon (SMR = 1.87; 95% CI = 1.29–2.59). Mortality rates for kidney cancer (SMR = 2.08; 95% CI = 1.00–3.82) and Hodgkin's disease (SMR = 3.13; 95% CI = 1.01–7.29) also were elevated. This study also conducted analyses based on years of police service. All malignant neoplasms and digestive and colon cancer were elevated after 1 to 9 years of employment. At 10 to 19 years of employment, all malignant neoplasms, cancers of the bladder and lymphatic and hematopoietic tissues, as well as leukemia were statistically significantly elevated. Increased SMRs for colon cancer were also observed with 30 or more years of police work (Violanti et al., 1998).

This dynamic retrospective cohort of the Buffalo Police Department was recently updated from a previous 1950 to 1990 cohort to include all new hires who worked a minimum of 5 years with follow-up to December 31, 2005. The time period during which black and female officers were selected for participation (i.e., for having worked ≥ 5 years) was January 1, 1980 through December 31, 2005. Officers who did not have either birth data or hire date (n = 44), and officers who worked < 5 years (n = 33) were excluded from this analysis. After all exclusions, the study sample consisted of 2,761 white male officers, 286 black officers, and 259 female officers. Analyses were conducted separately for each group. Mortality from all causes of death combined for white male police officers was higher than expected (SMR = 1.20; 95% CI = 1.14–1.26). Increased mortality was also observed for all malignant neoplasms combined (SMR = 1.32; 1.19–1.46), all benign neoplasms combined (SMR = 2.48; 1.17–4.89), and all diseases of the circulatory system combined (SMR = 1.11; 1.02–1.19). The elevated mortality for all malignant neoplasms was primarily due to excess cancers of the esophagus (SMR = 1.93; 1.08–3.18), colon (SMR = 1.83; 1.35–2.42), respiratory system (SMR = 1.24; 1.03–1.48), as well as Hodgkin's disease (SMR = 3.38; 1.23–7.36) and leukemia (SMR = 1.77; 1.08–2.73). Differences in mortality risk were noted for calendar year, years of employment, latency, and other related factors. Black police officers had significantly lower mortality than expected from all causes (SMR = 0.42; 0.17–0.88). While female officers had significantly elevated all-cause mortality (SMR = 2.17; 1.12–3.79). The cause-specific mortality experience of black and female officers was consistent with population rates (Vena et al., 2013).

A study by Forastiere and associates examined a total of 3,868 urban police officers in Rome who were investigated using a retrospective cohort design and analyzed using both cohort mortality and case-control analyses. Overall, officers had increased mortality rates from cancers of the colon, bladder, and kidneys, as well as non-Hodgkin's lymphoma. However, the mortality risk estimates were imprecise and not statistically significant (Forastiere et al., 1994). Of note was a statistically significant increase in male breast cancer mortality (SMR = 14.36; 95% CI = 1.73–51.90). Subjects with 20 to 29 years of employment duration had increased mortality risks from colon (SMR = 2.32; 95% CI = 1.32–3.76), breast (SMR = 21.82; 95% CI = 2.64–78.82), and endocrine gland cancers (SMR = 5.88; 95% CI = 1.21–17.19). There were no increases in any cancer mortality after 0 to 9, 10 to 19, or 30+ years of police work. Results from a case-control analysis by job category indicated bladder cancer mortality was elevated among car drivers (odds ratio [OR] = 4.17; 95% CI = 1.14–15.24), especially those with 10 or more years of experience (OR = 12.2; 95% CI = 2.93–51.32). Increased non-Hodgkin's lymphoma mortality was also observed among motor-cyclist officers with at least 10 years of experience, although the esti-mate was imprecise (OR = 24.0; 95% CI = 1.06–544) (Forastiere et al., 1994).

Feuer and Rosenman (1986) performed a proportional mortality study of New Jersey police officers and firefighters between 1974 and 1980 with at least 10 years of employment. A total of 567 officers were included, and all analyses were restricted to the white male population. An elevated proportional mortality ratio (PMR) was identified for di-gestive cancers (PMR = 1.58, p < 0.05) and for melanoma (PMR = 2.10, p < 0.05). The PMR for digestive cancer increased with increas-ing duration of employment, although the PMRs did not achieve sta-tistical significance.

Mortality among firefighters employed for at least 1 year in Seattle and Tacoma, Washington, and Portland, Oregon, was examined be-tween 1944 and 1979 with follow-up until 1989 in a retrospective co-hort study that examined whether smoke exposure among firefighters increased cancer risk (Demers, Heyer, & Rosenstock, 1992). In addition to using police as a comparison population for their study, however, Demers and colleagues also examined the mortality experience in this population of police officers compared to national rates. Inclusion cri-teria were not specified and little information was provided concerning the dynamics or characteristics of the 3,676-officer study population that yielded 714 deaths. Police officers had an SMR for all cancers com-bined of 0.95 (95% CI = 0.81–1.11), and a decreased colon cancer mor-tality (SMR = 0.50; 95% CI = 0.22–0.99) compared to white U.S. males. There were no statistically significant increases in mortality for other cancer types, although the point estimates for lymphosarcoma and leukemia were elevated. The primary focus of this study was lung cancer mortality. The SMR for lung cancer among police was 0.92 (95% CI = 0.69–1.19) (Demers et al., 1992).

Similarly, Rosenstock, Demers, Heyer, and Barnhart focused on res-piratory mortality in a subset of this population, with inclusion limited to those employed at least one day after January 1, 1980, and actively employed for at least one day after January 1, 1945, with follow-up through 1984. Due to the limited inclusion criteria, however, the police comparison cohort was limited to Portland and Tacoma because "Seat-tle records could not provide complete assessment of the police co-hort." There was a total of 2,074 police officers and 389 observed deaths. There was a nonsignificant elevation in mortality rates for malignant neoplasms of the trachea, bronchus, or lung among police officers compared to the U.S. population (SMR = 1.09; 95% CI = 0.75–1.26) (Rosenstock et al., 1990). No other cancer risks were assessed.

A 22-year span of mortality data was examined among officers in the Helsinki police force, which included 970 men 34 to 64 years old from 1971 to 1994 (Pyorala, Miettinen, Laakso & Pyorala, 2000). Previously, the Helsinki Policemen Study found associations between elevated insulin and either cardiovascular disease mortality or stroke (Pyorala, 1979; Pyorala et al., 1998). The authors then examined the relationship between plasma insulin levels and other categories of mortality, including cancer. Adjusted hazard ratios for cancer mortality were calculated for police officers with low (hazard ratios = 1.26; 95% CI = 0.65–2.44) or high insulin levels (hazard ratios = 1.32; 95% CI = 0.74–2.36) compared to combined quintiles 2 to 4. A risk comparison to the general population was not provided (Pyorala et al., 2000).

INCIDENCE AND CASE-CONTROL STUDIES

Gu and associates (2011) examined cancer incidence among 2,234 white male police officers with at least 5 years of police service in Buffalo, New York, between 1950 and 2005. The period of this retrospective investigation was January 1, 1976, until December 31, 2006. This cohort is the retrospective counterpart to the prospective BCOPS cohort that provides a prospective framework for examining biological processes through which stressors associated with police work may mediate adverse health outcomes. The protocol combines the characterization of stress biomarkers, subclinical CVD measures, psychosocial factors, and shift work to examine their potential associations with psychological disturbances and chronic diseases afflicting police officers (Violanti et al., 2006; Violanti et al., 2009). A total of 406 incident cancers were observed, similar to the U.S. white male population (standardized incidence ratio [SIR] = 0.94, 95% CI = 0.85–1.03). However, an elevated SIR for Hodgkin's lymphoma was observed (SIR = 3.34, 95% CI = 1.22–7.26). There also were statistically significant decreases in skin (SIR = 0.54, 95% CI = 0.26–0.98) and bladder cancer risk (SIR = 0.64, 95% CI = 0.39–0.99). When duration of employment was evaluated at 0 to 19 or 20 to 29 years, no statistically significant risks were observed for any cancers types. With 30 or more years of employment, however, officers had an increased risk of brain cancer (SIR = 2.92, 95% CI = 1.07–6.36) (Gu et al., 2011).

Using a retrospective cohort design, Finkelstein (1998) examined cancer risk among 22,197 Ontario police officers or retirees from 1964 to 1995. Data were obtained from department rosters with cancer incidence data from the Ontario Cancer Registry and mortality data from the Ontario Mortality Database (Finkelstein, 1998). A lower incidence of all cancers combined (SIR = 0.90; 90% CI = 0.83–0.98), lung cancer (SIR = 0.66; 90% CI = 0.52–0.82), or melanoma (SIR = 1.45; 90% CI = 1.10–1.88) was observed among male officers from the time of cohort entry to the end of 1995. In this study, there were a number of melanomas as well as testicular tumors diagnosed between the actual hire date and the date at which complete cohort identification was possible in their police department, possibly resulting in an underestimation of cases. When rates beginning in 1964 or the date of hire were examined to the end of 1995 among all police officers, the incidence of testicular cancer (SIR = 1.33; 90% CI = 1.0–1.74) or melanoma (SIR = 1.37; 90% CI = 1.08–1.72) was elevated, whereas the rate for all solid tumors was reduced (SIR = 0.83; 90% CI = 0.77–0.90) (Finkelstein, 1998). One limitation was that this study had relatively short latencies between cohort entry and diagnosis. An entry criterion was enrollment on the police roster in 1970; Toronto (n = 5,416) and Provincial police (n = 5,366), however, were not added until 1981 and 1987, respectively. Follow-up was to the end of 1995, thus a majority of the cohort had less than a 15-year follow-up.

Leukemia incidence was examined among various occupational groups in the Portland-Vancouver metropolitan area from 1963 through 1977. Usual occupation of the case was used to calculate SIRs for each occupational group based on the 1970 census by occupation. There was a statistically significant increase in total leukemia incidence (SIR = 2.6; p < 0.05) among police officers compared to the general population. This result was primarily driven by an elevated SIR for nonlymphatic leukemia (SIR = 3.4, p < 0.05). Although limited by time period (case ascertainment included the years 1963–1977), this incidence study contributes to the body of evidence that police officers may be at increased risk of leukemia (Morton & Marjanovic, 1984).

To examine prostate cancer risks, a population-based prospective cohort study of men employed in various occupations was performed in The Netherlands beginning in 1986 with follow-up until 1993 (Zeegers, Friesema, Goldbohm & van den Brandt, 2004). This study employed a case-cohort approach, collecting data on 830 cases and 1,525 subcohort members, who were grouped based on their occupation. Incident prostate cancers were ascertained through a cancer registry. Police work defined as the last occupation held at the time of the baseline questionnaire in September 1989, was associated with a substantial increase in prostate cancer risk (relative risk [RR] = 4.00; 95% CI = 1.59–10.02). In addition, police work for most of the career also was associated with an increased prostate cancer risk (RR = 3.91; 95% CI = 1.53–9.99). Ever having worked as a police officer was associated with a 67 percent increase in prostate cancer risk for each decade of work (Zeegers et al., 2004).

To examine the hypothesis that radar devices contribute to increases in testicular cancer, a retrospective cohort of 340 officers was examined in response to reports of a cancer cluster in two police departments in the state of Washington (Davis & Mostofi, 1993). There was a total of six cases of testicular cancer, which resulted in a SMR of 6.9 (p < 0.01). All those diagnosed with testicular cancer had been working as police officers for most of their occupational life and the average work duration as a police officer prior to diagnosis was 14.7 years (Davis & Mostofi, 1993).

Another cancer cluster in a British Columbia police detachment examined 20 current and 154 previous employees associated with the worksite since occupancy began in 1963 (van Netten et al., 2003). A total of 16 cancer cases were reported. The age at diagnosis was between 22 and 44 years. The total number of male cancer cases was 2.3 times higher than expected in the general British Columbia population (p < 0.05, based on a one-sided significance test). Specifically, excess cases of testicular, cervical, and colon cancer were identified, along with melanoma, leukemia, and lymphoma, although not all achieved statistical significance (van Netten et al., 2003)

The role of occupation as a risk factor for cancer among 58,134 male patients over 25 years of age was evaluated between 1980 and 1993 in the Swiss Cancer Registries of Basel, Geneva, St. Gall, Vaud, and Zurich (Bouchardy et al., 2002). A case-referent method was applied where cancers of interest were evaluated and all other cancer cases served as referents. Police officers were more likely to have cancer of the lung (small cell, OR = 1.5; 95% CI = 1.0–2.2), prostate (OR = 1.3; 95% CI = 1.0–1.5), or bladder (OR = 1.4; 95% CI = 1.0–1.9). Increased ORs were also noted among police officers for cancers of the colon, rectum, liver, lung, kidney, and thyroid gland, as well as Hodgkin's disease, acute leukemia, and melanoma, although none of these achieved statistical significance (Bouchardy et al., 2002). Use of cancer cases as controls could lead to an underestimation of risk if there was an unknown association between police work with one or more of the referent cancers.

Several other studies of cancer among Swedish police officers have been reported. For example, acoustic neuromas were examined in a case-control study that included 793 cases from the entire Swedish population from 1987 to 1999. Compared to all men, the OR for police officers was greater after 10 years of work experience prior to their diagnosis (OR = 2.5; 95% CI = 1.1–5.6). A similar effect was observed for those with more than 10 years of experience, but it was not statistically significant (OR = 1.9; 95% CI = 0.8–4.5) (Prochazka et al., 2010). A Swedish cohort study of occupation and thyroid cancer risk followed 2,845,992 persons over 19 years. Among police offices, there was an approximate doubling of thyroid cancer risk after adjustment for age, time period, and geographic area (RR = 2.12; 95% CI = 1.23–3.66) (Lope et al., 2005). In another Swedish cohort of 1,779,646 men employed at the time of the 1970 census, Pollán, Gustavsson, and Floderus (2001) found an elevated risk of male breast cancer among 12,107 male police officers compared to the entire cohort (RR = 2.90; 95% CI = 1.08–7.80). Only male breast cancers were examined, however, and there were only 4 cases reported among police officers, which limits the interpretation (Pollán et al., 2001).

Using populations from Chicago, Illinois, and Detroit, Michigan, Karami and associates (2012) examined the risk of renal cell carcinomas (RCC) among various occupations. This study included both whites and blacks, as well as both males and females. Only forty-two police officers (twenty-six diagnosed with RCC, sixteen controls) were included, however. After adjustment for sex, age, race, city location, history of hypertension, smoking status, BMI, and family history of cancer, police officers had a statistically significant increase in RCC risk (OR = 2.2, 95% CI = 1.0–4.8). This relationship was primarily observed among officers with 5 or more years of police experience (OR

= 2.4, 95% CI = 1.0–5.7) (Karami et al., 2012).

A case-control study of lung cancer examined the role of occupation among 550 black men and women and 386 controls matched by gender and age to within 5 years. Although no statistically significant associations with lung cancer were observed for any specific job category, the OR for police officers was elevated (OR = 2.0; 95% CI = 0.50–7.9). This was one of the few studies focusing on minority populations (Muscat, Stellman, Richie & Wynder, 1998).

Although they did not include a measure of cancer risk or mortality, Bagai and colleagues (2007) examined colon cancer risk factors among police officers. This was a cross-sectional study of 3,756 members of the Toronto Police Service. Participants were given a colorectal cancer risk assessment questionnaire containing questions about age; personal history of colorectal polyps or cancer; a family history of colorectal polyps or cancer; a personal history of inflammatory bowel disease; and for women a personal history of breast, ovarian, or uterine cancer. Results of the study showed that nearly one third of this population was at average or above-average risk for colorectal cancer (Bagai et al., 2007).

CONCLUSION

As mentioned in this chapter and described elsewhere in this book, police work is associated with exposure to a variety of carcinogenic agents, lifestyles, or risk factors, such as shift work, poor diets or a lack of physical activity leading to obesity, alcohol consumption, and air pollution exposure, among others (Berg, Hem, Lau, Haseth & Ekeberg, 2005; Burch, Yost, Johnson & Allen, 2005; Charles et al., 2007; Juster, McEwen & Lupien, 2010; Pilidis, Karakitsios, Kassomenos, Kazos & Stalikas, 2009; Ramey, Franke & Shelley, 2004; Richmond et al., 1998; Riediker et al., 2004; Violanti et al., 2009; Zukauskas, Ruksenas, Burba, Grigaliuniene & Mitchell, 2009). It is important to understand the complex web of potentially carcinogenic exposures among police officers and how these exposures modify processes in the human body to increase cancer susceptibility.

Among the epidemiological investigations that examined relationships between police work and cancer, statistically significant increases in mortality due to all cancer; digestive organ malignancies; and cancer of the esophagus, colon, kidney, bladder, brain, lymphatic and hematopoietic tissues, endocrine glands, and breasts; as well as testicular cancer, melanoma, and Hodgkin's disease have been reported (Davis & Mostofi, 1993; Feuer & Rosenman, 1986; Forastiere et al., 1994; Vena et al., 1986; Violanti et al., 1998). Evidence for dose-response with increasing years of police work was noted in a few studies (Forastiere et al., 1994; Vena et al., 1986). When cancer incidence was examined, some consistency with cancer mortality studies was observed. Statistically significant increases in cancer incidence have been reported for all cancer combined, and for cancers of the prostate, bladder, and thyroid, as well as testicular cancer, Hodgkin's lymphoma, and melanoma (Bouchardy et al., 2002; Finkelstein, 1998; Gu et al., 2011; van Netten et al., 2003; Zeegers et al., 2004). Studies of cancer among police have been subject to the several limitations, however, including the healthy worker effect or other forms of selection bias, a lack of characterization of confounding, and imprecise assessment of exposure to carcinogens and other occupational risk factors for police. All long-term studies used occupation as police officer as the exposure measure and only a few assessed length of employment. There are only two well-conducted retrospective cohort studies that quantified risk or incidence of cancer among police officers. None of the previous studies used direct measures of shift work, stress, and individual lifestyle and susceptibility factors. No long-term prospective studies with direct exposure measures have been conducted. Little is known of how multiple carcinogenic exposures combine or interact to elicit changes in cancer incidence or mortality. Despite these limitations, an ample literature describes biologically plausible pathways that can predispose or potentiate cancer risks among police officers. Thus, there is a clear need to more comprehensively evaluate these effects in this understudied occupation.

The law enforcement workplace is dynamic, and effective programs for disease or injury prevention require ongoing monitoring of hazards and health in order to ensure the adequacy of disease prevention strategies. Early diagnosis and prompt treatment should be a priority, especially for colon cancer. A review of forty-five worksite health promotion trials found an overall modest but positive effect of various interventions and health promotion programs, including ones focusing on cancer-related risk factors such as smoking, alcohol, physical activity, diet/obesity, and solar radiation (Janer, Sala, & Kogevinas, 2002). Other studies have described successful job-stress interventions (Lamontagne, Keegel, Louie, Ostry & Landsbergis, 2007). To optimize prevention efforts, potential carcinogenicity among police can be addressed more effectively by characterizing and controlling exposure or practices that elicit increased risks and by monitoring biological perturbations resulting from those activities. Future primary and secondary prevention interventions should focus on the most common cancers or cancer sites most strongly attributable to police work in order to prevent or ameliorate their impact.

REFERENCES

Arendt, J. (2005). Melatonin: Characteristics, concerns, and prospects. *Journal of Biological Rhythms, 20*, 291–303.

Bagai, A., Parsons, K., Malone, B., Fantino, J., Paszat, L., & Rabeneck, L. (2007). Workplace colorectal cancer-screening awareness programs: An adjunct to primary care practice? *Journal of Community Health, 32*, 157–167.

Berg, A. M., Hem, E., Lau, B., Haseth, K., & Ekeberg, O. (2005). Stress in the Norwegian police service. *Occupational Medicine, 55*, 113–120.

Bouchardy, C., Schüler, G., Minder, C., Hotz, P., Bousquet, A., Levi, F., . . . Raymond, L. (2002). Cancer risk by occupation and socioeconomic group among men – a study by the Association of Swiss Cancer Registries. *Scandinavian Journal of Work, Environment and Health, 28* Suppl 1, 1–88.

Breckenkamp, J., Berg, G., & Blettner, M. (2003). Biological effects on human health due to radiofrequency/microwave exposure: A synopsis of cohort studies. *Radiation and Environmental Biophysics, 42*, 141–154.

Burch, J. B., Wirth, M., & Yang, X. (2013). Disruption of circadian rhythms and sleep: Role in carcinogenesis. In C. A. Kushida (Ed.), *Encyclopedia of Sleep*. Oxford, UK: Elsevier.

Burch, J. B., Yost, M. G., Johnson, W., & Allen, E. (2005). Melatonin, sleep, and shift work adaptation. *Journal of Occupational and Environmental Medicine, 47*, 893–901.

Carere, A., Andreoli, C., Galati, R., Leopardi, P., Marcon, F., Rosati, M. V., . . . Crebelli, R. (2002). Biomonitoring of exposure to urban air pollutants: Analysis of sister chromatid exchanges and DNA lesions in peripheral lymphocytes of traffic policemen. *Mutation Research, 518*, 215–224.

Charles, L. E., Burchfiel, C. M., Fekedulegn, D., Vila, B., Hartley, T. A., Slaven, J., . . . Violanti, J. M. (2007). Shift work and sleep: The Buffalo Police health study. *Policing: An International Journal of Police Strategies and Management, 30*, 215–227.

Chida, Y., Hamer, M., Wardle, J., & Steptoe, A. (2008). Do stress-related psychosocial factors contribute to cancer incidence and survival? *Nature Clinical Practice Oncology, 5*, 466–475.

Davis, R. L., & Mostofi, F. K. (1993). Cluster of testicular cancer in police officers exposed to hand-held radar. *American Journal of Industrial Medicine, 24*, 231–233.

Demers, P. A., Heyer, N. J., & Rosenstock, L. (1992). Mortality among firefighters from three northwestern United States cities. *British Journal of Industrial Medicine, 49*, 664–670.

FBI. (2008). *Crime in the United States 2007.* Washington, DC: Federal Bureau of Investigation.

Feuer, E., & Rosenman, K. (1986). Mortality in police and firefighters in New Jersey. *American Journal of Industrial Medicine, 9*, 517–527.

Finkelstein, M. M. (1998). Cancer incidence among Ontario police officers. *American Journal of Industrial Medicine, 34*, 157–162.

Forastiere, F., Perucci, C. A., Di Pietro, A., Miceli, M., Rapiti, E., Bargagli, A., & Borgia, P. (1994). Mortality among urban policemen in Rome. *American Journal of Industrial Medicine, 26*, 785–798.

Franke, W. D., Cox, D. F., Schultz, D. P., & Anderson, D. F. (1997). Coronary heart disease risk factors in employees of Iowa's Department of Public Safety compared to a cohort of the general population. *American Journal of Industrial Medicine, 31*, 733–737.

Friedenreich, C. M., & Orenstein, M. R. (2002). Physical activity and cancer prevention: Etiologic evidence and biological mechanisms. *Journal of Nutrition, 132*(Suppl.), 3456S–3464S.

Gordon, N. P., Cleary, P. D., Parker, C. E., & Czeisler, C. A. (1986). The prevalence and health impact of shiftwork. *American Journal of Public Health, 76*, 1225–1228.

Greene, M. W. (2012). Circadian rhythms and tumor growth. *Cancer Letters, 318*, 115–123.

Gu, J. K., Charles, L. E., Burchfiel, C. M., Andrew, M. E., & Violanti, J. M. (2011). Cancer incidence among police officers in a U.S. northeast region: 1976–2006. *International Journal of Emergency Mental Health, 13*, 279–289.

Hastings, M., O'Neill, J. S., & Maywood, E. S. (2007). Circadian clocks: Regulators of endocrine and metabolic rhythms. *Journal of Endocrinology, 195*, 187–198.

Hu, Y., Bai, Z., Zhang, L., Wang, X., Yu, Q., & Zhu, T. (2007). Health risk assessment for traffic policemen exposed to polycyclic aromatic hydrocarbons (PAHs) in Tianjin, China. *Science of the Total Environment, 382*, 240–250.

IARC. (2010). Painting, firefighting, and shiftwork. *IARC Monographs on the Evaluation of Carcinogenic Risks to Humans, 98*, 806.

Janer, G., Sala, M., & Kogevinas, M. (2002). Health promotion trials at worksites and risk factors for cancer. *Scandinavian Journal of Work, Environment and Health, 28*, 141–157.

Juster, R. P., McEwen, B. S., & Lupien, S. J. (2010). Allostatic load biomarkers of chronic stress and impact on health and cognition. *Neuroscience and Biobehavioral Reviews, 35*, 2–16.

Karami, S., Colt, J. S., Schwartz, K., Davis, F. G., Ruterbusch, J. J., Munuo, S. S., . . . Purdre, M. P. (2012). A case-control study of occupation/industry and renal cell carcinoma risk. *BMC Cancer, 12*, 344.

Lamontagne, A. D., Keegel, T., Louie, A. M., Ostry, A., & Landsbergis, P. A. (2007). A systematic review of the job-stress intervention evaluation literature, 1990–2005. *International Journal of Occupational and Environmental Health, 13*, 268–280.

Lope, V., Pollán, M., Gustavsson, P., Plato, N., Pérez-Gómez, B., Aragones, N. . . . Abente, G. (2005). Occupation and thyroid cancer risk in Sweden. *Journal of Occupational and Environmental Medicine, 47*, 948–957.

Mitka, M. (2005). Meth lab fires put heat on burn centers. *Journal of American Medical Association, 294*, 2009–2010.

Morton, W., & Marjanovic, D. (1984). Leukemia incidence by occupation in the Portland-Vancouver metropolitan area. *American Journal of Industrial Medicine, 6*, 185–205.

Mukamal, K. J., & Rimm, E. B. (2008). Alcohol consumption: Risks and benefits. *Current Atherosclerosis Reports, 10*, 536–543.

Muscat, J. E., Stellman, S. D., Richie, J. P., Jr., & Wynder, E. L. (1998). Lung cancer risk and workplace exposures in black men and women. *Environmental Research, 76*, 78–84.

Ozlu, T., & Bulbul, Y. (2005). Smoking and lung cancer. *Tuberk Toraks, 53*, 200–209.

Pilidis, G. A., Karakitsios, S. P., Kassomenos, P. A., Kazos, E. A., & Stalikas, C. D. (2009). Measurements of benzene and formaldehyde in a medium sized urban environment. Indoor/outdoor health risk implications on special population groups. *Environmental Monitoring and Assessment, 150*, 285–294.

Pollán, M., Gustavsson, P., & Floderus, B. (2001). Breast cancer, occupation, and exposure to electromagnetic fields among Swedish men. *American Journal of Industrial Medicine, 39*, 276–285.

Prochazka, M., Feychting, M., Ahlbom, A., Edwards, C. G., Nise, G., Plato, N., . . . Forssén, U. M. (2010). Occupational exposures and risk of acoustic neuroma. *Occupational and Environmental Medicine, 67*, 766–771.

Pyorala, K. (1979). Relationship of glucose tolerance and plasma insulin to the incidence of coronary heart disease: Results from two population studies in Finland. *Diabetes Care, 2*, 131–141.

Pyorala, M., Miettinen, H., Laakso, M., & Pyorala, K. (1998). Hyperinsulinemia and the risk of stroke in healthy middle-aged men: The 22-year follow-up results of the Helsinki Policemen Study. *Stroke, 29*, 1860–1866.

Pyorala, M., Miettinen, H., Laakso, M., & Pyorala, K. (2000). Plasma insulin and all-cause, cardiovascular, and noncardiovascular mortality: The 22-year follow-up results of the Helsinki Policemen Study. *Diabetes Care, 23*, 1097–1102.

Ramey, S. L., Downing, N. R., & Franke, W. D. (2009). Milwaukee police department retirees: Cardiovascular disease risk and morbidity among aging law enforcement officers. *AAOHN Journal, 57*, 448–453.

Ramey, S. L., Franke, W. D., & Shelley, M. C., 2nd. (2004). Relationship among risk factors for nephrolithiasis, cardiovascular disease, and ethnicity: Focus on a law enforcement cohort. *AAOHN Journal, 52*, 116–121.

Richmond, R. L., Wodak, A., Kehoe, L., & Heather, N. (1998). How healthy are the police? A survey of life-style factors. *Addiction, 93*, 1729–1737.

Riediker, M., Devlin, R. B., Griggs, T. R., Herbst, M. C., Bromberg, P. A., Williams, R. W., & Cascio, W. E. (2004). Cardiovascular effects in patrol officers are associated with fine particulate matter from brake wear and engine emissions. *Particle and Fibre Toxicology, 1*, 2.

Roberts, D. L., Dive, C., & Renehan, A. G. (2010). Biological mechanisms linking obesity and cancer risk: New perspectives. *Annual Review of Medicine, 61,* 301–316.

Rosenstock, L., Demers, P., Heyer, N. J., & Barnhart, S. (1990). Respiratory mortality among firefighters. *British Journal of Industrial Medicine, 47,* 462–465.

Seitz, H., & Poschl, G. (1997). Alcohol and gastrointestinal cancer: Pathogenic mechanisms. *Addiction Biology, 2,* 19.

Thrasher, D. L., Von Derau, K., & Burgess, J. (2009). Health effects from reported exposure to methamphetamine labs: A poison center-based study. *Journal of Medical Toxicology, 5,* 200–204.

van Netten, C., Brands, R. H., Hoption Cann, S. A., Spinelli, J. J., & Sheps, S. B. (2003). Cancer cluster among police detachment personnel. *Environment International, 28,* 567–572.

Vena, J. E., Charles, L. E., Gu, J. K., Burchfiel, C. M., Andrew, M. E., Fekedulegn, D. (2013). Mortality of a Police Cohort 1950–2005. Manuscript submitted for publication.

Vena, J. E., Violanti, J. M., Marshall, J., & Fiedler, R. C. (1986). Mortality of a municipal worker cohort: III. Police officers. *American Journal of Industrial Medicine, 10,* 383–397.

Violanti, J. M., Andrew, M., Burchfiel, C. M., Hartley, T. A., Charles, L. E., & Miller, D. B. (2007). Post-traumatic stress symptoms and cortisol patterns among police officers. *Policing: An International Journal of Police Strategies & Management, 30,* 189–202.

Violanti, J. M., Burchfiel, C. M., Hartley, T. A., Mnatsakanova, A., Fekedulegn, D., Andrew, M. E., . . . Vila, B. J. (2009). Atypical work hours and metabolic syndrome among police officers. *Archives of Environmental and Occupational Health, 64,* 194–201.

Violanti, J. M., Burchfiel, C. M., Miller, D. B., Andrew, M. E., Dorn, J., Wactawski-Wende, J., . . . Trevisan, M. (2006). The Buffalo Cardio-Metabolic Occupational Police Stress (BCOPS) pilot study: Methods and participant characteristics. *Annals of Epidemiology, 16,* 148–156.

Violanti, J. M., Vena, J. E., & Petralia, S. (1998). Mortality of a police cohort: 1950–1990. *American Journal of Industrial Medicine, 33,* 366–373.

Wirth, M., Burch, J., Violanti, J., Burchfiel, C., Fekedulegn, D., Andrew, M., . . . Vena, J. E. (2011). Shiftwork duration and the awakening cortisol response among police officers. *Chronobiology International, 28,* 446–457.

Youngstedt, S. D., & Kripke, D. F. (2004). Long sleep and mortality: Rationale for sleep restriction. *Sleep Medicine Reviews, 8,* 159–174.

Zeegers, M. P., Friesema, I. H., Goldbohm, R. A., & van den Brandt, P. A. (2004). A prospective study of occupation and prostate cancer risk. *Journal of Occupational and Environmental Medicine, 46,* 271–279.

Zukauskas, G., Ruksenas, O., Burba, B., Grigaliuniene, V., & Mitchell, J. T. (2009). A study of stress affecting police officers in Lithuania. *The International Journal of Emergency Mental Health, 11,* 205–214.

Chapter 5

SHIFT WORK AND HEALTH CONSEQUENCES IN POLICING

Penelope Baughman, Desta Fekedulegn, Luenda E. Charles, Ja K. Gu, Claudia Ma, John M. Violanti, Michael Wirth, Anna Mnatsakanova, Tara A. Hartley, Michael E. Andrew, and Cecil M. Burchfiel

Shift work is complex and encompasses a wide variety of work schedules and circumstances.

> Shift work involves working outside the normal daylight hours. That is, outside the hours of around 7 a.m. to 6 p.m., the time period in which many people in our society work a 7- to 8-hour shift. Shift workers might work in the evening, in the middle of the night, overtime or extra-long workdays. They also might work regular days at one time or another. Many shift workers "rotate" around the clock, which involves changing work times from day to evening, or day to night. This might happen at different times of the week or at different times of the month" (National Institute for Occupational Safety and Health [NIOSH], 1997, pp. 1–2).

The U.S. Bureau of Labor Statistics' most recent reports about shift work in the United States are based on data from a supplement to the May 2004 Current Population Survey, a monthly household survey of national employment and unemployment. Nearly 15 percent of full-time workers usually worked an alternative shift (6.7% on evening shifts, 3.2% on night shifts, 3.1% on employer-arranged irregular schedules, and 2.5% on rotating shifts), a decrease from 18 percent in May 1991. A greater percentage of men worked an alternative shift than did women (16.7 vs. 12.4%). Blacks worked alternative shifts more often than did whites, Hispanics or Latinos, or Asians. Shift work was most common among workers in service occupations: 50.6 percent worked in protective service (police, firefighters, and guards), 40.4 percent in food preparation and serving, and 26.2 percent in production, transportation, and material moving (Bureau of Labor Statistics [BLS], 2005; McMenamin, 2007). Note that the preceding statistics are based on current work, which may underestimate the number of individuals who have ever worked alternative shifts. It could also be worthwhile to consider past work because the effects of shift work may be cumulative over time.

Police work necessarily entails shift work to help ensure public safety. "Police officers have reported that shift work and overtime are among the most difficult requirements of their job" (Violanti et al., 2009, p. 194). In this high-demand, high-stress occupation, shift work is a major contributor to stress and can present challenges in several ways – as the source of problems, hastening potential problems, or complicating existing ones.

Reasons for working an alternative shift among U.S. workers included "nature of the job" (54.6%), "personal preference" (11.5%), "better arrangements for family or child care" (8.2%), "could not get any other job" (8.1%), and "better pay" (6.8%). Personal preference was given as the reason many chose to work night and evening shifts (21.0 and 15.9%, respectively) or that working these shifts assisted with family or child care needs (15.9 and 11.0%, respectively). The "nature of the job" was the most common reason for working rotating, split, and employer-arranged irregular schedules (BLS, 2005; McMenamin, 2007).

Shift work is a recognized physical and psychological challenge to worker health and performance and is a far-reaching exposure in occupational health. Rearrangement of sleep and work time can have a vast impact not only on police officers but also on their families and the people that they seek to protect and serve. A number of health concerns are associated with shift work and police officers represent a large share of the affected working population. Results from a study of Buffalo, New York, police officers and studies of other law enforcement officers will be used to summarize health hazards associated with shift work.

METHODS USED TO ASSESS SHIFT WORK

From a research perspective, shift work is much like a "natural experiment." Groups of workers are naturally exposed to different shifts, similar to the different treatments received by groups of people in a planned scientific experiment. In order to evaluate this "natural experiment," researchers must gather data on work history (shift work exposure information). Studies of associations between work history and various health outcomes would help us to better understand the health hazards related to shift work, but a readily available source of national data on shift work is not available in the United States. In general, there are two approaches to capture shift work information. It can be collected directly from workers, through the use of questionnaires about work history, or indirectly from existing sources of work history information, such as payroll record-keeping systems.

Questionnaires can be a quick and inexpensive method to obtain work history data. They can be customized to the specific needs of the study and result in a rich source of information about shift work. An important limitation of questionnaires is that recall may be difficult for workers with long or complex work histories. Thus, questionnaires may be best used for collecting recent work history.

Because complete and accurate long-term work history can be difficult to obtain by questionnaire, a better source of long-term work history may be from existing information gathered in payroll record-keeping systems. These are very detailed records accumulated throughout the period of employment and are much more objective than are self-reported data. Another advantage of long-term work history data is that researchers can study the effects of shift work that occurred prior to the development of a particular health outcome. This allows investigation of causal relationships between exposure to shift work and development of disease. The main challenge is that the payroll information was originally collected for an administrative purpose. Preparing the existing data for the purposes of a research study can be costly and time consuming. These data are also often difficult to obtain and are rarely utilized for research on shift work by police officers.

In the BCOPS study of Buffalo, New York, police officers, both methods of data collection were used. The payroll records were a more reliable source of long-term work history (Violanti et al., 2006) and could be useful for studying conditions that take longer to develop, such as cancer. In contrast, questionnaires could capture specific details about recent work history that may be associated with changes in health that occur over shorter periods of time, such as sleep or psychological symptoms.

Daily computerized payroll records for Buffalo, New York, police officers were made available from 1994 to 2010 from the Buffalo payroll department and officers worked fixed shifts during this time. These records include the start time, shift length, hours worked, and type of activity performed (regular work, overtime, and court time work). Information regarding sick days and time off due to on-duty injury was also available. Prior to 1994, Buffalo police officers worked a schedule requiring two of the three shifts of officers to work 16 hours within a 24-hour period or "doubling back" (Vena, Violanti, Marshall & Fiedler, 1986). This work history was recorded using a paper-based system. Efforts are underway to capture information from these records to study the health effects of the earlier shift-scheduling pattern.

Preparation of the computerized payroll records included several steps. Type of work was classified as regular time, overtime, or court time work using information on the type of pay received and type of leave taken. The shift for each work day was determined using start times for the regular time work. The distribution of shift start times were consistent with those in other occupations involving shift work; typical start times were 7:00 or 8:00 AM, 4:00 PM, and 8:00 or 9:00 PM. The shift start times were then used to define the shift for each day as follows: day shift (4:00 AM through 11:59 AM), afternoon shift (12:00 PM through 7:59 PM), and night shift (8:00 PM through 3:59 AM). The number of hours worked per week was also determined for each type of work (regular time, overtime, or court time). Although officers were scheduled on permanent shifts since 1994, they occasionally worked on shifts other than their permanent shift to cover for other officers who might be on sick or injury leave or vacation in their districts or other districts. To account for this, a variable that represents the shift on which a participant spent the majority of his or her work hours (the dominant shift) was derived. The total hours worked by each participant during the time period spanning from 1994 to the date of examination in the study was partitioned into hours worked on the day, afternoon, and night shift. A dominant shift for each participant was defined as the shift that accounted for the largest percentage of the total hours worked.

There are limitations in any investigation of shift work. Regardless of the approach used to collect work history information, there remains an important methodological challenge in studying the effects of shift work, known as the healthy worker effect (Rothman, Greenland, & Lash, 2008). For example, a project is developed to investigate the association between shift work exposure and a health outcome among workers in a particular industry. This effect is created when some workers leave employment due to an inability to adjust to the shift or the adverse health effects of the shift work, leaving only the "healthy workers" in the study. These "healthy workers" would be those who were more resilient to the effects of shift work or who learned to tolerate it more successfully. Although it is important to study these workers, it is also important to understand the experiences of the workers who left due to the effects of shift work on their health. Because the final results would be based on the experience of the "healthier workers," there would likely be an underestimation of the effect of the shift work on the health outcome. The following sections describe some of health consequences related to shift work.

SHIFT WORK AND SLEEP DISORDERS

Scientific evidence shows that shift work is disruptive to acquiring a sufficient amount of and good sleep quality. As an occupational group, police officers have been a useful model for research on shift work, sleep, fatigue, and human performance (Charles et al., 2007; Vila, 2006). Police work involves exposure to both traumatic and nontraumatic (routine administrative and organizational aspects of police work) stressors and these may negatively affect sleep quality. Self-reported sleep quality was compared between police officers and individuals not involved in police, emergency, or security services. Those who worked variable work shifts and those who worked stable day shifts were considered separately. Compared to the nonpolice groups, police officers on variable shifts and stable day shifts reported poorer sleep quality and fewer hours of sleep on average. Among police officers, exposure to traumatic incidents was connected mainly with nightmares. Nontraumatic stress was strongly associated with poor global sleep quality (Neylan et al., 2002).

Associations of shift work with sleep quantity and quality were investigated among Buffalo police officers. Charles and colleagues (2007) found that night shift work was significantly associated with snoring and decreased sleep duration among police officers. Shift workers may also experience breathing disturbances, such as obstructive sleep apnea. Police officers did not show a significant difference in sleep apnea severity after working the night shift as compared with working the day shift. Several breathing characteristics, however, were increased (worsened) on polysomnography during sleep after night work (Tafil-Klawe, Laudencka, Klawe & Miskowiec, 2005). In another sleep study, results from overnight polysomnography were compared between shift-working and non–shift-working police officers. In this study, however, shift work was not significantly associated with obstructive sleep apnea since the disorder was identified in equal numbers in both groups of officers (Klawe, Laudencka, Miskowiec & Tafil-Klawe, 2005).

Undiagnosed sleep disorders among police officers may pose health and safety risks. In a screening of a group of North American police officers, 40 percent had at least one sleep disorder, including 34.6 percent with obstructive sleep apnea, 6.5 percent with moderate to severe insomnia, and 5.4 percent with shift work disorder. On a sleepiness scale, 28.5 percent reported excessive sleepiness and 26.1 percent reported sleepiness while driving at least monthly. Police officers with obstructive sleep apnea or a sleep disorder had increased reports of physical and mental health conditions such as diabetes, depression, and CVD. Using information from monthly follow-up surveys, police officers who were identified as having a sleep disorder reported making a serious administrative error, falling asleep while driving, making an error or safety violation due to fatigue, showing uncontrolled anger toward suspects, absenteeism, and falling asleep during meetings more frequently when compared to police officers who were not identified as having a sleep disorder (Rajaratnam et al., 2011).

Sleep duration may influence blood levels of leptin, a hormone that regulates appetite and metabolism. Higher levels of leptin are associated with CVD. In an investigation of police officers, those who reported having short (< 5 hours) and long (≥ 8 hours) sleep duration had higher levels of leptin compared to police officers who reported an average of 5 to 7 hours of sleep (Charles et al., 2011). These associations between sleep duration and leptin were stronger among female officers with a normal BMI (24.9 kg/m or less), officers (male or female) with smaller abdominal height (less than 20 cm), and those who primarily worked on the day shift (Charles et al., 2011). The relationship between shift work, sleep, and wellness was evaluated at three U.S. midwestern police departments (Ramey et al., 2012). Comparisons were made for officers who worked primarily day shifts with those who worked primarily nonday shifts and for officers who slept less than six hours per day with those who slept at least six hours per day. Officers who primarily worked nonday shifts were fourteen times more likely to sleep less than six hours compared with officers who worked day shifts. Officers who slept less than six hours per day were twice as likely to experience poor sleep quality compared to those who slept more hours (Ramey et al., 2012).

Police officers who are shift workers may require a longer recovery time and longer sleep duration than police officers who are not shift workers. A group of state police officers in Italy had their sleep patterns, sleep disorders, sleepiness at work, and hypnotic drug intake assessed by self-administered questionnaire (Garbarino, Nobili, et al., 2002). The shift workers had more frequent difficulty in initiating sleep, with sleep latency (time it took to fall asleep exceeded 20 minutes) and with early awakenings than did nonshift workers. Daytime sleepiness and hypnotic drug intake were similar between the groups; however, shift workers reported requiring longer sleep duration (Garbarino, Nobili, et al., 2002).

The natural tendency to fall asleep and sleep deprivation due to lengthy waking hours may reduce vigilance and contribute to the danger of night shift work. Napping before working a night shift may be an effective countermeasure to the deterioration of alertness and performance associated with night work. In a group of Italian shift-working police drivers, naps were studied as a countermeasure to understand how they may help in preventing sleep-related accidents (Garbarino et al., 2004). Using highway accident data from 1993 to 1997, the accident risk was influenced most by the natural tendency for sleep. Using 2003 data, it was estimated that drivers who did not take naps had a 38 percent increase in accidents. The number of accidents per hour increased with sleep deprivation. Napping was associated with a 48 percent decrease in accidents (Garbarino et al., 2004).

Using a combined field and laboratory research design, the effect of consecutive night shift work on the sleepiness, vigilance, and driving performance of police officers was studied (Waggoner, Grant, Van

Dongen, Belenky & Vila, 2012). Officers worked their regular night shift cycles followed by measurements takes of driving performance and psychomotor vigilance in a laboratory on the morning following the fifth consecutive night shift and on the morning after three consecutive days off. Comparing results for the two observation periods, sleepiness, vigilance, and simulated driving performance were significantly degraded following five consecutive night shifts (Waggoner et al., 2012).

Evidence suggests that occupational health physicians should be attentive to possible sleep disorders in shift-working police officers because these may be associated with or result in health problems and accidents. Results from a cross-sectional study showed that sleep-related accidents were increased among shift workers and related to the presence of indicators of sleep disorders (Garbarino et al., 2001).

SHIFT WORK AND INJURIES

Long and erratic work hours and insufficient sleep may result in fatigue that could impair the performance and decision-making ability of police officers, potentially threatening their health and safety and that of the public they serve and protect (Vila, 2006). Work history and workplace injury records were used to study the association of shift work and injury occurrence among Buffalo police officers. Violanti and colleagues (2012) examined the association between shift work and injury occurrence. Compared to police officers who worked the day shift, occurrence of first injury was significantly elevated in officers working the night (by 72%) and afternoon (by 66%) shifts. On the first day back to work after being off duty, injury occurrence was elevated for those on the night shift compared with those working the day (by 69%) or afternoon shift (by 54%). The joint combination of working the night shift and having a heavy workload (very busy, frequent complaints, high crime area) was associated with a 2.3-fold greater occurrence of injury compared with officers working the day shift and having a light workload (precinct not busy, low crime area) (Violanti et al., 2012).

SHIFT WORK AND CARDIOVASCULAR DISEASE

Comparisons of CVD morbidity between police populations and the general population have revealed elevated rates among police officers. For example, CVD morbidity was more common in Iowa law enforcement officers than in the Iowa general population (31.5 vs. 18.4%) (Franke, Collins & Hinz, 1998). Results such as these suggest that employment as a law enforcement officer is associated with an increased risk for CVD and stimulate interest in the relationship between occupational stress and early signs for CVD among police officers.

Because shift work is a key source of occupational stress for police officers and shift work may increase the risk of chronic disease (Wang, Armstrong, Cairns, Key & Travis, 2011), the association between shift work and metabolic syndrome was studied among Buffalo police officers. Metabolic syndrome is a subclinical disorder associated with increased risk for development of CVD. It is defined as the presence of three or more of five metabolic syndrome components: elevated blood pressure (BP at or over 130/85 mmHg or on medication to treat elevated BP), elevated glucose (at or over 100 mg/dL or on medication to treat elevated glucose), elevated triglycerides (at or over 150 mg/dL or on medication to treat elevated triglycerides), reduced HDL-C (under 40 mg/dL in men, under 50 mg/dL in women, or on medication to treat cholesterol imbalance), elevated waist circumference (at or over 102 cm [40 in] in men, and 88 cm [35 in] in women) (Grundy et al., 2005). Metabolic syndrome is preventable, treatable, and can also be a reversible condition through healthy lifestyle choices and behaviors.

Officers who worked night shift and either had less than six hours of sleep or worked more overtime had a four-fold greater number of metabolic syndrome components than did officers working the day shift. Although age can be associated with an increasing number of metabolic syndrome components, these results were not explained merely by age differences. In fact, officers working the night shift were younger on average than officers working the day or afternoon shifts (Violanti et al., 2009).

Perceived stress can be an indicator of the effect of shift work and other occupational stressors. A study of law enforcement officers investigated whether perceived stress contributes to CVD (Franke, Ramey & Shelley, 2002). They found the best predictors of CVD were time in the profession (even after adjustment for the effects of aging), perceived stress, and hypertension. Three CVD risk factors were affected by perceived stress: cholesterol, hypertension, and physical activity (Franke, Ramey & Shelley, 2002).

Short-term effects of shift work have also been studied in policemen. The short-term effect of a change in shift rotation on cardiovascular risk factors was investigated by Orth-Gomer (1983). The officers worked four weeks in their customary counter-clockwise rotation and then switched to a clockwise rotation. Measurements of "serum lipids, glucose, uric acid, blood pressure, nocturnal urinary excretion of catecholamines, the quality and quantity of sleep, and tobacco consumption" were collected before, during, and after each of the two schedules. Although tobacco consumption was similar between the two schedules, clockwise rotation was associated with several measures of improved health including lower serum levels of triglycerides, glucose, systolic blood pressure, and urinary excretion of catecholamines, and there were reports of better and longer sleep (Orth-Gomer, 1983, p. 409).

Fatigue resulting from the demands of shift work may have an impact on the level and amount of physical activity that police officers can maintain. Occupational, sport, and household physical activity was collected for the BCOPS study by self-report from the officers. Shift work was associated with the prevalence of hard-intensity occupational and sport physical activity among male police officers and with very hard-intensity sport physical activity among female officers. Afternoon shift workers were the most active (Ma et al., 2011). Long work hours may also be associated with increased health risks for police officers. In Buffalo, working longer hours was significantly associated with larger waist circumference and higher BMI among male police officers working the night shift. These measures were not associated with work hours among women on any shift (Gu et al., 2012).

SHIFT WORK AND CANCER

Excess risk for specific types of cancer (colon, male breast, and endocrine glands) may be linked to certain occupations and occupational exposures. For example, a higher risk of bladder cancer, kidney cancer, and non-Hodgkin's lymphoma may exist for professional drivers (Forastiere et al., 1994). Scientific evidence suggests an association between night work and development of breast cancer. The IARC has classified shiftwork as a probable human carcinogen, with most of the research focused on breast cancer (IARC Working Monograph Group, 2010). There is limited and inconsistent evidence related to other forms of cancer and all cancers combined (Wang et al., 2011).

Scientific literature also suggests that there is a possibility that stress may influence the risk for certain types of cancer. In Buffalo police officers, increased risk of digestive cancer and cancer of the lymphatic and blood-forming tissues was identified with 10 to 19 years of service. Officers with this length of service had been previously identified as having the highest stress scores among Buffalo police officers. At the time of the cancer mortality study, Buffalo police officers also worked a difficult schedule requiring two of the three shifts of officers to work 16 hours within a 24-hour period or "doubling back" (Vena et al., 1986; Violanti, 1983).

Various cancers were represented in a 40-year mortality study of male police officers in Buffalo. The results showed higher than expected rates for all malignant cancers in officers with 1 to 9 years of service, for bladder cancer and leukemia in officers with 10 to 19 years of service, and colon cancer in officers with over 30 years of service (Violanti, Vena & Petralia, 1998).

Records for Buffalo police officers who worked between 1950 and 2005 were matched with cancer registry records. Among white male officers, 18.2 percent developed cancer between 1976 and 2006. Their overall cancer risk was similar to that of the U.S. white male population, but an elevated risk of Hodgkin's lymphoma was observed. The risk of brain cancer was slightly elevated and was significantly increased for officers with 30 or more years of police service (Gu, Charles, Burchfiel, Andrew & Violanti, 2011).

SHIFT WORK AND CORTISOL

Cortisol is a well-known "stress hormone," and an abnormal pattern of secretion has been associated with immune system dysregulation and may serve as an early sign of disease. The association of short-term shift work duration with awakening cortisol response was studied among Buffalo police officers using cortisol extracted from saliva samples. Short-term duration was characterized as 3-, 5-, 7-, or 14-day exposures determined from the work history records. The cortisol awakening response pattern was constructed from samples collected on first awakening, and at 15-, 30-, and 45-minute intervals thereafter. Based on work during the previous two weeks, night and afternoon shift workers had a significantly diminished awakening salivary cortisol levels (dysregulation) compared with day shift workers (Wirth et al., 2011).

Associations of long-term shift work (6–8 years) with waking salivary cortisol concentration and patterns during the first hour following awakening were also studied among Buffalo police officers. Long-term night shift work was associated with decreased average level and total volume of cortisol released over the waking period compared to the afternoon and day shift. However, the pattern of cortisol secretion was similar across shift (Fekedulegn et al., 2012).

Lower levels of basal cortisol on awakening have been associated with greater symptoms of PTSD, a severe anxiety disorder. This finding has been extended to urban police officers (Neylan et al., 2005). Apart from traumatic incidents on the job that may contribute to the development of PTSD, exposure to routine occupational stress also appears to be a risk factor for psychological distress among police officers, as well as a strong predictor of PTSD symptoms (Liberman et al., 2002).

SHIFT WORK AND SUICIDE IDEATION

In a 40-year study of mortality among male police officers in Buffalo, New York, a significantly higher than expected mortality rate was found for suicide (Violanti et al., 1998). To better understand the processes that lead to suicide among police officers, a study focused on the relationships among psychologically traumatic work experiences, the development of PTSD symptoms, and increased use of alcohol associated with PTSD. Traumatic work experiences increased the risk of PTSD symptoms followed by an increase in the risk of excessive alcohol use and suicide ideation. A ten-fold increased risk for suicide ideation was observed among Buffalo police officers with PTSD and increased alcohol use (Violanti, 2004).

The stress of shift work has been associated with suicide ideation among Buffalo police officers. Suicide ideation was more prevalent among policewomen with increased depressive symptoms and an increasing percentage of hours worked on the day shift and among policemen with higher PTSD symptoms and an increasing percentage of afternoon shift hours (Violanti et al., 2008). Of note are the differing psychological symptoms between women and men: women generally work the day shift, and the afternoon shift is generally the busiest shift, which may explain the results for men.

A nationwide study on suicidal ideation and suicide attempts among Norwegian police officers found a low occurrence of suicide ideation and attempts and identified marital status, subjective health complaints, traits associated with severe personality disorders, anxiety, and depression as independent predictors of serious suicidal ideation. Interestingly, female officers attributed personal problems as a greater influence on suicide ideation, whereas male officers attributed work problems as a greater influence on suicide ideation and attempts (Berg, Hem, Lau, Loeb & Ekeberg, 2003).

Putting the occurrence of workplace suicide mortality into perspective, a study compared workplace injury deaths among U.S. law enforcement officers between 1992 and 2002. There were 2,280 fatalities over the period, of which 122 (5%) were workplace suicides (Tiesman, Hendricks, Bell & Amandus, 2010). Although suicide was a small percentage of all workplace mortality, it represented a large number of opportunities to intervene with police officers who were having serious difficulties.

SHIFT WORK AMONG AN AGING WORKFORCE

Economic and demographic changes have created a general push toward increasing the legal retirement age. Two groups of German police officers participated in a study of the potential health and safety consequences that could be associated with later retirements. Data from one group were collected by questionnaire and data for the second group were collected from employment records. These sources were used to assess the "effects of lifetime exposure to shift work on health impairments and fitness for duty." Results indicated an increase in the risk of reduced fitness for duty as the number of years in shift work increased, in both groups. Health impairments increased rapidly beyond 20 years of shift work exposure (Wirtz & Nachreiner, 2012, p. 596).

It is important to understand how aging affects police officers' ability to tolerate shift work because changes in the workforce are resulting in an increasing number of shift workers over age 45. In a study of police officers in three age groups (20–32.9, 33–39.9, and 40 and above), "better attitudes towards their shift work, better adjustment to night-bound shifts, greater job satisfaction and organizational commitment, lower fatigue and longer sleep durations" were found among younger officers; older officers reported "higher morningness and lower sleep" as compared to younger officers. Older officers also had greater caffeine intake on all shifts (Smith & Mason, 2001a, p. 312).

REDUCING THE HEALTH CONSEQUENCES OF SHIFT WORK

Shift work is a challenge that cannot be eliminated and must instead be dealt with through individual and organizational responses to lessen its effect on workers. Because shift work is ever present in policing, use of coping strategies is needed to tolerate the demands of shift work and offset its toll. For example, individuals can work to practice healthy sleep habits, such as maintaining a regular sleep schedule, eliminating noise and light from their sleeping area, avoiding caffeine close to bedtime, and avoiding alcohol because it can disturb sleep (National Sleep Foundation, 2011). To help ensure adequate family and social interaction, family and social gatherings could be scheduled to best accommodate the work-sleep schedule. A structured diary could be completed for a period of two or more shift cycles, including officer responses to questions regarding patterns and disturbances in sleep duration, sleep quality, food intake, appetite, health complaints, recovery, and family issues. This could be used to increase individual awareness of the daily impact of shift work or it could be part of an overall organizational assessment, in which permanent day shift officers could also complete the diary and serve as a comparison group (Attia, Mustafa, Khogali, Mahmoud & Arar, 1985).

Institutions and industries can implement organizational changes such as rotating shifts to periodically give workers the opportunity to work more desirable shifts. With the physiological challenges associated with traditional night or rotating shifts and also with extended shifts and nonstandard hours, comprehensive fatigue management programs may be of benefit to police officers and organizations. These programs may include education, screening for sleep disorders, and interventions to lessen negative consequences associated with shift work (Barger,

Lockley, Rajaratnam & Landrigan, 2009).

Information was gathered using a group of methods to help develop interventions to reduce CVD and its risk factors in the Milwaukee Police Department. These methods included a health promotion planning model, survey data, and focus group data. Barriers and motivators to a healthy lifestyle emerged from the focus groups with police officers. Survey results were compared between police officers and the general population as a benchmark for overweight and hypertension (Ramey, Downing & Knoblauch, 2008). These methods could be adapted to explore problems associated with shift work.

Police officers with differing lengths of shift work exposure were studied to examine whether patterns in complaints change with increasing length of exposure. After 15 years of shift work exposure, health complaints associated with disruptions of circadian-controlled functions tended to be more dominant. This may suggest that shift-specific health impairment may be distinct from other non-shift-specific health issues (Nachreiner, Lubeck-Ploger & Grzech-Sukalo, 1995). This distinction could be important in designing support programs for shift-working officers.

The type of shift could also be considered, including fixed (permanent) shifts; rotating shifts, such as forward-rotating (day to afternoon then to night) and backward-rotating shifts (night to afternoon then to day); as well as the speed of rotation (slow or fast). These different types of rotation may be associated with different health effects. For example, the impact of rotation and timing of shifts on military police was studied to identify promising methods to lessen the negative consequences of shift work. The worker's shift could be predicted based on "work-home conflict, job attitudes, health, and absenteeism." In this case, rotation was related to unfavorable job attitudes and timing was related to increased work-home conflict. Avoiding fixed nonday shifts including weekends was suggested to reduce conflict between work and home, as was a high degree of flexibility in rotation rosters (Demerouti, Geurts, Bakker & Euwema, 2004, p. 987).

Police departments may also choose to change from rotating to permanent shift assignments. This change was made in the Lexington, Kentucky, Police Department in 1989. Following the change, sleep quality and sleep hygiene improved. Psychological well-being improved and absenteeism dropped from 1,400 hours in the six months prior to the change to 883 hours during the 6 months following the change (Phillips, Magan, Gerhardstein & Cecil, 1991).

Understanding individual differences may also be important to helping police officers tolerate the demands of shift work. For example, because shift work may influence worker health in many ways, further effects may be observed in workers who have health conditions or require use of prescription medications. Alterations that shift work may have upon how the body and brain process medications may be critical to the well-being of these workers and require specific medical attention (Garbarino et al., 2002).

Personality characteristics may also influence how well workers tolerate shift work. Locus of control, or the extent to which individuals believe that they can control events that affect them, has been used to examine the relationship between internal locus of control and commonly reported outcomes of shift work, such as "sleep disturbance, alertness on shift, psychological well-being, disturbance of social and family life, and fatigue." Higher internal locus of control was associated with fewer problems with shift work. This concept may be useful to consider in targeting interventions (Smith & Mason, 2001b, p. 217). Other personality traits that may be important to consider in the tolerance of shift work are "anxiety, emotional control, positive and negative affect, health complaints, sleep quality, difficulties in social and domestic life, and perceptions about shift work." Results suggest that tolerance of shift work, including shift and rotation, varies by personality traits, and understanding these may be useful in matching workers to appropriate shifts (Tamagawa, Lobb & Booth, 2007, p. 635).

Although we may often think of shift work as a fairly simple concept to understand, existing results demonstrate that it is an exposure with complex implications, particularly for the large proportion of police officers who serve the public outside of daytime hours. Although shift work cannot be eliminated, diligent individual and organizational efforts may reduce its impact on morbidity, mortality, injury, and disability among police officers. Police officers and the services they provide are clearly tremendous assets in our communities. Additional investment in the promotion of police officer health and safety related to the challenge of shift work not only would provide a direct benefit for officers and law enforcement organizations, but also would spill over in both subtle and important ways into our daily lives.

Disclaimer: The findings and conclusions in this report are those of the authors and do not necessarily represent the views of the National Institute for Occupational Safety and Health.

REFERENCES

Attia, M., Mustafa, M. K., Khogali, M., Mahmoud, N. A., & Arar, E. I. (1985). Optimization of night and shiftwork plans among policemen in Kuwait: A field experiment. *International Archives of Occupational and Environmental Health, 56*, 81–90.

Barger, L. K., Lockley, S. W., Rajaratnam, S. M., & Landrigan, C. P. (2009). Neurobehavioral, health, and safety consequences associated with shift work in safety-sensitive professions. *Current Neurology and Neuroscience Reports, 9*, 155–164.

Berg, A. M., Hem, E., Lau, B., Loeb, M., & Ekeberg, O. (2003). Suicidal ideation and attempts in Norwegian police. *Suicide & Life-threatening Behavior, 33*, 302–312.

Bureau of Labor Statistics (BLS). (2005). *Workers on flexible and shift schedules in 2004 summary.* Retrieved March 25, 2013, from http://www.bls.gov/news.release/flex.nr0.htm

Charles, L. E., Burchfiel, C. M., Fekedulegn, D., Vila, B., Hartley, T. A., Slaven, J., . . . Violanti, J. M. (2007). Shift work and sleep: The Buffalo Police health study. *Policing, 30*, 215–227. doi: 10.1108/13639510710753225

Charles, L. E., Gu, J. K., Andrew, M. E., Violanti, J. M., Fekedulegn, D., & Burchfiel, C. M. (2011). Sleep duration and biomarkers of metabolic function among police officers. *Journal of Occupational and Environmental Medicine, 53*, 831–837. doi: 10.1097/JOM.0b013e31821f5ece

Demerouti, E., Geurts, S. A., Bakker, A. B., & Euwema, M. (2004). The impact of shiftwork on work-home conflict, job attitudes and health. *Ergonomics, 47*, 987–1002. doi: 10.1080/00140130410001670408

Fekedulegn, D., Burchfiel, C. M., Violanti, J. M., Hartley, T. A., Charles, L. E., Andrew, M. E., & Miller, D. B. (2012). Associations of long-term shift work with waking salivary cortisol concentration and patterns among police officers. *Industrial Health, 50*, 476–486.

Forastiere, F., Perucci, C. A., Dipietro, A., Miceli, M., Rapiti, E., Bargagli, A., & Borgia, P. (1994). Mortality among urban policemen in Rome. *American Journal of Industrial Medicine, 26*, 785–798. doi: 10.1002/ajim.4700260607

Franke, W. D., Collins, S. A., & Hinz, P. N. (1998). Cardiovascular disease morbidity in an Iowa law enforcement cohort, compared with the general Iowa population. *Journal of Occupational and Environmental Medicine, 40*, 441–444.

Franke, W. D., Ramey, S. L., & Shelley, M. C., 2nd. (2002). Relationship between cardiovascular disease morbidity, risk factors, and stress in a law enforcement cohort. *Journal of Occupational and Environmental Medicine, 44*, 1182–1189.

Garbarino, S., De Carli, F., Mascialino, B., Beelke, M., Nobili, L., Squarcia, S., . . . Ferrillo, F. (2001). Sleepiness in a population of Italian shiftwork policemen. *Journal of Human Ergology, 30*, 211–216.

Garbarino, S., Mascialino, B., Penco, M. A., Squarcia, S., De Carli, F., Nobili, L., . . . Ferrillo, F. (2004). Professional shift-work drivers who adopt prophylactic naps can reduce the risk of car accidents during night work. *Sleep, 27*, 1295–1302.

Garbarino, S., Nobili, L., Beelke, M., Balestra, V., Cordelli, A., & Ferrillo, F. (2002). Sleep disorders and daytime sleepiness in state police shiftworkers. *Archives of Environmental Health, 57*, 167–173. doi: 10.1080/00039890209602932

Grundy, S. M., Cleeman, J. I., Daniels, S. R., Donato, K. A., Eckel, R. H., Franklin, B. A., . . . Blood, I. (2005). Diagnosis and management of the metabolic syndrome: An American Heart Association/National Heart, Lung, and Blood Institute Scientific Statement. *Circulation, 112*, 2735–2752. doi: 10.1161/CIRCULATIONAHA.105.169404

Gu, J. K., Charles, L. E., Burchfiel, C. M., Andrew, M. E., & Violanti, J. M. (2011). Cancer incidence among police officers in a U.S. northeast region: 1976–2006. *International Journal of Emergency Mental Health, 13*, 279–289.

Gu, J. K., Charles, L. E., Burchfiel, C. M., Fekedulegn, D., Sarkisian, K., Andrew, M. E., . . . Violanti, J. M. (2012). Long work hours and adiposity among police officers in a U.S. northeast city. *Journal of Occupational and Environmental Medicine, 54*, 1374–1381. doi: 10.1097/JOM.0b013e31825f2bea

IARC Working Monographs Group. (2010). IARC Monographs on the Evaluation of Carcinogenic Risks to Humans. Vol. 98: *Painting, Firefighting and Shiftwork*. Lyon, France: International Agency for Research on Cancer.

Klawe, J. J., Laudencka, A., Miskowiec, I., & Tafil-Klawe, M. (2005). Occurrence of obstructive sleep apnea in a group of shift worked police officers. *Journal of Physiology and Pharmacology: An Official Journal of the Polish Physiological Society, 56* (Suppl 4), 115–117.

Liberman, A. M., Best, S. R., Metzler, T. J., Fagan, J. A., Weiss, D. S., & Marmar, C. R. (2002). Routine occupational stress and psychological distress in police. *Policing, 25*, 421–439. doi: 10.1108/13639510210429446

Ma, C. C., Burchfiel, C. M., Fekedulegn, D., Andrew, M. E., Charles, L. E., Gu, J. K., . . . Violanti, J. M. (2011). Association of shift work with physical activity among police officers: The Buffalo Cardio-metabolic Occupational Police Stress study. *Journal of Occupational and Environmental Medicine, 53*, 1030–1036. doi: 10.1097/JOM.0b013e31822589f9

McMenamin, T. (2007). A time to work: Recent trends in shift work and flexible schedules. *Monthly Labor Review, December 2007*. Retrieved from http://www.bls.gov/opub/mlr/2007/12/art1full.pdf

Nachreiner, F., Lubeck-Ploger, H., & Grzech-Sukalo, H. (1995). Changes in the structure of health complaints as related to shiftwork exposure. *Work and Stress, 9*, 227–234. doi: 10.1080/02678379508256558

National Institute for Occupational Safety and Health [NIOSH]. (1997). *Plain Language About Shiftwork*. DHHS (NIOSH) Publication No. 97–145.

National Sleep Foundation. (2011). Shift work and sleep. Retrieved March 25, 2013, from http://www.sleepfoundation.org/article/sleep-topics/shift-work-and-sleep

Neylan, T. C., Brunet, A., Pole, N., Best, S. R., Metzler, T. J., Yehuda, R., & Marmar, C. R. (2005). PTSD symptoms predict waking salivary cortisol levels in police officers. *Psychoneuroendocrinology, 30*, 373–381. doi: 10.1016/j.psyneuen.2004.10.005

Neylan, T. C., Metzler, T. J., Best, S. R., Weiss, D. S., Fagan, J. A., Liberman, A., . . . Marmar, C. R. (2002). Critical incident exposure and sleep quality in police officers. *Psychosomatic Medicine, 64*, 345–352.

Orth-Gomer, K. (1983). Intervention on coronary risk factors by adapting a shift work schedule to biologic rhythmicity. *Psychosomatic Medicine, 45*, 407–415.

Phillips, B., Magan, L., Gerhardstein, C., & Cecil, B. (1991). Shift work, sleep quality, and worker health: A study of police officers. *Southern Medical Journal, 84*, 1176–1184, 1196.

Rajaratnam, S. M., Barger, L. K., Lockley, S. W., Shea, S. A., Wang, W., Landrigan, C. P., . . . Safety, G. (2011). Sleep disorders, health, and safety in police officers. *Journal of the American Medical Association, 306*, 2567–2578. doi: 10.1001/jama. 2011.1851

Ramey, S. L., Downing, N. R., & Knoblauch, A. (2008). Developing strategic interventions to reduce cardiovascular disease risk among law enforcement officers: The art and science of data triangulation. *American Association of Occupational Health Nurses Journal, 56*, 54–62.

Ramey, S. L., Perkhounkova, Y., Moon, M., Budde, L., Tseng, H. C., & Clark, M. K. (2012). The effect of work shift and sleep duration on various aspects of police officers' health. *Workplace Health & Safety, 60*, 215–222. doi: 10.3928/21650799-20120416-22

Rothman, K. J., Greenland, S., & Lash, T. L. (2008). *Modern Epidemiology* (3rd ed.). Philadelphia: Lippincott Williams & Wilkins.

Smith, L., & Mason, C. (2001a). Age and the subjective experience of shiftwork. *Journal of Human Ergology, 30*, 307–313.

Smith, L., & Mason, C. (2001b). Shiftwork locus of control effects in police officers. *Journal of Human Ergology, 30*, 217–222.

Tafil-Klawe, M., Laudencka, A., Klawe, J. J., & Miskowiec, I. (2005). Does night work favor sleep-related accidents in police officers? *Journal of Physiology and Pharmacology: An Official Journal of the Polish Physiological Society, 56* (Suppl 4), 223–226.

Tamagawa, R., Lobb, B., & Booth, R. (2007). Tolerance of shift work. *Applied Ergonomics, 38*, 635–642. doi: 10.1016/j.apergo.2006.05.003

Tiesman, H. M., Hendricks, S. A., Bell, J. L., & Amandus, H. A. (2010). Eleven years of occupational mortality in law enforcement: The census of fatal occupational injuries, 1992–2002. *American Journal of Industrial Medicine, 53*, 940–949. doi: 10.1002/ajim.20863

Vena, J., Violanti, J., Marshall, J., & Fiedler, R. (1986). Mortality of a municipal worker cohort: III. Police officers. *American Journal of Industrial Medicine, 10*, 383–397.

Vila, B. (2006). Impact of long work hours on police officers and the communities they serve. *American Journal of Industrial Medicine, 49*, 972–980. doi: 10.1002/ajim.20333

Violanti, J. (1983). Stress patterns in police work. *Journal of Police Science and Administration, II*, 211–216.

Violanti, J. M. (2004). Predictors of police suicide ideation. *Suicide & Life-Threatening Behavior, 34*, 277–283. doi: 10.1521/suli.34.3.277.42775

Violanti, J. M., Burchfiel, C. M., Hartley, T. A., Mnatsakanova, A., Fekedulegn, D., Andrew, M. E., . . . Vila, B. J. (2009). Atypical work hours and metabolic syndrome among police officers. *Archives of Environmental & Occupational Health, 64*, 194–201. doi: 10.1080/19338240903241259

Violanti, J. M., Burchfiel, C. M., Miller, D. B., Andrew, M. E., Dorn, J., Wactawski-Wende, J., . . . Trevisan, M. (2006). The Buffalo Cardio-metabolic Occupational Police Stress (BCOPS) pilot study: Methods and participant characteristics. *Annals of Epidemiology, 16*, 148–156. doi: S1047-2797(05)00252-8 [pii] 10.1016/j.annepidem.2005.07.054

Violanti, J. M., Charles, L. E., Hartley, T. A., Mnatsakanova, A., Andrew, M. E., Fekedulegn, D., . . . Burchfiel, C. M. (2008). Shift-work and suicide ideation among police officers. *American Journal of Industrial Medicine, 51*, 758–768. doi: 10.1002/ajim.20629

Violanti, J. M., Fekedulegn, D., Andrew, M. E., Charles, L. E., Hartley, T. A., Vila, B., & Burchfiel, C. M. (2012). Shift work and the incidence of injury among police officers. *American Journal of Industrial Medicine, 55*, 217–227. doi: 10.1002/ajim.22007

Violanti, J. M., Vena, J. E., & Petralia, S. (1998). Mortality of a police cohort: 1950–1990. *American Journal of Industrial Medicine, 33*, 366–373.

Waggoner, L. B., Grant, D. A., Van Dongen, H. P., Belenky, G., & Vila, B. (2012). A combined field and laboratory design for assessing the impact of night shift work on police officer operational performance. *Sleep, 35*, 1575–1577. doi: 10.5665/sleep.2214

Wang, X., Armstrong, M., Cairns, B., Key, T., & Travis, R. (2011). Shift work and chronic disease: The epidemiological evidence. *Occupational Medicine, 61*, 78–89. doi: 10.1093/occmed/kqr001

Wirth, M., Burch, J., Violanti, J., Burchfiel, C., Fekedulegn, D., Andrew, M., . . . Vena, J. E. (2011). Shiftwork duration and the awakening cortisol response among police officers. *Chronobiology International, 28*, 446–457. doi: 10.3109/07420528.2011.573112

Wirtz, A., & Nachreiner, F. (2012). Effects of lifetime exposure to shiftwork on fitness for duty in police officers. *Chronobiology International, 29*, 595–600. doi: 10.3109/07420528.2012.675844

Chapter 6

STRESSORS AND ASSOCIATED HEALTH EFFECTS FOR WOMEN POLICE OFFICERS

Tara A. Hartley, Anna Mnatsakanova, Cecil M. Burchfiel,
and John M. Violanti

A BRIEF HISTORY OF POLICE WOMEN

Women have been a part of law enforcement for more than 100 years (Kruger, 2007). The New York City prison system hired "police matrons" in 1845 to protect female prisoners, prepare paperwork, and answer telephones (Kruger, 2007). In the 1910s, the first female police officers were hired (Kruger, 2007). With the passage of Title VII of the 1964 Civil Rights Act and subsequent amendments, state and local governments provided more equal opportunities for women in law enforcement (Kruger, 2007). As a result, a steady increase in the number of women officers was found from 1972 to 1999 with female officers gaining approximately half a percent each year in large agencies: 2.0 percent to 14.3 percent, followed by a slight decline from 1999 to 2001 (down to 12.7%) (National Center for Women and Policing [NCWP], 2002). The latest statistics (1987–2007) from the U.S. Department of Justice, Bureau of Justice Statistics, provides a more in-depth picture by type of agency. Representation of female officers in local police departments (regardless of population size) gained about half a percent each year from 1987 to 2007 from 7.6 percent to almost 12 percent (Langton, 2010). However, over the same time period, a nominal increase occurred in state police departments and federal agencies (3.8% to 6.5%), while a slight decline occurred in sheriffs' departments (approximately 12.5% to 11.2%) (Langton, 2010). Most of the largest local police departments in the U.S. and the largest federal law enforcement agencies reported steady but small increases in the percentage of female officers over a 10-year period from 1997 to 2007 (Langton, 2010).

The representation of female racial minorities in policing is relatively low. In 2003, approximately 11.3 percent of police officers in local police departments were female, 7.0 percent of which were white, 2.7 percent were black, 1.3 percent Hispanic, and 0.3 percent other (includes Asian, Native Hawaiian, Pacific Islander, American Indian, Alaska Native, and any other race) (Hickman & Reaves, 2006). The number of female officers decreased with decreasing population size; the same trend is true for minority female representation. In the largest local police departments (serving 1 million or more residents), the percentage of female officers was 17.3 percent 9.4 percent of which were minority women. For medium-sized local police departments (50,000–99,999), the percentage of female officers was 8.8 percent 2.1 percent of which were minority women. In the smaller-sized local police departments (2,500–9,999), the percentage of female officers was 6.2 percent; 0.9 percent of that proportion was composed of minority women (Hickman & Reaves, 2006). By comparison, women compose nearly 50

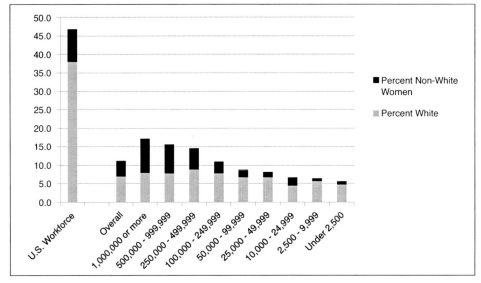

Figure 6-1. Female racial minorities in the U.S. workforce and in law enforcement by population size served in 2003. Source: Bureau for Labor Statistics (2003) and Bureau of Justice Statistics (2006).

percent of the general U.S. workforce, with 8.8 percent being minority women (U.S. Bureau of Labor Statistics, 2004).

Few women officers are in the top policing positions. According to a report from the NCWP (2002), women are more likely to hold lower-ranking positions than men were: line operations, 13.5 percent women, 86.5 percent men; supervisory, 9.6 percent women, 90.4 percent men; and top command, 7.3 percent women, 92.7 percent men. Of the 247 agencies surveyed, 56 percent had no women in the top command positions and 88 percent had no women of color in the top command positions (NCWP, 2002). These data represent the large police agencies (100 or more sworn officers). Because women officers represent an even smaller percentage of officers in small agencies (fewer than 100 sworn officers), the percentage of women holding top positions is also likely to be much smaller. Of the women in 235 small and rural police agencies surveyed, 9.7 percent held line operation positions, 4.6 percent of supervisory positions and 3.4 percent of top command positions (NCWP, 2002). The overwhelming majority (97.4%) had no women in the top command positions (NCWP, 2002).

Given the lack of female officers in law enforcement agencies, it is not surprising that policing has long been labeled a "male-dominated occupation." Prior research has identified specific sources of stress as-

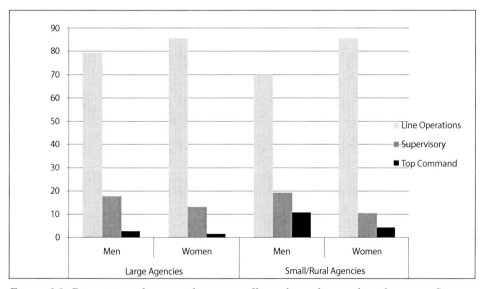

Figure 6-2. Percentage of men and women officers by police rank and agency. Source: NCWP (2002).

sociated with being female in a male-dominated workplace. We will discuss several of these stressors.

SOURCES OF STRESS FOR FEMALE POLICE OFFICERS

Regardless of gender, there are well-documented aspects of policing that are stressful, including erratic work hours, mandatory night shift, confronting death and violence, the threat of physical danger, and working with the public (Gershon, Barocas, Canton, Li & Vlahov, 2009; Violanti & Aron, 1994). Research to identify sources of workplace stress specific to female officers is limited. In their study of Norwegian police officers, Berg and colleagues (2005) found that female officers experienced fewer job stressors than their male counterparts did; however, they appraised these stressors as being more severe than men did. Gershon and associates (2009) reported similar levels of perceived work stress among 1,072 male and female officers from the Baltimore, Maryland, Police Department. The sources of stress may be different. Morash, Kwak, and Haarr (2006) found that female officers reported significantly higher levels of harassment, bias, underestimation of physical abilities, and lack of influence than their male counterparts did. These and other potential sources of stressors specific to police women are described in the following.

Are police women as skilled and able to perform the same policing duties as police men?

Despite research confirming that women are as capable as men to serve as police officers (Dejong, 2005), early debates centered on their physical strength and their skills and abilities to maintain authority (Morash, Kwak & Haarr, 2006).

"Simply stated, the presence of women in law enforcement indicated that the profession cannot be that demanding and physically challenging if females can successfully do the job" (Seklecki & Paynich, 2007).

Much of this criticism against women in policing has come from their male counterparts. More recently, the focus of this criticism seems to have shifted from lack of physical abilities to psychological and emotional weakness (Gosset & Williams, 1998; Seklecki & Paynich, 2007). Either criticism creates unnecessary stress for female officers.

Seklecki and Paynich (2007) surveyed more than 500 female officers from randomly selected police agencies across the United States using the National Directory of Law Enforcement Administrators, Correctional Institutions, and Related Agencies database. They found that nearly 40 percent of women felt they were made to feel less welcome than were men and over 30 percent said they were treated worse than men were during their rookie years. Gossett (1996) reported that female officers in the Dallas-Fort Worth area identified stressors on the job as treatment by male officers and supervisors, the need to prove themselves, and difficulties with promotion.

In their study of Australian female police officers, Thompson, Kirk, and Brown (2006) found that interpersonal stressors, including lack of colleague support, contributed significantly to their stress levels. Lack of colleague support is particularly problematic in terms of psychological well-being. Families and nonpolice friends may not understand the types of situations an officer experiences and describing these experiences may create additional fear and worry for their loved ones. A fellow officer is in the best position to comprehend and support his or her colleague (Waters & Ussery, 2007).

In addition to the psychological reaction, not "fitting in" can also be a safety issue in policing. Female officers have reported that their male counterparts fail to provide adequate backup and protection and have questioned their abilities as a police officer (Haarr, 1997). Police solidarity is an important component of safety, yet female officers may feel isolated from coworker support (Shelley, Morabito & Tobin-Gurley, 2011).

The need to fit in creates a dilemma for female officers. On the one hand, women are not expected to act like men because this would be seen as breaking away from the traditional female stereotype. On the other hand, women must perform duties as well as or better than their male counterparts (Seklecki & Paynich, 2007). Female officers may become fearful of making mistakes and develop a fear of failure (Wertsch, 1998). Also, a mistake by one female officer may be extended to all female officers in that unit or department (Martin & Jurik, 1996).

In addition, the duties for female officers are likely to be different than those for male officers. Female officer duties are more likely to include paperwork, community relations, training, and nonemergencies (Brown & Fielding, 1993; Dick & Jankowicz, 2001), and they have become the unofficial subject matter experts on domestic and child abuse

(Wertsch, 1998; Westmarland, 2001). Male officers are assigned to more danger-prone situations, including violent crime and emergency response (Brown & Fielding, 1993; Dick & Jankowicz, 2001; Wertsch, 1998). This imbalance provides fewer opportunities for female officers to gain experience and advance in their policing career (Brown & Fielding, 1993; Dick & Jankowicz, 2001).

Police officers are public servants; their job requires considerable "face time" with the community. Although few in number, prior research has shown that, in general, the public is supportive of female officers (Schuck & Rabe-Hemp, 2007). This may be true for two different reasons. Perpetrators may be more fearful of a female officer's reaction to a potentially dangerous situation than they are of a male officer's reaction. According to Johnson (1991),

> (S)everal police women remarked that when a male perpetrator is arrested by a male officer the male ego is challenged – battle lines are immediately drawn. . . . It was also noted that some male offenders comply because they assume that since the woman officer does not have the body strength, she is more likely to use the gun or they believe that women with guns are unpredictable.

Conversely, some have suggested that women may be better at policing than men are due to fewer citizen complaints, excessive force liability lawsuits, and allegations of excessive force (Schuck & Rabe-Hemp, 2007). In interviews with female officers, Johnson (1991) found that women felt having better communication skills compensated for their lack of physical skills. Schuck and Rabe-Hemp (2007) raised caution in suggesting that women are better than men because that perception creates unrealistic expectations for female officers, which may have similar consequences as the earlier assumptions that women could not perform police work.

Do police women experience harassment and sexism during recruitment, hiring, and promotion?

Sexual harassment and sexual discrimination may be two sources of stress for female officers (Chaiyavej & Morash, 2008; Deschamps, Paganon-Badinier, Marchand & Merle, 2003; Greene & del Carmen, 2002; Liberman et al., 2002; Morash et al., 2006; Thompson et al., 2006). Previous research on stress and gender indicates that interpersonal issues, that is, lack of coworker support, sexual harassment, discrimination, conflict, and lack of confidentiality, are significant stressors for women officers, who rate emotional support as more important than men do (Deschamps et al., 2003; Thompson et al., 2006).

In their study of police officers from New York City, New York; Oakland, California; and San Jose, California, Liberman and associates (2002) found that, although routine work stressors were similar among male and female officers, women and minority officers reported a more discriminatory work environment. Morash and colleagues (2006) found that female officers experienced significantly more problems with sexual harassment, bias, and underestimation of their physical ability than did male officers. Prior studies have reported that most female officers have experienced sexual discrimination (Chaiyavej & Morash, 2008; Greene & del Carmen, 2002). Even more troublesome is that this behavior is often tolerated, ignored, or endorsed among organizational subcultures (NCWP, 1999). When Hassell and Brandl (2009) found that the least common workplace stressor for officers in their study was sexually offensive behavior, they offered potential explanations for this contradictory finding: police women may view sexual harassment as "the price of fitting in," or they may simply handle the situation.

Are the expectations for police women different than those for police men?

Policing requires some of the longest and most inflexible work hours during childbearing and child-raising years. Consequently, female officers may postpone or forgo having children (Mason & Goulden, 2004), or they may choose to forgo career advancement in order to start and care for a family (Whetstone, 2001).

Women officers who decide to have children may qualify for the Family and Medical Leave Act of 1993 (FMLA). There is no standard national policy in place for police women during their pregnancy, however (Schulze, 2010). Under FMLA, the officer may qualify if she develops complications during pregnancy (i.e. serious health condition). Otherwise, she may be expected to continue in her current position. Schulze (2010) found that only 13 percent of police agencies surveyed had a leave policy in place for pregnant officers and these policies varied considerably. For example, 5 of the 203 agencies surveyed permit additional time off in excess of the FMLA,; the New York City Police Department provides up to 1 year of unpaid child care, up to 8 weeks of paid leave, and an optional maternity uniform for pregnant officers (Schulze, 2010).

Certain exposures aligned with policing may pose significant health risks to the officer and her unborn child. Shift work and long work hours have been associated with preterm birth (Bodin, Axelsson & Ahlborg, 1999). Pregnant officers are more susceptible to adverse health effects from occupational chemical exposure (i.e., heavy metals, organic solvents, pesticides) and physical hazards (radiation, trauma, noise) (Czarnecki, 2003). For example, lead exposure during pregnancy is associated with preeclampsia, spontaneous abortion, premature membrane rupture, and neurobehavioral effects in children (Gardella, 2001; Winder, 1993). Firearms training exposes officers not only to lead but also to other metals such as copper, arsenic, and barium, which could lead to harmful health effects (Dams et al., 1988), and to firearms cleaning products, which often contain organic solvents known to have teratogenic effects (Czarnecki, 2003). Police officers are exposed to high noise levels during firearms training, when using vehicle sirens, and in traffic. The known effects of noise exposure on pregnancy are well-documented and include preterm delivery (Nurminen, 1995; Zhan et al., 1991), miscarriage (Zhan et al., 1991; Zhang, Cai & Lee, 1992), intrauterine growth retardation (Nurminen, 1995), and hypertension (Zhan et al., 1991).

To reduce these potential exposures and related health effects, some agencies either place pregnant officers on "light duty," administrative duties that do not require them to perform the typical physical duties and mandatory overtime, or prohibit pregnant officers from working in a "uniformed capacity" (Schulze, 2010). Still other agencies deny work limitations or light duty to pregnant officers. Officers in advanced pregnancies may have difficulty wearing their bullet-proof vest or reaching for their weapon (Shelley et al., 2011).

Returning to work following the birth of a child may also be a source of stress for female officers. Considerable attention has been raised regarding the issue of work-life balance (positive) or work-life conflict (negative). Being a police officer requires availability and flexibility. Shift work and long working hours can disrupt an officer's ability to have a normal family life (Davey, Obst & Sheehan, 2001). Women who have traditionally had more domestic responsibilities may find the "balance" to be their greatest stressor (He, Zhao & Archbold, 2002). Women may be more likely to experience feelings of abandonment and neglect (mother's guilt) and pressure from coworkers and the public to conform to traditional family roles (i.e., staying at home) (Schulze,

2010). Police women who are already mothers may face discrimination when applying for employment, because police work requires substantial flexibility in scheduling (Correll & Benard, 2007).

Among all police women, are there certain groups who may be more adversely affected by occupational stressors?

The stressors discussed previously represent examples for all police women. In our review of the literature, two groups of police women were identified who may be more adversely affected by these stressors. We will discuss each briefly.

As described earlier, many of the smaller and more rural police departments have a low percentage of women officers (6.2%). Krimmel and Gormley (2003) found that when the percentage of women in a department is less than 15 percent, female officers have lower levels of job satisfaction, higher levels of work-related depression, and lower self-esteem. This may be due to the fact that the frequencies of stressors are increased or because they lack support from coworkers and the administration. Belknap and Shelley (1992) commented that

> [P]olicewomen in departments in which policewomen make up a smaller percentage of the department are expected to face more resistance than policewomen in departments where policewomen make up a larger percentage of the department.

Women in smaller police agencies were more likely to perceive gender differences in policing styles, and the percentage of women officers is significantly related to these perceptions (Belknap & Shelley, 1992; Greene & del Carmen, 2002).

Minority police women experience both sexual and racial discrimination (Dodge & Pogrebin, 2001; Haarr, 1997; Hassell & Brandl, 2009; Taylor Greene, 2000). In their study of 1,191 police officers from the Milwaukee Police Department, Hassell and Brandl (2009) found that white, black, and Latina female officers had more negative workplace experiences than white male officers. In addition, black and Latina female officers had higher stress levels than white male officers had. In a qualitative study of urban police officers, Dodge and Pogrebin (2001) found a variety of stressors experienced by black female officers. Among these were struggles to fit in with other women officers or other black officers. Black women felt they needed to work twice as hard as their white female counterparts did for recognition (Dodge & Pogrebin, 2001). They also felt unsupported by their black male counterparts, who seemed interested in fitting in with white male officers and who thought showing support for black females would prohibit their own inclusion (Dodge & Pogrebin, 2001).

HEALTH EFFECTS OF STRESS ON FEMALE POLICE OFFICERS

Research investigations examining the association between police stressors and health outcomes, including psychological and physical health, in female police officers are rare. Many studies have included only male officers (Garbarino et al., 2011) or did not compare differences in men and women (Arial, Gonik, Wild & Danuser, 2010; Collins & Gibbs, 2003; Davey et al., 2001; Gershon et al., 2009). In studies including only male officers, the interpretation of associations of interest may be extended to women officers. In studies including both men and women, the sample size for female officers tends to be small, which makes detecting significant differences problematic.

Stress and Psychological Health

In general, stress-related mental ill health has worsened for police officers over the past two decades (Collins & Gibbs, 2003). Results from studies examining sex differences in the association between stress and psychological health are mixed.

Yoo and Franke (2011) compared measures of psychological distress between female and male police officers in Iowa. Female officers had significantly higher levels of perceived stress, higher job demand with lower job control (i.e., job strain), and more fatigue and exhaustion (i.e., vital exhaustion) and felt they put forth more effort with fewer rewards (i.e., effort-reward imbalance) than the male officers did (Yoo & Franke, 2011). In a study of Baltimore, Maryland, police officers, He and colleagues (2002) found that female officers had significantly higher levels of somatization (i.e., psychological distress from perception of cardiovascular, gastrointestinal, or respiratory disorders) and depression compared to male officers. For male officers, both work environment and work-family conflict were significant predictors of somatization, anxiety, and depression, yet for female officers, only work–family conflict significantly predicted these health outcomes (He et al., 2002).

Prolonged occupational stress due to emotional and interpersonal interactions can lead to symptoms of burnout symptoms, such as depersonalization, emotional exhaustion, and reduced professional efficacy. These symptoms may in turn have negative consequences for both the individual and the organization (Maslach, Schaufeli & Leiter, 2001). Martinussen, Richardsen, and Burke (2007) examined work and non-work stressors and their association with burnout in a sample of Norwegian police officers. Burnout scores were similar for male and female officers; both work-home pressures and lack of support were associated with all three dimensions of burnout (Martinussen et al., 2007). As described earlier, both work-family balance and lack of coworker support are substantial sources of stress for female police officers.

Another negative health outcome that female officers may experience is PTSD. PTSD is an anxiety disorder that occurs following a tragic event (National Institute of Mental Health [NIMH], 2013b). Symptoms of PTSD must occur for at least 1 month and include reexperiencing symptoms (i.e., flashbacks, bad dreams), avoidance symptoms (i.e., feeling emotionally numb, losing interest in activities), and hyperarousal symptoms (i.e., easily startled, having trouble sleeping) (NIMH, 2013b). Several studies of PTSD in the general population have reported that women have higher rates of PTSD when compared to men (Breslau et al., 1997; Kessler et al., 1995); the difference is not entirely due to greater exposure to sexual assault in women (Pole et al., 2001).

PTSD can be a reality for police officers who are confronted with violent and tragic events in their jobs, a situation somewhat similar to that of the military. Reports on gender differences in PTSD among the military are somewhat mixed. Some studies indicate that female veterans have higher rates of PTSD than male veterans have (Stretch, Knudson & Durand, 1998; Wolfe, Brown & Kelley, 1993), whereas others report no gender differences (Sutker, Davis, Uddo & Ditta, 1995) or even lower prevalence rates of PTSD among female veterans when compared with their male counterparts (Kulka et al., 1990). Studies have examined the association between traumatic police events and PTSD, but very few have examined whether there are differences between male and female officers. Following the 1998 fire at a gathering place in Sweden that claimed the lives of sixty-three teens, Renck, Weisæth, and Skarbö (2002) measured PTSD symptoms in forty-one police officers who were either at the scene of the fire or at the hospitals where the injured were transported. They found that female officers, although small in number (n = 5), had higher levels of intrusive thoughts (one component of PTSD) than did male officers (Renck et al., 2002).

Among 655 police officers (519 men and 136 women) from three large U.S. metropolitan areas, there were no significant differences in PTSD symptoms by sex (Pole et al., 2001). Pole and colleagues suggest that training factors along with selection into policing may help protect female officers from the increased vulnerability to PTSD found in the general female population. In addition to this inoculation factor, coping mechanisms may also play an important role in reducing the risk. Whereas in general male and female officers may have similar levels of police stress, the way in which they cope with stress may be different (Haarr & Morash, 1999; He et al., 2002). Martinussen and colleagues (2007) suggest that female police officers may use more active coping mechanisms to help them deal with negative situations. He and colleagues (2002) found that female officers used significantly more constructive coping than male officers did: making a plan of action and following it, 48 percent versus 44 percent; talking with family and friends, 52 percent versus 37 percent; praying for guidance and strength, 59 percent versus 29 percent; and relying on faith, 62 percent versus 35 percent. Use of constructive coping was found to reduce depression in female officers (He et al., 2002).

Stress and Cardiovascular Disease

CVD has been and continues to be the leading cause of death for women in the United States (Department of Health and Human Services [DHS], 2009). Psychological stress has been independently associated with increased risk for CVD (Rozanski, Blumenthal & Kaplan, 1999; Tennant, 2000). Like other health effects, the association between work stress and CVD is understudied in female officers. What follow are brief summaries from the few published studies we identified with CVD, CVD risk factors, and subclinical CVD as the outcome.

One of the more recent studies of the health effects of policing on women was by Yoo and Franke (2011). Using self-report questionnaires, police women had a significantly increased prevalence of hypercholesterolemia, a known independent CVD risk factor (Ridker, Rifai, Cook, Bradwin & Buring, 2005), compared to a civilian cohort matched on age, race, and socioeconomic status (46% vs. 29%) (Yoo & Franke,

2011). Yoo and Franke (2011) found that both occupation and gender were significant predictors of perceived future ill health. Two thirds (68%) of the female officers surveyed felt that being a police officer and 42 percent felt that being both a police officer *and* being female increased their risk of chronic disease. Importantly, those female officers who reported that being an officer contributed to their chronic disease risk were more likely to be overweight or obese; have higher levels of perceived stress, job strain, and effort-reward imbalance; and lower social support than those who reported the opposite (Yoo & Franke, 2011). The findings were similar for those who reported being a female officer contributed to chronic disease risk with the addition of significantly higher CVD symptoms or history than those who reported the opposite (Yoo & Franke, 2011).

In the BCOPS study, a significant association was found between workplace stress and the metabolic syndrome (MetSyn) in female but not in male officers (Hartley, Burchfiel, et al., 2011). The MetSyn is a group of risk factors, including abdominal obesity, elevated triglycerides, hypertension, glucose intolerance, and reduced HDL-C, that has been shown to increase risk for developing CVD and diabetes (Grundy et al., 2005). MetSyn scores range from zero to five, with scores of three or more indicating presence of MetSyn (Grundy et al., 2005). Using the Spielberger Police Stress Survey, positive and significant associations were found for all three types of police stressors in women – organizational stressors, physical and psychological threats, and lack of support – with the number of MetSyn components, and specifically with higher odds of having abdominal obesity and reduced HDL-C (i.e., "good" cholesterol).

Adding to the findings of this study, the association between MetSyn and subclinical CVD was examined in the same BCOPS study cohort. Carotid intima media thickness (IMT), measured noninvasively with B-mode ultrasound, was used as the measure of sublinical CVD (Riley, 2002). Prior studies have indicated that the association between MetSyn and carotid IMT is stronger in women than in men (Iglseder, Cip, Malaimare, Ladurner & Paulweber, 2005; Kawamoto, Tomita, Inoue, Ohtsuka & Kamitani, 2007). A positive and significant association was found between MetSyn and carotid IMT in female but not male officers (Hartley, Shankar, et al., 2011). Importantly, carotid IMT was significantly higher among women officers who had either hypertension or reduced HDL-C (Hartley, Shankar, et al., 2011).

In addition to using questionnaires, psychological stress can also be assessed objectively through analysis of salivary cortisol. Cortisol is an important glucocorticoid hormone that can measure the body's physiological reaction to stress. Cortisol levels rise when the body reacts to an environmental or physiological event, like waking up in the morning, or when it is exposed to a potentially stressful situation, such as being involved in a high-speed chase. Once the situation is over, the increased secretion of cortisol ends and cortisol output returns to normal. Cortisol can be measured noninvasively from samples of saliva. In the BCOPS study, the association between salivary cortisol levels at awakening and brachial artery reactivity (BAR) was examined. BAR measures the function of the endothelium or lining of blood vessels using flow-mediated dilation via ultrasound (Corretti et al., 2002). Dysfunction of the endothelium is a marker of early or subclinical CVD (Widlansky, Gokce, Keaney & Vita, 2003). Results indicated that elevated cortisol secretion after awakening was significantly and inversely associated with impaired flow-mediated dilation in female but not male officers (Violanti et al., 2009). Violanti and colleagues (2009) suggested that this association might have been more easily detected in women because women may experience greater stress due to responsibilities outside police work, conflict with colleagues, and social isolation.

Health Outcomes of Depression

In the United States, the lifetime prevalence of depression among adults is 16.5 percent with an average age of onset at 32 years (NIMH, 2013a). Women are 70 percent more likely than men to experience depression during their lifetime (NIMH, 2013a), and this increased prevalence may be due to hormonal or biological factors (NIMH, 2013c).

The risk of developing CVD in those with depression is approximately 1.7 times higher than in those without depression (Keyes, 2004). Kinder, Carnethon, Palaniappan, King, and Fortmann (2004) found that young women with a history of depression were twice as likely to have MetSyn as those without depression; yet, there was no association in young men. In the BCOPS study, female officers had a higher prevalence of depression than did male officers (16.0% vs. 10.2%) (Hartley et al., 2012). The results for the association between depressive symptoms and subclinical CVD are mixed. Violanti and colleagues (2013) found a significant inverse association between depressive symptoms and

BAR, a subclinical measure of CVD. Although this association was not gender specific, the association was significant among those who were current cigarette smokers. This may be particularly important for women officers, because the percentage of current smokers in the BCOPS study was twice as high for women than it was for men: 26.0 percent versus 13.1 percent (Violanti et al., 2013). Other studies utilizing the same sample found no association between depressive symptoms and carotid IMT (Violanti et al., 2012) or the MetSyn (Hartley, Shankar, et al., 2011). Hartley, Shankar, and colleagues (2011) found a significant association between depressive symptoms and MetSyn in a sample of male police officers from Spokane, Washington. This cohort was significantly older than the BCOPS study participants were, however, and age is a risk factor for subclinical CVD.

Prior studies have suggested a link between depression and osteoporosis. Eskandari and colleagues (2007) found the prevalence of low bone mineral density to be higher in premenopausal women with depression than in those without depression. Osteoporosis, also known as porous bone, is a disease characterized by reduced bone mineral density and deterioration of bone tissue leading to increased risk of fracture (National Institute of Arthritis and Musculoskeletal and Skin Diseases [NIAMS], 2012). Risk factors for osteoporosis include being female, of older age, of small body size, Caucasian or Asian and having a family history of osteoporosis and a host of modifiable risk factors including low levels of sex hormones, low calcium and vitamin D levels, certain medications and lifestyle (i.e., alcohol abuse, cigarette smoking, physical inactivity) factors (NIAMS, 2012). In the BCOPS study, higher levels of self-reported depressive symptoms were significantly associated with lower levels of bone mineral density among female officers but not among male officers (Charles et al., 2012). The authors suggested the inverse association found in female officers may be due to additional stressors experienced by women, including many discussed earlier: racial discrimination, sexual harassment, and childcare and household responsibilities (Charles et al., 2012).

CONCLUSIONS

In summary, female police officers comprise a small yet slowly increasing percentage of police departments today, even though policies have been in existence for decades to increase their representation. Prior research suggests that female officers face unique stressors as a result of working in a male-dominated occupation, including work factors, such as perception of inadequate physical ability, sexual harassment and discrimination, and nonwork stressors, such as family responsibilities and pregnancy. The proportion of female officers tends to decrease with decreasing police department size. In the smaller police departments, women officers in general and minority women in particular may have less coworker support and be more affected by these stressors. Prior investigations, including the study of police officers in Buffalo, New York, have found significant cross-sectional associations between police stressors and psychological and physiological health. These include associations with burnout, depression, MetSyn, and subclinical (or early) cardiovascular disease.

Future research studies of police officers should strive to include more female police officers, particularly women in the smaller police agencies. Increased participation by female officers in research studies will help to identify specific biological mechanisms driving the sex differences, such as differences in hormone levels or inflammation. Additionally, research studies with prospective designs are highly desirable and will help to determine causal associations (i.e., does depression lead to MetSyn).

Disclaimer: The findings and conclusions in this report are those of the authors and do not necessarily represent the views of the National Institute for Occupational Safety and Health.

REFERENCES

Arial, M., Gonik, V., Wild, P., & Danuser, B. (2010). Association of work related chronic stressors and psychiatric symptoms in a Swiss sample of police officers: A cross sectional questionnaire study. *International Archives of Occupational and Environmental Health, 83*, 323–331.

Belknap, J., & Shelley, J. K. (1992). The new Lone Ranger: Policewomen on patrol. *American Journal of Police, 12*, 47–76.

Berg, A. M., Hem, E., Lau, B., Håseth, K., & Ekeberg, Ø. (2005). Stress in the Norwegian police service. *Occupational Medicine, 55*, 113–120.

Bodin, L., Axelsson, G., & Ahlborg, G. Jr. (1999). The association of shift work and nitrous oxide exposure in pregnancy with birth weight and gestational age. *Epidemiology, 10*, 429–436.

Breslau, N., Davis, G. C., Andreski, P., Peterson, E. L., & Schultz, L. R. (1997). Sex differences in posttraumatic stress disorder. *Archives of General Psychiatry, 54*, 1044.

Brown, J., & Fielding, J. (1993). Qualitative differences in men and women police officers' experience of occupational stress. *Work & Stress, 7*, 327–340.

Chaiyavej, S., & Morash, M. (2008). Dynamics of sexual harassment for policewomen working alongside men. *Policing: An International Journal of Police Strategies & Management, 31*, 485–498.

Charles, L. E., Fekedulegn, D., Miller, D. B., Wactawski-Wende, J., Violanti, J. M., Andrew, M. E., & Burchfiel, C. M. (2012). Depressive symptoms and bone mineral density among police officers in a northeastern US city. *Global Journal of Health Science, 4*, 39–50.

Collins, P. A., & Gibbs, A. C. C. (2003). Stress in police officers: A study of the origins, prevalence and severity of stress-related symptoms within a county police force. *Occupational Medicine, 53*, 256–264.

Correll, S., & Benard, S. (2007). Getting a job: Is there a motherhood penalty? *American Journal of Sociology, 112*, 1297–1388.

Corretti, M. C., Anderson, T. J., Benjamin, E. J., Celermajer, D., Charbonneau, F., Creager, M. A., . . . Vogel, R. (2002). Guidelines for the ultrasound assessment of endothelial-dependent flow-mediated vasodilation of the brachial artery: A report of the International Brachial Artery Reactivity Task Force. *Journal of the American College of Cardiology, 39*, 257–265.

Czarnecki, F. (2003). The pregnant officer. *Clinics in Occupational and Environmental Medicine, 3*, 641–648.

Dams, R., Vandecasteele, C., Desmet, B., Helsen, M., Nagels, M., Vermeir, G., & Yu, Z. Q. (1988). Element concentrations in the air of an indoor shooting range. *Science of the Total Environment, 77*, 1–13.

Davey, J. D., Obst, P. L., & Sheehan, M. C. (2001). Demographic and workplace characteristics which add to the prediction of stress and job satisfaction within the police workplace. *Journal of Police and Criminal Psychology, 16*, 29–39.

Dejong, C. (2005). Gender differences in officer attitude and behavior. *Women & Criminal Justice, 15*, 1–32.

Department of Health and Human Services, CDC (DHHS). (2009). *Leading cause of death in females*. Retrieved on March 21, 2013, from http://www.cdc.gov/women/lcod/

Deschamps, F., Paganon-Badinier, I., Marchand, A., & Merle, C. (2003). Sources of assessment of occupational stress in the police. *Journal of Occupational Health, 45*, 358–364.

Dick, P., & Jankowicz, D. (2001). Social constructionist account of police culture and its influence on the representation and progression of female officers: A repertory grid analysis in a UK police force. *Policing: An International Journal of Police Strategies & Management, 24*, 181–199.

Dodge, M., & Pogrebin, M. (2001). African-American policewomen: An exploration of professional relationships. *Policing: An International Journal of Police Strategies & Management, 24*, 550–562.

Eskandari, F., Martinez, P. E., Torvik, S., Phillips, T. M., Sternberg, E. M., Mistry, S., . . . Cizza, G. (2007). Low bone mass in premenopausal women with depression. *Archives of Internal Medicine, 167*, 2329–2336.

Garbarino, S., Magnavita, N., Elovainio, M., Heponiemi, T., Ciprani, F., Cuomo, G., & Bergamaschi, A. (2011). Police job strain during routine activities and a major event. *Occupational Medicine, 61*, 395–399.

Gardella, C. (2001). Lead exposure in pregnancy: A review of the literature and argument for routine prenatal screening. *Obstetrical & Gynecological Survey, 56*, 231–238.

Gershon, R. R., Barocas, B., Canton, A. N., Li, X., & Vlahov, D. (2009). Mental, physical, and behavioral outcomes associated with perceived work stress in police officers. *Criminal Justice and Behavior, 36*, 275–289.

Gossett, J. (1996). *Perceived Discrimination Among Women in Law Enforcement in the Dallas, Fort Worth Metroplex.* (Unpublished master's thesis). Texas Woman's University, Denton, TX.

Gossett, J. L., & Williams, J. E. (1998). Perceived discrimination among women in law enforcement. *Women & Criminal Justice, 10*, 53–73.

Greene, H. T., & del Carmen, A. (2002). Female police officers in Texas: Perceptions of colleagues and stress. *Policing: An International Journal of Police Strategies & Management, 25*, 385–398.

Grundy, S. M., Cleeman, J. I., Daniels, S. R., Donato, K. A., Eckel, R. H., Franklin, B. A., . . . Costa, F. (2005). Diagnosis and management of the metabolic syndrome: An American Heart Association/National Heart, Lung, and Blood Institute Scientific Statement. *Circulation, 112*, 2735–2752.

Haarr, R. (1997). Patterns of interaction in a police bureau: Race and gender barriers to integration. *Justice Quarterly, 14*, 53–85.

Haarr, R. N., & Morash, M. (1999). Gender, race and strategies of coping with occupational stress in policing. *Justice Quarterly, 16*, 303–336.

Hartley, T. A., Burchfiel, C. M., Fekedulegn, D., Andrew, M. E., Knox, S. S., & Violanti, J. M. (2011). Associations between police officer stress and the metabolic syndrome. *International Journal of Emergency Mental Health, 13*, 243–256.

Hartley, T. A., Knox, S. S., Fekedulegn, D., Barbosa-Leiker, C., Violanti, J. M., Andrew, M. E., & Burchfiel, C. M. (2012). Association between depressive symptoms and metabolic syndrome in police officers: Results from two cross-sectional studies. *Journal of Environmental and Public Health, 2012*, 2012: 861219.

Hartley, T. A., Shankar, A., Fekedulegn, D., Violanti, J. M., Andrew, M. E., Knox, S. S., & Burchfiel, C. M. (2011). Metabolic syndrome and carotid intima media thickness in urban police officers. *Journal of Occupational and Environmental Medicine, 53*, 553–561.

Hassell, K. D., & Brandl, S. G. (2009). An examination of the workplace experiences of police patrol officers: The role of race, sex, and sexual orientation. *Police Quarterly, 12*, 408–430.

He, N., Zhao, J., & Archbold, C. A. (2002). Gender and police stress: The convergent and divergent impact of work environment, work-family conflict, and stress coping mechanisms of female and male police officers. *Policing: An International Journal of Police Strategies & Management, 25*, 687–708.

Hickman, M., & Reaves, B. (2006). *Local police departments, 2003*. U.S. Department of Justice, Office of Justice Programs, Bureau of Justice Statistics. Retrieved on February 19, 2013, from http://bjs.ojp.usdoj.gov/index.cfm?ty=pbdetail&iid =1045

Iglseder, B., Cip, P., Malaimare, L., Ladurner, G., & Paulweber, B. (2005). The metabolic syndrome is a stronger risk factor for early carotid atherosclerosis in women than in men. *Stroke, 36,* 1212–1217.

Johnson, L. B. (1991). Job strain among police officers: Gender comparisons. *Police Studies: International Review of Police Development, 14,* 12–16.

Kawamoto, R., Tomita, H., Inoue, A., Ohtsuka, N., & Kamitani, A. (2007). Metabolic syndrome may be a risk factor for early carotid atherosclerosis in women but not in men. *Journal of Atherosclerosis and Thrombosis, 14,* 36–43.

Kessler, R. C., Sonnega, A., Bromet, E., Hughes, M., & Nelson, C. B. (1995). Posttraumatic stress disorder in the National Comorbidity Survey. *Archives of General Psychiatry, 52,* 1048.

Keyes, C. L. (2004). The nexus of cardiovascular disease and depression revisited: The complete mental health perspective and the moderating role of age and gender. *Aging & Mental Health, 8,* 266–274.

Kinder, L. S., Carnethon, M. R., Palaniappan, L. P., King, A. C., & Fortmann, S. P. (2004). Depression and the metabolic syndrome in young adults: Findings from the Third National Health and Nutrition Examination Survey. *Psychosomatic Medicine, 66,* 316–322.

Krimmel, J. T., & Gormley, P. E. (2003). Tokenism and job satisfaction for policewomen. *American Journal of Criminal Justice, 28,* 73–88.

Kruger, K. J. (2007). Pregnancy & policing: Are they compatible? Pushing the legal limits on behalf of equal employment opportunities. *Wisconsin Women's Law Journal, 22,* 61–90.

Kulka, R. A., Schlenger, W. E., Fairbank, J. A., Hough, R. L., Jordan, B. K., & Marmar, C. R., (1990). *Trauma and the Vietnam War Generation: Report of Findings From the National Vietnam Veterans Readjustment Study*. New York: Brunner/Mazel.

Langton, L. (2010). *Women in law enforcement, 1987–2008*. U.S. Department of Justice, Office of Justice Programs, Bureau of Justice Statistics. Retrieved on February 19, 2013, from http://bjs.ojp.usdoj.gov/index.cfm?ty=pbdetail&iid=2274

Liberman, A. M., Best, S. R., Meltzer, T. J., Fagan, J. A., Weiss, D. S., & Marmar, C. R. (2002). Routine occupational distress in police. *Policing: An International Journal of Police Strategies & Management, 25,* 421–441. http://dx.doi.org/10.1108/136395 10210429446.

Martin, S. E., & Jurik, N. C. (1996). *Doing Justice, Doing Gender: Women in Legal and Criminal Justice Occupations*. Thousand Oaks, CA: Sage.

Martinussen, M., Richardsen, A. M., & Burke, R. J. (2007). Job demands, job resources, and burnout among police officers. *Journal of Criminal Justice, 35,* 239–249.

Maslach, C., Schaufeli, W. B., & Leiter, M. P. (2001). Job Burnout. *Annual Review of Psychology, 52,* 397–422.

Mason, M. A., & Goulden, M. (2004). Marriage and baby blues: Redefining gender equity in the academy. *The Annals of the American Academy of Political and Social Science, 596,* 86–103.

Morash, M., Kwak, D. H., & Haarr, R. (2006). Gender differences in the predictors of police stress. *Policing: An International Journal of Police Strategies & Management, 29*, 541–563.

National Center for Women and Policing (NCWP). (1999). *Equality Denied: The Status of Women in Policing: 1998.* Retrieved on March 21, 2013, from http://www.womenandpolicing.org/Final_1999StatusReport.htm

National Center for Women and Policing (NCWP). (2002). *Equality Denied: The Status of Women in Policing: 2001.* New York: Columbia University.

National Institute of Arthritis and Musculoskeletal and Skin Diseases (NIAMS). (2012). *Osteoporosis Overview.* Retrieved on February 19, 2013, from http://www.niams.nih.gov/Health_Info/Bone/Osteoporosis/overview.asp

National Institute of Mental Health (NIMH). (2013a). *Major Depressive disorder Among Adults.* Retrieved on February 19, 2013, from http://www.nimh.nih.gov/statistics/1MDD_ADULT.shtml

National Institute of Mental Health (NIMH). (2013b). *Post-Traumatic Stress Disorder (PTSD).* NIH Publication No. 08.6388. U.S. Department of Health and Human Services. National Institutes of Health. Retrieved on February 19, 2013, from http://www.nimh.nih.gov/health/publications/post-traumatic-stress-disorder-ptsd/nimh_ptsd_booklet.pdf

National Institute of Mental Health (NIMH). (2013c). *What Causes Depression?* Retrieved on February 19, 2013, from http://www.nimh.nih.gov/health/publications/depression/what-causes-depression.shtml

Nurminen, T. (1995). Female noise exposure, shift work, and reproduction. *Journal of Occupational and Environmental Medicine, 37*, 945–950.

Pole, N., Best, S. R., Weiss, D. S., Metzler, T., Liberman, A. M., Fagan, J., & Marmar, C. R. (2001). Effects of gender and ethnicity on duty-related posttraumatic stress symptoms among urban police officers. *The Journal of Nervous and Mental Disease, 189*, 442–448.

Renck, B., Weisæth, L., & Skarbö, S. (2002). Stress reactions in police officers after a disaster rescue operation. *Nordic Journal of Psychiatry, 56*, 7–14.

Ridker, P. M., Rifai, N., Cook, N. R., Bradwin, G., & Buring, J. E. (2005). Non–HDL cholesterol, apolipoproteins AI and B100, standard lipid measures, lipid ratios, and CRP as risk factors for cardiovascular disease in women. *Journal of the American Medical Association, 294*, 326–333.

Riley, W. A. (2002). Carotid intima-media thickness: Risk assessment and scanning protocol. *European Heart Journal, 23*, 916–918.

Rozanski, A., Blumenthal, J. A., & Kaplan, J. (1999). Impact of psychological factors on the pathogenesis of cardiovascular disease and implications for therapy. *Circulation, 99*, 2192–2217.

Schuck, A. M., & Rabe-Hemp, C. (2007). Women police. *Women & Criminal Justice, 16*, 91–117.

Schulze, C. (2010). Institutionalized masculinity in U.S. police departments: How maternity leave policies (or lack thereof) affect women in policing. *Criminal Justice Studies, 23*, 177–193.

Seklecki, R., & Paynich, R. (2007). A national survey of female police officers: An overview of findings. *Police Practice and Research, 8*, 17–30.

Shelley, T., Morabito, M., & Tobin-Gurley, J. (2011). Gendered institutions and gender roles: Understanding the experience of women in policing. *Criminal Justice Studies: A Critical Journal of Crime, Law and Society, 24,* 351–367.

Stretch, R. H., Knudson, K. H., & Durand, D. (1998). Effects of premilitary and military trauma on the development of post-traumatic stress disorder symptoms in female and male active duty soldiers. *Military Medicine, 163,* 466–470.

Sutker, P. B., Davis, J. M., Uddo, M., & Ditta, S. R. (1995). Assessment of psychological distress in Persian Gulf troops: Ethnicity and gender comparisons. *Journal of Personality Assessment, 64,* 415–427.

Taylor Greene, H. (2000). Black females in law enforcement. *Journal of Contemporary Criminal Justice, 16,* 230–239.

Tennant, C. (2000). Work stress and coronary heart disease. *Journal of Cardiovascular Risk, 7,* 273–276.

Thompson, B. M., Kirk, A., & Brown, D. (2006). Sources of stress in policewomen: A three factor model. *International Journal of Stress Management, 13,* 309–328.

U.S. Bureau of Labor Statistics. (2004). *Employment and Earnings 2003.* Retrieved on March 20, 2013, from http://www.bls.gov/cps/cpsa2003.pdf

Violanti, J. M., & Aron, F. (1994). Ranking police stressors. *Psychological Reports, 75,* 824–826.

Violanti, J. M., Burchfiel, C. M., Fekedulegn, D., Andrew, M. E., Dorn, J., Hartley, T. A., . . . Miller, D. B. (2009). Cortisol patterns and brachial artery reactivity in a high stress environment. *Psychiatry Research, 169,* 75–81.

Violanti, J. M., Charles, L. E., Gu, J. K., Burchfiel, C. M., Andrew, M. E., Joseph, P. N., & Dom, J. M. (2012). Depressive symptoms and carotid artery intima-media thickness in police officers. *International Archives of Occupational and Environmental Health, November 25,* 1–12.

Violanti, J. M., Charles, L. E., Gu, J. K., Burchfiel, C. M., Andrew, M. E., Joseph, P. N., & Dom, J. M. (2013). Associations of depressive symptoms and brachial artery reactivity among police officers. *Safety and Health at Work, 4,* 27–36.

Waters, J. A., & Ussery, W. (2007). Police stress: History, contributing factors, symptoms, and interventions. *Policing: An International Journal of Police Strategies & Management, 30,* 169–188.

Wertsch, T. L. (1998). Walking the thin blue line: Policewomen and tokenism today. *Women and Criminal Justice, 9,* 23–61.

Westmarland, L. (2001). *Gender and Policing: Sex, Power and Police Culture.* Cullompton, UK: Willan Publishing.

Whetstone, T. S. (2001). Copping out: Why police officers decline to participate in the sergeant's promotional process. *American Journal of Criminal Justice, 25,* 147–159.

Widlansky, M. E., Gokce, N., Keaney, J. F., & Vita, J. A. (2003). The clinical implications of endothelial dysfunction. *Journal of the American College of Cardiology, 42,* 1149–1160.

Winder, C. (1993). Lead, reproduction and development. *Neurotoxicology, 14,* 303–317.

Wolfe, J., Brown, P. J., & Kelley, J. M. (1993). Reassessing war stress: Exposure and the Persian Gulf War. *Journal of Social Issues, 49,* 15–31.

Yoo, H., & Franke, W. D. (2011). Stress and cardiovascular disease risk in female law enforcement officers. *International Archives of Occupational and Environmental Health, 84,* 279–286.

Zhan, C., Lu, Y., Li, C., Wu, Z., Long, Y., Zhou, L., & Zhou, B. (1991). A study of textile noise influence on maternal function and embryo-growth [Chinese]. *Hua Xi Yi Ke Da Xue Xue Bao, 22,* 394–398.

Zhang, J., Cai, W. W., & Lee, D. J. (1992). Occupational hazards and pregnancy outcomes. *American Journal of Industrial Medicine, 21,* 397–408.

Chapter 7

POLICE SUICIDE: A DETRIMENTAL OUTCOME OF PSYCHOLOGICAL WORK EXPOSURES

JOHN M. VIOLANTI

Police work is precarious not only to one's physical health but also to one's mental well-being. Officers are often placed in situations of severe emotional stress. Additionally, police officers are exposed to traumatic work events. Such events may involve shootings; seeing dead bodies or severely injured persons; seeing abused children; and other threatened or actual violence (Violanti & Paton, 1999).

Police officers often have difficulty in expressing emotions; there is a lack of an outlet to vent feelings outside of work and a lack of diversion from the police role (Laufersweiler-Dwyer, & Dwyer, 2000). Other mental health risk factors include inadequate social support networks and emotional exhaustion. Paton, Violanti, and Schmuckler (1999) discuss the long-term implications and consequences of repetitive exposure to high-risk and duty-related traumatic incidents, exploring implications for behavioral addiction and separation from active police duties. Figley (1999) developed a model of "police compassion fatigue," suggesting that if police officers are empathic, have sufficient concern for others, and are exposed to traumatized people on a continuous basis, they may develop a debilitating psychological fatigue.

POLICE SUICIDE

It is very possible that the chronic stress, life circumstances, inability to cope, and traumatic police work exposures increase the risk for psychological difficulties. Likely the most devastating maladaptation to these factors is suicide. One would expect that the police suicide rates should be lower than they are, given that they are an employed, healthy, and psychologically tested group (McMichael, 1976). Certainly, they should be lower than the U.S. general population, because this reference group includes the institutionalized, mentally ill, and unemployed. Despite these circumstances, a good amount of epidemiological evidence suggests that there is an elevated rate of suicide within law enforcement.

Vena, Violanti, Marshall, and Fiedler (1986) found male officers to have an age-adjusted mortality ratio for suicide of approximately three times that of male municipal workers in the same cohort. Lester (1992) found that seven of twenty-six countries for the decade of 1980 to 1989 had police suicide rates above the general population. A mortality study of police officers in Rome, Italy, found the suicide ratio among male police officers to be 1.97 times as high as the general male Italian population (Forastiere et al., 1994). Violanti, Vena, and Marshall (1996) found that male police officers had a suicide rate of 8.3 times that of homicide and 3.1 times that of work accidents. Compared to male municipal workers, male police officers had a 53 percent increased rate of suicide over homicide, a three-fold rate of suicide over accidents, and a 2.65-fold rate of suicide over homicide and accidents combined.

Darragh (1991) conducted an epidemiological analysis on factors based on 558 consecutive cases of self-inflicted death in the United Kingdom that revealed a dramatic increase in suicide among security force personnel. Helmkamp (1996), in a study of suicide among males in the U.S. Armed Forces, found military security and law enforcement specialists had a significant increased rate ratio for suicide. Hartwig and Violanti (1999) found that the frequency of police suicide occurrence in Westphalia, Germany, has increased over the past 7 years, particularly in the 21 to 30 and 51 to 60 years of age categories. Most of suicides were male officers (92%). Cantor, Tyman, and Slatter (1999) found the high rate of suicide among Australian police that was attributable to stress, health, and domestic difficulties. Occupational problems were more intense than personal ones were. Charbonneau (2000), in a study in Quebec, Canada, found police suicide rates to be almost twice that of the general population. Rates were elevated mostly among young officers (20–39 years of age).

In a nationwide study on suicide ideation and attempts among 3,272 Norwegian police, Berg, Hem, Lau, Loeb, and Ekeberg (2003) found that 24 percent felt that life was not worth living, 6.4 percent seriously considered suicide, and 0.7 percent attempted suicide. Serious suicide ideation was mainly attributed to personal and family problems. Violanti (2004) found that certain traumatic police work exposures increased the risk of having a high level of PTSD symptoms, which subsequently increased the risk of alcohol use and suicide ideation. The combined impact of PTSD and increased alcohol use led to a ten-fold increased risk of suicide ideation.

Violanti and colleagues (2008) found that for each standard deviation increase in depression symptoms, the prevalence ratio (PR) of suicide ideation increased 73 percent in women officers and 67 percent in men officers. In a national study utilizing National Occupational Mortality Surveillance (NOMS) data, Violanti (2010) found the police suicide rate to be four times that of firefighters. Minority officers had 4.5 times and policewomen 12 times the number of suicides than did firefighters. Police suicides outnumbered homicides by 2.36 times.

In a national web surveillance of 119,000 media reports on police suicide, O'Hara and Violanti (2009) found that officers in the age category 30 to 35 years are at a higher risk for suicide. Suicide among officers of lower rank and the use of firearms were prevalent. Violanti and associates (2012) examined the risk of retired officers compared to those still working. Adjusted for age and years of service, suicide rates were 8.4 times higher in working officers versus separated and retired officers. Survival time to suicide was significantly lower for current working officers, suggesting suicide in a significantly shorter time span. Violanti, Hartley, Mnatsakanova, Andrew, and Burchfiel (in press) examined police suicide rates according to department size. Those police departments smallest in size had significantly higher suicide rates than did those classified as small and large (p < 0.0001). Possible reasons included lack of availability for mental health assistance, increased workload and danger, and community visibility.

ETIOLOGY OF POLICE SUICIDE

Early Theoretical Models of Police Suicide

Freud's concept of aggression and self-destruction served as the basis for early theories of police suicide (Freud, 1954). According to Freud, societal limitation of aggression undermined the psychic health of individual members and threatened each of them with suicide (Litman, 1970). Freud's concept was first applied to the police by Friedman (1968) in his analysis of ninety-three New York City police suicides in 1934. At that time in history, police officers worked under an edict of "social license" and often committed acts of aggression without penalty. When the government controlled such police behavior, some officers could not adjust and committed suicide.

Bonafacio (1991) proposed a contemporary psychodynamic approach to police suicide. Bonafacio's consensus was that the officer's id has overwhelmed the ego's capacity to maintain a balance between external reality and the superego. Suicide is the police officer's attempt to restore the self concept as moral and decent. In paying the ultimate penance for surrendering to impulses, the police officer seeks to reclaim the superego's approval.

Henry and Short (1954) added a social dimension to Freud's model by relating aggression to societal as well as individual frustration. Suicide, as an act of aggression, could not be differentiated from the source of the frustration that generates the aggression (society). Heiman (1977) viewed social factors as covariates of aggression and police suicide. Officers were viewed as being regularly exposed to human misery and in constant demand for "interpersonal giving." Demands on police officers were often beyond their ability to respond, which led to extreme frustration sometimes followed by suicide.

Social isolation explanations of police suicide have also been suggested. Nelson and Smith (1970) hypothesized that officers are continuously disintegrated from society by their jobs and that such isolation increases the potential for suicide. Heiman (1977) found London bobbies to have lower suicide rates than New York City police officers had. Heiman concluded that London bobbies are more socially accepted than are American police officers, thus having more stable social relationships and fewer suicides. Loo (1986), in his study of Royal Canadian Mounted Police, concluded that, similar to most suicides, RCMP officers committed suicide in response to life situations that were intolerable.

Violanti (1997) developed a theoretical model of police suicide based on the premise that officers adopt the police role as a principal mode for dealing with psychological strain. The stringent acquisition and maintenance of the police role restricts cognitive flexibility and the use of other life roles by police officers, thus impairing their ability to deal with psychological distress. As a result, the potential for suicide among police officers may increase. This process likely involves a complex interaction of the individual, police organization, social relationships, and society. Dominant use or perhaps overlearning of the police role constricts cognitive coping style and affects the use of other roles to deal with life strain. As a result, the potential for suicide may increase. Figure 7-1 illustrates this model.

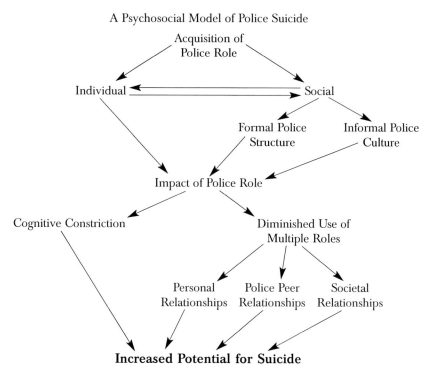

Figure 7-1. Etiology of suicide in context of the police role. Source: Violanti, J. M. (1997). Suicide and the police role: A psychosocial model. *An International Journal of Police Strategies & Management, 20*, 698–715. doi.org/10.1108/13639519710368107. Used with permission.

- **Acquisition of the police role.** Acquisition refers to the rookie officer's adaptation of a new work role and appears to occur interactively at individual and social levels (Harris, 1973). The acquisition process is very strong in initial police training and continues to dominate officers' lives throughout their careers. The police role isolates officers from other life roles. Cognitive, social, and inflexible styles associated with the police role hinder efficacious coping with stressful interpersonal interactions and precipitate risk factors associated with the potential for suicide.
- **Diminished use of other social roles.** Adherence to the police role may affect the self-representational structure of officers, which defines the self as having purpose and meaning in the social environment. When meaning is lost, or the officer becomes isolated through role restriction, the potential for suicide may increase (Turner & Roszell, 1994).
- **The police role and relationships.** Police officers appear to have problems with relationships. Ivanoff (1994) found that relationships were a primary factor in 57.6 percent of police suicides in New York City over the past 10 years. Officers were involved in extramarital affairs, were recently separated or divorced, or had conflict with supervisors at work. One reason for relational difficulties may be an emotional detachment from others. The role of a police officer calls for depersonalization; interpersonal relationships, on the other hand, call for human emotion (Violanti & Paton, 1999). In some respects, the police role becomes a safe place to hide but at the same time does not allow for an outlet of emotions. The inability for police officers to use other roles to solve problems with a family person, friend, or lover may be behind many police relationship problems (Reiser, 1974).

This model is somewhat restrictive because the police role may be but one of many circumstances that increase the potential for suicide. Suicide is a complex phenomenon that involves the interaction of many risk factors. In a study of lifetime variables in persons between the ages of 15 and 85 years, factors such as gender, age, race, personality, life experiences, prior socialization, and psychological disposition all contributed in varying degrees to completed suicide (Vaillant & Blumenthal, 1990). Also, one cannot clearly determine causal direction in this model. It is possible that preexisting selection processes are operative; incoming officers with higher levels of psychological well-being may be resistant to cognitive constriction and more willing to become involved in other life roles (Thoits, 1983; Verbugge, 1983).

PREVENTION

There are challenges in police suicide prevention. We have not yet learned the prevalence and incidence of suicide in law enforcement. We only know that, in most cases, the rate is higher than in other working or general populations. There is also a lack of sufficient information as to why police suicide occurs, calling for a more in-depth research into the lives and experiences of those officers who do commit suicide. The obvious solution is to conduct further and more careful research on a wider scale. It appears through the efforts of groups like the International Association of Chiefs of Police (IACP), Badge of Life (BOL), and Survivors of Law Enforcement Suicide (SOLES) that police agencies are beginning to understand the seriousness of suicide risk in police work.

What happens in a department after a suicide can be devastating. Quite often, entire departments succumb to a depressed mood and productivity falls. There is often a grief wave in the department when an officer suicides. Police administrators have commented that somehow their officers do not seem the same after a suicide; supervisors notice an effect on morale, happiness, and work. This emphasizes the need to recognize and prevent suicides among police personnel. *Postvention* involves a designed plan to help reduce the negative impact on departments and family. Postvention is essential because it allows for the proper grieving of survivors and departments and shows that someone cares enough to be concerned about those who survive suicide. Police leaders should arrange for psychological debriefings after the suicide of an officer that will help individual survivors and the department deal with the crisis.

Prevention Considerations

The Emotional Self-Care (ESC) training program is a recent prevention effort by the BOL group (O'Hara, 2011) based on two simple principles:

- That each officer will be responsible for his or her own emotional well-being
- That a department is responsible for providing the career-long training, tools, and resources with which an officer can meet that responsibility

ESC training is a form of aggressive prevention that involves every officer – not just officers that are suicidal and not just officers that are "in trouble." The ESC program involves annual training in recognition of trauma, stress management, resilience, and healthy lifestyles. An additional suggestion is an annual "mental health check" that is voluntary and confidential (O'Hara, 2011).

Psychological autopsies may be an important research tool in determining police suicide precedents (Knoll, 2009). The issues of stress, PTSD, alcohol use, depression, and relationship problems must be further explored. This research design will allow us to examine risk factors reportedly associated with police suicide. Most previous studies on police suicide provide evidence of high risk but fall short in explaining precipitant individual and social factors involved in police suicide. This lack of information impedes efforts at suicide prevention among the police, other similar occupations, and specific age groups. The psychological autopsy is an established means for obtaining comprehensive retrospective information about victims of completed suicide.

POLICE SUICIDE SURVIVORS

For suicide survivors, the sudden or unexpected death of a loved can be a traumatic life event. Although most duty-related deaths are distressful, suicide may create even more trauma for survivors. It is unfortunate that survivors of police suicide must deal not only with their own grief but also with negative reactions of police peers, the organization, and the public. The police work group has the potential to provide a supportive set of conditions in reducing psychological distress, because it provides environmental structure, leadership, companionship, and a source of motivation for recovery. Quite often, however, survivors of police suicide are abandoned more quickly than those of officers who died from other causes. Police officials may not place much emphasis on assisting survivors of police suicide due to the stigma associated with such deaths. The actions and reactions of the police chief down to the patrol officer will forever be remembered by a survivor. The trauma that survivors experience may vary from visual effects to improper notification, to department speculation, and to lack of compassion toward survivors. The survivor, as well as the police department, may embark on a painful journey for years to come (Tate, 2011).

CONCLUSION

A number of medical, psychological, and social influences appear to be associated with police suicide, and knowledge of these influences is necessary in order to reach that goal. All too often the operational dangers of police work are emphasized, leading to a neglect of the hidden psychological danger in this profession. Suicide is a consequence of that hidden danger. In the least, we should adequately address this problem and provide methods and means to prevent future tragedies, for fear that more officers may fall from the edge.

REFERENCES

Berg, A. M., Hem, E., Lau, B., Loeb, M., & Ekeberg, O. (2003). Suicidal ideation and attempts in Norwegian police. *Suicide and Life Threatening Behavior 33*, 302–312.

Bonafacio, P. (1991). *The Psychological Effects of Police Work: A Psychodynamic Approach* (pp. 169–174). New York: Plenum Press.

Cantor, C. H., Tyman, R., & Slater, P. J. (1995). A historical survey of police in Queensland, Australia, 1843–1992. *Suicide and Life Threatening Behavior, 25*, 499–507.

Charbonneau, F. (2000). Suicide among the police in Quebec. *Population, 55*, 367–378.

Darragh, P. M. (1991). Epidemiology of suicide in Northern Ireland. *Irish Journal of Medical Science, 160*, 354–357.

Figley, C. R. (1999). Police compassion fatigue (PCF): Theory, research, assessment, treatment, and prevention. In J. M. Violanti & D. Paton (Eds.), *Police Trauma: Psychological Aftermath of Civilian Combat* (pp. 37–53). Springfield, IL: Charles C Thomas Publishing.

Forastiere, F., Perucci, C. A., DiPietro, A., Miceli, M., Rapiti, E., Bargagli, A., & Borgia, P. (1994). Mortality among urban policemen in Rome. *American Journal of Industrial Medicine, 26*, 785–798.

Freud, S. (1954). *The Origins of Psychoanalysis*. New York: Basic Books.

Friedman, P. (1968). Suicide among police: A study of 93 suicides among New York City policemen 1934–1940. In E. S. Shneidman (Ed.), *Essays of Self Destruction* (pp. 414–419). New York: Science House.

Harris, R. N. (1973). *The Police Academy: An Inside View* (pp. 45–78). New York: Wiley Publishing.

Hartwig, D., & Violanti, J. M. (1999). Suicide by police officials in North Rhine-West-phalia. An evaluation of 58 suicides between 1992–1998. *Archives of Kriminologie, 204,* 129–142.

Heiman, M. F. (1977). Suicide among police. *American Journal of Psychiatry, 134,* 1286–1290.

Helmkamp, J. C. (1996). Occupation and suicide among males in the U.S. Armed Forces. *Annals of Epidemiology, 6,* 83–88.

Henry, A., & Short, J. (1954). *Suicide and Homicide.* Glencoe, IL: Free Press.

Ivanoff, A. (1994). *The New York City Police Suicide Training Project* (pp. 5–15). New York: The Police Foundation.

Knoll, J. L. (2009). The psychological autopsy protocol. *Law and Psychiatry, 15,* 57–67.

Laufersweiler-Dwyer, D. L., & Dwyer, R. G. (2000). Profiling those impacted by organizational stressors at the macro, intermediate and micro levels of several police agencies. *Justice Professional, 12,* 443–469.

Lester, D. (1992). Suicide in police officers: A survey of nations. *Police Studies, 15,* 146–148.

Litman, R. E. (1970). *The Psychology of Suicide* (pp. 565–586). New York: Science House.

Loo, R. (1986). Suicide among police in a federal force. *Suicide and Life Threatening Behavior, 16,* 379–388.

McMichael, A. J. (1976). Standardized mortality ratios and the "healthy worker effect": Scratching beneath the surface. *Journal of Occupational Medicine, 18,* 165–168.

Nelson, Z., & Smith, W. E. (1970). The law enforcement profession: an incidence of high suicide. *Omega, 1,* 293–299.

O'Hara, A. F. (2011). Looking for new prevention alternatives: The badge of life emotional self-care training. In J. M. Violanti, A. F. O'Hara, & T. Tate (Eds.), *On the Edge: Recent Perspectives on Police Suicide* (pp. 77–94). Springfield, IL: Charles C Thomas.

O'Hara, A. F., & Violanti, J. M. (2009). Police suicide: A web surveillance of national data. *International Journal of Emergency Mental Health, 11,* 17–24.

Paton, D., Violanti, J. M., & Schmuckler, G. (1999). Chronic exposure to risk and trauma: Addiction and separation issues in police officers. In J. M. Violanti & D. Paton (Eds.), *Police Trauma: Psychological Aftermath of Civilian Combat* (pp. 78–87). Springfield, IL: Charles C Thomas.

Reiser, M. (1974). Some organizational stressors on police officers. *Journal of Police Science and Administration, 2,* 156–159.

Tate, T. T. (2011). Survivors: The personal tragedy of police suicide. In J. M. Violanti, A. F. O'Hara, & T. T. Tate (Eds.), *On the Edge: Recent Perspectives on Police Suicide* (pp. 95–131). Springfield, IL: Charles C Thomas.

Thoits, P. A. (1983). Multiple identities and psychological well-being: A reformulation and test of the social isolation hypothesis. *American Sociological Review, 48,* 174–187.

Turner, R. J., & Roszell, P. (1994). Psychosocial resources and the stress process. In W. R. Avison & I. H. Gotlib (Eds.), *Stress and Mental Health* (pp. 179–210). New York: Plenum Press.

Vaillant, G. E., & Blumenthal, S. J. (1990). Suicide over the life cycle: Risk factors and span-life development. In S. J. Blumenthal & D. J. Kupfer (Eds.), *Suicide Over the Life Cycle* (pp. 1–17). Washington, DC: American Psychiatric Press.

Vena, J. E., Violanti, J. M., Marshall, J., & Fiedler, R. C. (1986). Mortality of a municipal worker cohort: III. Police officers. *American Journal of Industrial Medicine, 10*, 383–397.

Verbugge, L. M. (1983). Multiple roles and physical health of women and men. *Journal of Health and Social Behavior, 24*, 16–30.

Violanti, J. M. (1997). Suicide and the police role: A psychosocial model. *An International Journal of Police Strategies & Management, 20*, 698–715. doi: org/10.1108/13639519710368107

Violanti, J. M. (2004). Predictors of police suicide ideation. *Suicide and Life Threatening Behavior, 4*, 277–283.

Violanti, J. M. (2010). Police suicide: A national comparison with fire-fighter and military personnel. *International Journal of Police Strategies & Management, 33*, 270–286. doi: 10.1108/13639511011044885

Violanti, J. M., Fekedulegn, D., Charles, L. E., Andrew, M. E., Hartley, T. A., Mnatsakanova, A., & Burchfiel, C. M. (2008). *Depression and Suicidal Ideation Among Police Officers.* Presented at the Work, Stress, and Health Conference, March 2008, Washington, DC.

Violanti, J. M., Gu, J. K., Charles, L. E., Fekedulegn, D., Andrew, M. E., & Burchfiel, C. M. (2012). Is suicide higher among separated/retired police officers? An epidemiological investigation. *International Journal of Emergency Mental Health, 13*, 221–228.

Violanti, J. M., Hartley, T. A., Mnatsakanova, A., Andrew, M. E., & Burchfiel, C. M. (2013). Police suicide in small departments: A comparative analysis. *International Journal of Emergency Mental Health.*

Violanti, J. M., & Paton, D. (1999). *Police Trauma: Psychological Aftermath of Civilian Combat* (pp. 78–87). Springfield, IL: Charles C Thomas Publishing.

Violanti, J. M., Vena, J. E., & Marshall, J. R. (1996). Suicides, homicides, and accidental deaths: A comparative risk assessment of police officers and municipal workers. *American Journal of Industrial Medicine, 30*, 99–104.

Chapter 8

VULNERABILITY TO WORK-RELATED POSTTRAUMATIC STRESS: FAMILY AND ORGANIZATIONAL INFLUENCES

Douglas Paton and Kim Norris

Protective and emergency services officers (e.g., police officers, firefighters) can experience critical incidents capable of eliciting acute and chronic posttraumatic stress reactions repeatedly over the course of careers that can span decades (North et al., 2002; Paton, 2005, 2008; Paton & Violanti, 2007; Paton, Violanti, Burke & Gherke, 2009; Violanti & Paton, 2006). The fact that such studies reveal considerable diversity in traumatic stress outcomes, even among officers who faced the same event, makes it pertinent to explain this diversity, however. Many factors can be implicated in explaining this diversity. Some of these are summarized in Figure 8-1.

Figure 8-1 draws attention to the fact that a comprehensive understanding of traumatic stress vulnerability must accommodate not only the critical incident experience but also the personal and organizational characteristics that describe the social and organizational context in which such experiences are situated. This chapter takes an ecological approach to exploring how organizational and family environments and processes can be implicated in understanding traumatic stress risk. Furthermore, it argues that family and organizational influences exercise an interdependent influence on vulnerability. These factors are introduced in terms of how they can interact with critical incident experiences through their influence on meaning and support.

Critical incidents create a sense of psychological disequilibrium that results when the interpretive frameworks or schemata that guide officers' expectations and actions have lost their capacity to organize novel experiences in meaningful and manageable ways (Dunning, 2003; Janoff-Bulman, 1992; Paton, 1994). One goal of critical incident risk management that emerges from this view is identifying the contextual (e.g., family, or-

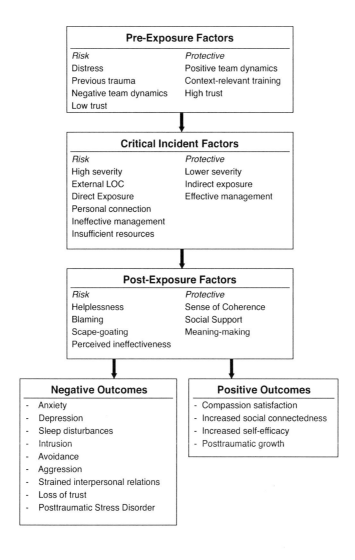

Figure 8-1. Preexposure, even, and postexposure influences on traumatic stress vulnerability (Adapted from Norris, Paton & Ayton, 2012).

ganizational) and process (e.g., managerial procedures) influences on how officers can render unpredictable and challenging work experiences coherent, meaningful, and manageable (Dunning, 2003; Frederickson, Tugade, Waugh & Larkin, 2003; Paton, 1994, 2006). The rationale for pursuing this line of inquiry derives from empirical findings that identified the potential for organizational and family characteristics to exercise significant influences in posttrauma outcomes (Eränen, Millar & Paton, 2000; Paton, Smith, Ramsay & Akande, 1999; Paton, Smith, Violanti & Eränen, 2000; Paton, Violanti, Burke & Gherke, 2009). The discussion is framed using earlier work on traumatic stress vulnerability in emergency responders involved in rescue following the sinking of the Baltic Sea ferry Estonia to introduce how family, work–family interface, and organizational characteristics influence posttraumatic stress vulnerability (Eränen et al., 2000; Paton et al., 2000). Discussion with an introduction to family influences.

FAMILY

The analysis that is summarized in Figure 8-2 revealed a prominent role for family characteristics and dynamics in posttraumatic stress risk. An interesting finding from the structural equation modeling analysis was that the receipt of psychological debriefing did not have a direct effect on posttraumatic stress. However, for example, by increasing people's understanding of the benefits of emotional disclosure and social support in recovering from traumatic experiences, the debriefing experience acted as a type of context-relevant training (*see* Figure 8-1) that translated into higher quality social support skills (e.g., increased emotional disclosure, ability to seek and use support from others). Improved social and emotional competence, in turn, enriched the quality of family functioning and facilitated the ability of the family experience to influence on posttrauma outcome (Figure 8-2). Thus, the family became a resource that assisted assimilation of experience and facilitated the management of posttrauma symptoms.

A role for social skills and family relationships in trauma mitigation has been reported in other studies (Paton & Kelso, 1991; Scotti, Beach, Northrop, Rode & Forsyth, 1995; Wraith, 1994). Paton and Kelso reported that the partners of emergency responders who had been involved in disaster response roles were keen to know more about traumatic stress syndromes and in what they could do to assist their partner's recovery from traumatic stress. If they are to pursue this goal effectively, they need to be supported by the emergency services organization. The benefits of the latter are also indicated in Figure 8-2, which illustrates how the positive perception of organizational climate had correspondingly positive influences on the quality of family life. This introduces a need to consider the work–family interface in comprehensive conceptualizations of traumatic stress risk.

THE WORK–FAMILY INTERFACE

The work–family interface refers to the interdependence between work and nonwork roles in the individual employee experience. The interrelationships between work and nonwork (i.e., family) roles are reciprocal in nature; work-related demands can interfere with family-related responsibilities (work interference with family, e.g., working late precludes spending time with family) and family-related responsibilities can interfere with work-related demands (family interference with work, e.g., caring for a sick child precludes attending work) (Greenhaus, Collins, Singh & Parasuraman, 1997; Netemeyer, Boles & McMurrian, 1996).

Work by Norris (2010) identified the importance of the work–family interface. Specifically, Norris argued that in addition to organizational influences, family processes (including the dynamics of an intimate relationship and family-level coping strategies) can act to mediate the relationship between the experience of a critical incident and traumatic stress outcomes. Of particular importance is the degree of perceived familial involvement in the employment experience (which can be readily facilitated by organizational culture; *see* later). Higher levels of perceived familial involvement in the employment experience promote greater communication, trust, and availability of resources (at the level of the individual, organization, and family), facilitating enhanced capacity for the employee to manage the traumatic sequelae of experiencing work-related traumatic events.

In contrast, lower levels of perceived familial involvement can engender a situation in which the individual is forced to balance the competing and incongruent demands of the organization with those of the family. The result is that the individual's personal resources are deplet-

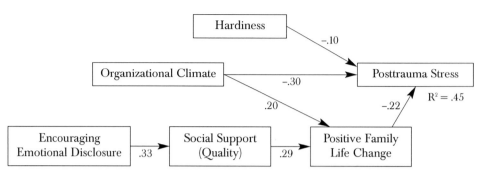

Figure 8-2. Organizational and family influences on posttraumatic stress risk (Adapted from Eränen et al., 2000; Paton et al., 2000).

ed and are therefore not available to be directed toward dealing with critical incident experiences. In turn, this increases the traumatic stress risk faced by officers. Thus it can also contribute to increasing the likelihood of officers' forming turnover intentions (or even leaving the organization) and/or relationship dissolution. Both of these factors contribute toward a negative spiral of traumatic stress risk. They increase the probability of officers disengaging from relationships (e.g., with colleagues, *see* later) that serve to impose meaning on critical incident experience and/or offer (e.g., with colleagues and family) support (from colleagues and family) (Paton et al., 2009). It is not always possible for people to act on turnover intentions (e.g., lack of alternative employment opportunities in an area). If officers remain despite forming such intentions, this can increase the likelihood of their disengaging from organizational life and entering a negative spiral of vulnerability.

Further emphasizing the complex interplay between individual, familial, and organizational influences on critical incident responses are findings by Norris, Paton, and Ayton (2012). Adopting a qualitative ecological approach, the authors examined factors prior to, during, and after critical incident exposure (Figure 8-2) that predicted positive or negative adaptation to the event within a sample of Australian Antarctic expeditioners. Their research identified that risk and protective factors included person, team, organization, and family level constructs throughout the process and were not merely the inverse of one another. Of note, previous critical incident exposure in this context was found to be a risk factor for traumatic stress outcomes in this population. Discussion with participants regarding this finding indicated that negative team dynamics and organizational culture associated with the previous critical incident experience had placed strain on the expeditioners' personal resources and negatively affected familial relationships (Norris et al., 2012). In turn, this appeared to have influenced schema development regarding critical incidents insofar as expecting the same (i.e., negative outcome) should future exposure occur. This provides another example of how family-person-organization interdependencies can lead an officer into a vulnerability spiral.

In addition, Norris and colleagues (2012) concurrently examined partner responses to the same events and found that expeditioner well-being and their own relationship with the organization (i.e., organizational influence and culture) were primary determinants of partner adaptation to the event. Partner adaptation is relevant to this discussion because partners were identified as a protective factor (and thereby facilitative of positive adaptation) in provision of social support to expeditioners post incident. Partners experiencing negative trauma reactions following the event (suggested to occur as a result of poor familial–organizational interplay) are less able to provide social support to expeditioners, rendering them at greater risk of developing negative trauma responses themselves. In this context, the interplay between person, team, organization, and family level constructs further emphasizes the argument for adopting an ecological approach to develop a comprehensive understanding of adaptation to critical incident exposure. How work–family relationships can make independent contributions to traumatic stress risk can be illustrated using shift work as a context.

Shift Work

Shift work is a common component of emergency service work and one with a well-documented history of being an organizational practice capable of influencing family functioning (Shakespeare-Finch, Paton & Violanti, 2003). Because it significantly influences officers' ability to participate in family life, shift work represents a phenomenon that can affect the quality of family well-being. Any work-related practice that affects the quality of family life has the potential to affect the quality of support available with the posttrauma environment, particularly in relation to the implications of the spillover effects introduced earlier for reducing access to meaning making and support resources. The importance of understanding this relationship takes on greater importance when it is understood that organizational factors such as shift work can have a greater influence on family relationships than the traumatic nature of officers' work experiences can (Wraith, 1994).

Shakespeare-Finch and colleagues (2003) discussed how, when shift work was controlled for, there was no difference in family functioning between an emergency services shift-work group and a control group comprised of nonemergency shift workers. This suggests that shift work, rather than officers' traumatic experience per se, affected family functioning. This finding provides a vivid illustration of how organizational choices (e.g., regarding family friendly shift-work policies) can affect the quality of officers' relationship with their families and consequently influence the capacity of the family to act as a recovery resource following a traumatic event and reduce officers' capacity to respond effectively to future critical incidents (*see* earlier). Thus decisions emergency service agencies make regarding elements of the work–family relationship can contribute to the proactive management of stress risk. Emergency organizations have the capacity to offer the information and training required to facilitate the realization of the benefits that can arise from developing the competencies (e.g., facilitate emotional disclosure, social skills) of family members as support and recovery resources.

Organizations also have a direct influence on how officers render critical incident experience meaningful and coherent and thus on their traumatic stress vulnerability. The argument for giving the organization a pivotal role in this process derives from how experience in and of organizations defines the context within which officers experience and interpret critical incidents and their sequelae and within which future capabilities are nurtured or restricted (Paton et al., 2009).

ORGANIZATIONAL INFLUENCES

Officers respond to incidents as members of an agency whose organizational culture influences their thoughts, actions, and responses. This occurs as a result of how, for example, socialization, context-relevant training, and management and organizational practices (e.g., the degree to which organizational culture engages in blaming and scapegoating) shape the way officers think and behave (using schema whose nature derives from the ensuing patterns of interaction with colleagues, senior officers, and organizational procedures over time and that en-culturate officers into organizational life). These factors interact to de-scribe the social and organizational context in which challenging expe-riences are made sense of (Paton et al., 1999, 2009; Weick & Sutcliffe, 2007) (*see also* Figure 8-2).

In the context of arguing that organizational characteristics be af-forded a prominent position as predictor of resilience, it is necessary to provide evidence to support this view. Evidence is offered here from two perspectives. The first discusses how organizational life influences officers' interpretation of traumatic experiences. The second explores how perceptions of organizational characteristics can have a direct ef-fect on posttrauma outcomes.

Paton and colleagues (1999) explored how organizational experience influences traumatic reactivity by examining the psychometric struc-ture of responses to traumatic events assessed using the Impact of Event Scale (IES) (Horowitz, Wilner & Alvarez, 1979). If a scale is accessing a latent construct that is a robust measure of the experience of traumatic stress, the structural relations between items should hold irrespective of, for example, the professional or organizational membership of those being tested. To test this using the IES, Paton and colleagues compared the structural dimensions of traumatic reactivity across organizations (e.g., human service and emergency service organizations), professions (e.g., firefighters versus social services), and countries (e.g., by compar-ing Scottish, Nigerian, and Australian firefighters).

The ensuing multidimensional scaling analysis of traumatic stress data (Figure 8-3) revealed a two-dimensional solution on which the rel-ative positions of each agency could be plotted. An important aspect of this analysis was its focusing on traumatic stress symptoms rather than on officers' perceptions of their organization. This reduced the possi-bility of officers' perceptions of their organization confounding the analysis.

The social services samples, whose members regularly deal with crit-ical incidents, were tested twice (6 months apart, SocServ1 and Soc-Serv2, respectively; *see* Figure 8-3) to assess the reliability of the analy-sis (Paton et al., 1999). No significant differences were found between them (Figure 8-3), suggesting that the organizational issues were exer-cising a consistent influence on traumatic stress experiences. The social services and Australian firefighter samples were both from the same Australian city. Significant differences between the social services populations and the Australian firefighter population on Dimension 1 (Figure 8-3), but not on Dimension 2, make it possible to argue that nationality (Australian) introduces some consistency (Dimension 2) into how traumatic experiences are interpreted but professional or organizational membership does (Dimension 1). Similarly, the failure to find significant difference between the firefighter samples (Dimension 1) suggests that "being a firefighter" may introduce some similarity into how traumatic events are experienced. However, differences between the Australian (AusFire, Figure 8-3) and the Scottish and Nigerian (ScotFire and NigeriaFire, Figure 8-3) samples on Dimension 2 again point to their being unique national or cultural influences on interpretative processes. The latter argument raises issues regarding the failure to find significant differences between the Scottish and Nigerian samples, however (Figure 8-3). One tentative explanation for this derives from the fact that training for both takes place in the United Kingdom and thus instills in officers similar ways of thinking. The latter remains tentative until a more searching analysis of the issues can be conducted. Nonetheless, this idea is consistent with the process of enculturation discussed earlier.

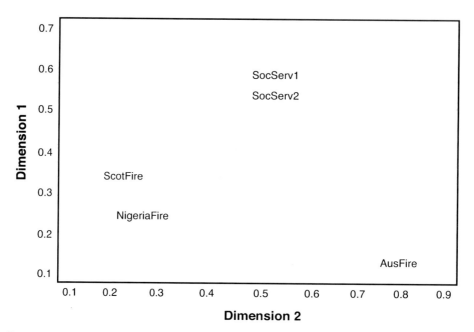

Figure 8-3. Summary of multidimensional scaling analysis of national and organizational influence on traumatic stress reactions (Adapted from Paton et al., 1999).

The differences evident can be attributed to organizational and cultural factors influencing the structure of officers' traumatic stress reactions. That is, organizational experience (which is assumed to be captured in organizational culture and transmitted via the beliefs and actions of senior managers and other officers; *see* below) can be implicated in how traumatic experiences were being interpreted (Paton et al., 1999, 2009; Weick & Sutcliffe, 2007). This is reinforced by the contents of Figure 8-2. It is not enough to be able to identify the existence of organizational differences, however. It is also necessary to identify how this translates into organizational characteristics and practices that influence traumatic stress risk.

ORGANIZATIONAL CHARACTERISTICS

Organizational characteristics can influence how officers interpret traumatic events and their consequences. At a distal level, organizations exert an influence on how meaning is attributed to traumatic experience as a consequence of the recruitment, selection, and training processes they develop (*see* earlier). These processes, as a result of their influence on officer socialization and acculturation into the emergency services organization, influence how all aspects of organizational life, including critical incidents and their consequences, are responded to and interpreted (Paton et al., 2009). At a proximal level, the interpretive structures that emerge are influenced by how officers interact with other members (personal connections; *see* Figure 8-1) of the organization in the context of experiencing critical incidents that often fall outside the normal operating parameters of emergency and protective services life. Thus, one approach to understanding organizational influence on traumatic stress involves understanding the dynamics of these organizational relationships and how they influence the meaning attributed to critical incidents and the actions taken to manage their consequences. When dealing with atypical challenging events, officers rely more on others for information and guidance about how to respond. The atypical nature of the events makes it difficult for officers to independently assess the veracity or utility of the information provided (which as alluded to previously can represent content that is embedded in the organizational culture), however, and this makes trust an important interpersonal dynamic in this context. Thus levels of trust are influenced by the organizational culture and the dynamics of interpersonal relationships (Barker & Camarata, 1998; Norris, 2010; Paton & Stephens, 1996; Siegrist & Cvetkovich, 2000).

Trust

Trust is a prominent determinant of the effectiveness of interpersonal relationships, group processes, and organizational relationships (Barker & Camarata, 1998; Herriot, Hirsh & Reilly, 1998), particularly when individuals face some potential or actual risk (Coleman, 1990). When dealing with critical incidents, agencies and officers alike have to deal with risk and uncertainty, and trust has been identified as a predictor of people's ability to deal with complex, high-risk events (Siegrist & Cvetkovich, 2000), especially when relying on others to provide information or assistance about atypical experiences or circumstances.

Trust influences perception of other's motives, their competence, and the credibility of the information they provide (Earle, 2004). The perceived credibility of information will influence the extent to which the information available will contribute to officers' sense of meaning and purpose. Individuals are more willing to commit to acting cooperatively in high-risk situations when they believe those with whom they must collaborate or work under are competent, dependable, and likely to act with integrity (in the present and in the future) and to care for their interests (Dirks, 1999; Paton & Stephens, 1996). Officers functioning in trusting, reciprocal relationships are left feeling empowered and are more likely to experience meaning in their work.

Organizational cultures that value openness create opportunities for officers to engage in the kind of learning required to facilitate the development of their ability to deal with novel events (Barker & Camarata, 1998). In the absence of this openness, existing cultural precepts prevail and, if these are prescriptive, deny the reality of traumatic experience, and blame officers for operational problems, then traumatic stress vulnerability is increased (Paton et al., 2009; *see also* Figure 8-1).

The learning and support benefits that can reduce traumatic stress risk are enhanced when organizational openness and communication extends to involve officers' partners and families who are then more trusting and supportive of the organization and employee's engagement in the work role. This has the effect of minimizing tension between work and nonwork roles (Norris, 2010) and increasing the availability of the family as an enduring support resource. Those with a major role to play in creating and sustaining a climate of trust are the senior officers who translate organizational culture into the day-to-day values and procedures that sustain the schema officers engage to plan for and respond to critical incidents (Paton & Stephens, 1996; Paton et al, 2009).

Senior Officer Support

The actions of senior officers play a central role in developing and sustaining empowering environments that affect vulnerability (Liden, Wayne, & Sparrow, 2000; Paton & Stephens, 1996). Leadership practices such as positive reinforcement, positive feedback, encouragement, and constructive discussion of response problems and how they can be resolved in future from both coworkers and senior officers empower employees act to reduce stress risk (Paton, 1994; Quinn & Spreitzer, 1997). It does so by reducing the likelihood that officers' attribute stress and response problems to personal weakness and replacing it with an active approach that focuses on anticipating how to exercise control in future critical incidents (MacLeod & Paton, 1999; Raphael, 1986).

A high level of senior officer support enhances feelings of competence and informs officers that they are allowed and encouraged to exercise choice (self-determination) about how they conduct some of their work (Langfried, 2000). Quality supervisor–subordinate relationships, for which supportive supervisor behavior is a crucial factor (Liden, Sparrow & Wayne, 1997) creates a supportive culture and enhances general feelings of competence (Cogliser & Schriesheim, 2000). Additionally, quality supervisor–subordinate relationships instigates the creation of similar value structures between individuals (Cogliser & Schriesheim, 2000), building shared schema, enabling officers to find increased meaning in critical incident experiences and contributes to the development of a sense of cohesion between colleagues (Paton et al., 2009).

Peer Relationships and Team Cohesion

The quality of peer relationships and team cohesion influences the informational and emotional social support available to officers and so influences levels of traumatic stress risk. The improved coordination resulting from a high level of peer cohesion increases the likelihood of officers experiencing more intrinsic value (meaning) in the performance of a task (Mullen & Copper, 1994; Paton & Stephens, 1996; Perry, 1997).

Members of cohesive work teams are more willing to share their knowledge and skills, so contributing to the development and maintenance of the kind of learning culture that reduces stress vulnerability because it focuses on learning from events. Cohesive networks are less dependent on senior officers for obtaining important resources, because reciprocal peer relationships are an alternative source for such resources (Liden et al., 1997), contributing to a greater sense of self-determination in one's work. Relations with coworkers predict officers' sense of psychological empowerment, particularly with regard to creating a level of fit in the relationship between an individual's values and attitudes and those of a work role (i.e., it contributes to meaningfulness and coherence) (Liden et al., 2000; Major, Kozlowski, Chao & Gardner, 1995).

PSYCHOLOGICAL EMPOWERMENT

Empowerment describes a process of facilitating competencies using organizational strategies to remove conditions that foster powerlessness (e.g., the organizational and operational hassles that increase traumatic stress vulnerability) and develop formal organizational practices and informal techniques for developing learned resourcefulness (e.g., self-efficacy information and competencies) that reduce stress risk (Conger & Konungo, 1988; Hart & Wearing, 1995; Norris et al., 2012; Paton et al., 2009). Placing the development of competencies in an organizational context provides a foundation for the development of organizational strategies to manage posttraumatic stress risk.

The empowerment construct is an important one for officers whose professional life makes repeated exposure to critical incidents an occupational reality. For example, according to empowerment theorists, environmental events (e.g., critical incidents) provide information to officers about both the consequences of their previous task behavior and the conditions they can expect to experience in future task behavior (Conger & Konungo, 1988; Conger, 1989). If positively reviewed (e.g., senior officers facilitate opportunities to learn from critical incidents), future vulnerability is reduced. In addition to its emanating from their own experiences, officers' understanding of critical incidents and their implications can also come from peers, subordinates, and superiors at work in the context of, for example, performance appraisals, training programs, and meetings (Paton & Jackson, 2002). Thus, through each progressive cycle of event (e.g., following a challenging critical incident), assessment, and feedback, officers construct the operational schema they use to respond to, plan for, and interpret critical incidents and so reduce traumatic stress vulnerability.

A crucial issue here is identifying how organizational life affects vulnerability. Several have been identified and include context-relevant training and positive feedback and reviews of performance that facilitate learning (Paton, 1994; Paton & Jackson, 2002; Spreitzer, 1997). Training and positive reviews enhance self-efficacy which, in turn, increases the quality of the planning, effort, and persistence invested in confronting significant physical and psychological demands. A second element relates to the degree to which officers perceive that their behavior is self-determined (Spreitzer, 1997). This is assessed in terms of the degree to which officers believe they are actively involved in defining how they perform their critical incident response role, are given responsibility for making decisions, and are not just passive actors (e.g., in the case of organizational hassles, such as dealing with excessive red tape, that increase stress vulnerability) (Hart & Wearning, 1995; Paton & Jackson, 2002; Paton et al., 2009).

A sense of choice is particularly important for dealing with emergent, contingent emergency demands. By definition, the specific nature or demands of critical incidents cannot be predicted in advance and thus create a need for innovative and creative approaches and planning and responding to critical incidents (Paton & Flin, 1999). For this to happen, organizations must devolve authority to officers when responding to complex critical incidents rather than prescribing what they should do (which increases vulnerability because the response is more likely to be inappropriate). Organizations that are highly prescriptive in this regard are also more likely to sustain a blaming and scapegoating culture (*see* Figure 8-1) that contributes to greater traumatic stress risk. An ability to exercise choice also facilitates learning from training and operational experiences and transmitting the lessons learned to others. Spreitzer (1997) also argues for organizational culture and procedures to facilitate officers' beliefs that they can influence important organizational outcomes. That is, to engender the belief through, for example, training, management practices, incident reviews, and so on that actively demonstrate that officers' work is valued and plays crucial role in the attainment of important organizational outcomes. These cultural attributes influence traumatic stress vulnerability by influencing how officers interpret critical incident experiences via two interpretive styles, envisioning and evaluation (Spreitzer, 1995, 1997).

Envisioning refers to how officers anticipate or envision future events and outcomes and derives from how empowerment – manifested through senior officer and team relationships (which themselves manifest dominant aspects of organizational culture) – influences the kinds of attributions officers make about critical incident experiences. Officers who anticipate positive rather than negative outcomes are more likely to approach critical incidents as learning experiences, and this predisposition reduces stress risk (e.g., because both successes and problems become stimuli for developing future personal and team learning) (Paton et al., 2009). Given that officers face the prospect of experiencing novel events or events with novel characteristics and thus inevitably have to confront complex, dynamic incidents, the kind of learning culture that can ensue from creating the environmental conditions to encourage envisioning increases the likelihood that response problems and challenges will be perceived as catalysts for future development and not as failure (Paton, 2006; Paton & Stephens, 1996).

A second interpretive style is evaluation. This refers to how officers evaluate success or failure. Thomas and Velthouse (1990) argue that officers who adopt less absolutist and more realistic standards experience greater levels of empowerment. This observation is reinforced by findings that officers who approach critical incidents with realistic performance expectations and acknowledge environmental limitations on their outcomes, more readily adapt to challenging circumstances (Paton, 1994; Raphael, 1986). The organizational influence in this regard can be discerned through, for example, the socialization, training. and review processes that represent the interpersonal and organizational context in which critical incidents are experienced (Paton et al., 2009). The more the interpersonal and organizational context promotes learning and support (in officers, families, and teams), the more stress risk, and thus officers' vulnerability to traumatic stress, is reduced.

CONCLUSION

The work discussed in this chapter illustrates how organizational culture, enacted through senior officers, team relationships, and the work–family interface, influences traumatic stress risk. The variables discussed – peer support, supervisor support, organizational culture, trust, empowerment, and family dynamics – are amenable to change (Cogliser & Schriesheim, 2000; Hart, Wearing & Headey, 1993; Hart & Cooper, 2001; Herriot et al., 1998; Perry, 1997; Quinn & Spreitzer, 1997; Shakespeare-Finch et al., 2003; Wraith, 1994) and so offer the potential for being managed as part of a proactive organizational traumatic stress risk management strategy.

REFERENCES

Barker, R. T., & Camarata, M. R. (1998). The role of communication in creating and maintaining a learning organization: Preconditions, indicators, and disciplines. *The Journal of Business Communication, 35*, 443–467.

Cogliser, C. C., & Schriesheim, C. A. (2000). Exploring work unit context and leader-member exchange: A multi-level perspective. *Journal of Organizational Behaviour, 21*, 487–511.

Coleman, J. S. (1990). *Foundations of Social Theory.* Cambridge, MA: Belknap Press.

Conger, J. A. (1989). Leadership: The art of empowering others. *The Academy of Management Executive, 3*, 17–24.

Conger, J. A., & Konungo, R. (1988). The empowerment process: Integrating theory and process. *Academy of Management Review, 13*, 471–482.

Dirks, K. T. (1999). The effects of interpersonal trust on work group performance. *Journal of Applied Psychology, 84*, 445–455.

Dunning, C. (2003). Sense of coherence in managing trauma workers. In D. Paton, J. M. Violanti & L. M. Smith (Eds.), *Promoting Capabilities to Manage Posttraumatic Stress: Perspectives on Resilience* (pp. 119–135). Springfield, IL: Charles C Thomas.

Earle, T. C. (2004). Thinking aloud about trust: A protocol analysis of trust in risk management. *Risk Analysis, 24*, 169–183.

Eränen, L., Millar, M., & Paton, D. (2000). *Organizational Recovery From Disaster: Traumatic Response Within Voluntary Disaster Workers.* Presented at the International Society for Stress Studies Conference, June 2000, Istanbul, Turkey.

Fredrickson, B. L., Tugade, M. M., Waugh, C. E., & Larkin, G. R. (2003). What good are positive emotions in crises? A prospective study of resilience and emotions following the terrorist attacks on the United States on September 11th, 2001. *Journal of Personality and Social Psychology, 84*, 365–376.

Greenhaus, J., Collins, K., Singh, R., & Parasuraman, S. (1997). Work and family influences on departure from public accounting. *Journal of Vocational Behavior, 50*, 249–270.

Hart, P. M., & Cooper, C. L. (2001). Occupational Stress: Toward a more integrated framework. In N. Anderson, D. S. Ones, H. K. Sinangil, & C. Viswesvaren (Eds.), *International Handbook of Work and Organizational Psychology. Vol. 2: Organizational Psychology.* London: Sage Publications.

Hart, P. M., & Wearing, A. J. (1995). Occupational stress and well-being: A systematic approach to research, policy and practice. In P. Cotton (Ed.), *Psychological Health in the Workplace.* Carlton: Australian Psychological Society.

Hart, P. M., Wearing, A. J., & Headey, B. (1993). Assessing police work experiences: Development of the Police Daily Hassles and Uplifts Scales. *Journal of Criminal Justice, 21*, 553–572.

Herriot, P., Hirsh, W., & Reilly, P. (1998). *Trust and Transition: Managing Today's Employment Relationship.* Chichester, UK: John Wiley & Sons.

Horowitz, M., Wilner, M., & Alvarez, W. (1979). Impact of Event Scale: A measure of subjective stress. *Psychosomatic Medicine, 41*, 209–218.

Langfried, C. W. (2000). The paradox of self-management: Individual and group autonomy in work groups. *Journal of Organizational Behaviour, 21*, 563–585.

Liden, R. C., Sparrow, R. T., & Wayne, S. J. (1997). Leader-member exchange theory: The past and potential for the future. *Research in Personnel and Human Resources Management, 15*, 47–119.

Liden, R. C., Wayne, S. J., & Sparrow, R. T. (2000). An examination of the mediating role of psychological empowerment on the relations between the job, interpersonal relationships, and work outcomes. *Journal of Applied Psychology, 85*, 407–416.

MacLeod, M. D., & Paton, D. (1999). Police officers and violent crime: Social psychological perspectives on impact and recovery. In J. M. Violanti & D. Paton (Eds.), *Police Trauma: Psychological Aftermath of Civilian Combat* (pp. 25–36). Springfield, IL: Charles C Thomas.

Major, D. A., Kozlowski, S. W., Chao, G. T., & Gardner, P. D. (1995). A longitudinal investigation of newcomer expectations, early socialization outcomes, and the moderating effects of the role development factors. *Journal of Applied Psychology, 80*, 418–431.

Mullen, B., & Copper, C. (1994). The relation between group cohesiveness and performance: An integration. *Psychological Bulletin, 115*, 210–227.

Netemeyer, R. G., Boles, J. S., & McMurrian, R. (1996). Development and validation of work-family conflict and family-work conflict scales. *Journal of Applied Psychology, 81*, 400–410.

Norris, K. (2010). Breaking the ice: Developing a model of expeditioner and partner adaptation to Antarctic employment. (Unpublished doctoral dissertation). University of Tasmania, Australia.

Norris, K., Paton, D., & Ayton, J. (2012). *Expeditioner and Partner Responses to Critical Incidents in Antarctica.* Poster session presented at the 32nd meeting of the SCAR Open Science Conference, Portland, Oregon.

North, C. S., Tivis, L., McMillen, J. C., Pfefferbaum, B., Cox, J., Spitznagel, E. L., . . . Smith, E. M. (2002). Coping, functioning, and adjustment of rescue workers after the Oklahoma City bombing. *Journal of Traumatic Stress, 15*, 171–175.

Paton, D. (1994). Disaster relief work: An assessment of training effectiveness. *Journal of Traumatic Stress, 7*, 275–288.

Paton, D. (2005). Critical incidents and police officer stress. In H. Copes (Ed.), *Policing and Stress* (pp. 25–40). Upper Saddle River, NJ: Prentice-Hall.

Paton, D. (2006). Posttraumatic growth in emergency professionals. In. L. Calhoun & R. Tedeschi (Eds.), *Handbook of Posttraumatic Growth: Research and Practice.* Mahwah, NJ: Lawrence Erlbaum Assoc.

Paton, D. (2008). Critical incidents. In B. L. Cutler (Ed.), Encyclopedia of Psychology and Law (Vol. 2, pp. 171–172) Thousand Oaks, CA.: Sage.

Paton, D., & Flin, R. (1999). Disaster stress: An emergency management perspective. *Disaster Prevention and Management, 8*, 261–267.

Paton, D., & Jackson, D. (2002). Developing disaster management capability: An assessment centre approach. *Disaster Prevention and Management, 11*, 115–122.

Paton, D., & Kelso, B. A. (1991). Disaster stress: The impact on the wives and family. *Counselling Psychology Quarterly, 4*, 221–227.

Paton, D., Smith, L. M., Ramsay, R., & Akande, D. (1999). A structural re-assessment of the Impact of Event Scale: The influence of occupational and cultural contexts. In R. Gist & B. Lubin (Eds.), *Response to Disaster.* Philadelphia, PA: Taylor & Francis.

Paton, D., Smith, L. M., Violanti, J., & Eränen, L. (2000). Work-related traumatic stress: Risk, vulnerability and resilience. In D. Paton, J. M. Violanti & C. Dunning (Eds.), *Posttraumatic Stress Intervention: Challenges, Issues and Perspectives* (pp. 187–204). Springfield, IL: Charles C Thomas.

Paton, D., & Stephens, C. (1996). Training and support for emergency responders. In D. Paton & J. Violanti (Eds.), *Traumatic Stress in Critical Occupations: Recognition, Consequences and Treatment.* Springfield, IL: Charles C Thomas.

Paton, D., & Violanti, J. M. (2007). Terrorism stress risk assessment and management. In B. Bonger, L. Beutler & P. Zimbardo (Eds.), *Psychology of Terrorism.* San Francisco: Oxford University Press.

Paton, D., Violanti, J. M., Burke, K., & Gherke, A. (2009). *Traumatic Stress in Police Officers: A Career Length Assessment From Recruitment to Retirement.* Springfield, IL: Charles C Thomas.

Perry, I. (1997). Creating and empowering effective work teams. *Management Services, 41*, 8–11.

Quinn, R. E., & Spreitzer, G. M. (1997). The road to empowerment: Seven questions every leader should consider. *Organisational Dynamics, Autumn*, 37–49.

Raphael, B. (1986). *When Disaster Strikes.* London: Hutchinson.

Ripley, R. E., & Ripley, M. J. (1992). Empowerment, the cornerstone of quality: Empowering management in innovative organizations in the 1990's. *Management Decision, 30*, 20–43.

Scotti, J. R., Beach, B. K., Northrop, L. M. E., Rode, C. A., & Forsyth, J. P. (1995). The psychological impact of accidental injury. In J. R. Freedy & S. E. Hobfoll (Eds.), *Traumatic Stress: From Theory to Practice.* New York: Plenum Press.

Siegrist, M., & Cvetkovich, G. (2000). Perception of hazards: The role of social trust and knowledge. *Risk Analysis, 20,* 713–719.

Shakespeare-Finch, J., Paton, D., & Violanti, J. (2003). The family: Resilience resource and resilience needs. In D. Paton, J. Violanti & L. Smith (Eds.), *Promoting Capabilities to Manage Posttraumatic Stress: Perspectives on Resilience.* Springfield, IL: Charles C Thomas.

Spreitzer, G. M. (1995). An empirical test of a comprehensive model of intrapersonal empowerment in the workplace. *American Journal of Community Psychology, 23,* 601–629.

Spreitzer, G. M. (1997). Toward a common ground in defining empowerment. *Research in Organizational Change and Development, 10,* 31–62.

Thomas, K. W., & Velthouse, B. A. (1990). Cognitive elements of empowerment: An "interpretive" model of intrinsic motivation. *Academy of Management Review, 15,* 666–681.

Violanti, J. M., & Paton, D. (2006). *Who Gets PTSD? Issues of Vulnerability to Posttraumatic Stress.* Springfield, IL: Charles C Thomas.

Weick, K. E., & Sutcliffe, K. M. (2007). *Managing the Unexpected: Resilient Performance in an Age of Uncertainty* (2nd ed.). San Francisco, CA.: Jossey-Bass.

Wraith, R. (1994). The impact of major events on children. In R. Watts & D. J. de la Horne (Eds.), *Coping With Trauma.* Brisbane: Australian Academic Press.

Chapter 9

PROTECTIVE ATTRIBUTES: RESILIENCE IN POLICING

MICHAEL E. ANDREW, JANIE L. HOWSARE, TARA A. HARTLEY,
ERIN M. MCCANLIES, CECIL M. BURCHFIEL, AND JOHN M. VIOLANTI

A recent newspaper article heralds results from studies on social environment and development of trauma (Dobbs, 2012). These studies claim that the social environment, after exposure to traumatic events, may determine whether or not individuals develop PTSD. The influence of social support as a protective factor for development of longer term symptoms is well known (Brewin, Andrews & Valentine, 2000; Marmar et al., 2006; Ozer, Best, Lipsey & Weiss, 2003; Wu et al., 2013; Yuan et al., 2011). The strength of social environment as a protective or risk factor points out that resilience goes beyond individual characteristics. This chapter provides an overview of current thinking and issues concerning resilience as it might be applied in law enforcement.

DEFINING RESILIENCE

Reviewing the literature for a specific definition of the term resilience leads to the observation that it has been defined in numerous ways and that the definition has evolved over time. These definitions can be grouped into three forms as follows: (1) resilience as an individual characteristic like hardiness (Maddi, 2004, 2005; Wu et al., 2013), (2) resilience as a process of adaptation operationalized as a trajectory (Bonanno, 2012; Bonanno, Westphal & Mancini, 2011; Norris, Stevens, Pfefferbaum, Wyche & Pfefferbaum, 2008; Norris, Tracy & Galea, 2009), and (3) resilience as an outcome related to the ability to return to a symptom-free state after exposure to stress or trauma (Southwick, Litz, Charney & Friedman, 2011). In a recent commentary, Bonanno and associates (2011) point out that "resilience is not the result of a few dominant factors, but rather that there are multiple independent predictors of resilient outcomes." This chapter addresses some of the factors thought to be predictors of resilience, but the list of proposed factors is long and diverse – and there is too little agreement in the literature to address them all.

Resilience as an Individual Characteristic

Resilience as an individual characteristic different from recovery has been defined as the ability "to maintain a stable equilibrium" in the face of loss or trauma (Bonanno, 2004). Individual characteristics thought to be components of resilience are introduced in the following sections.

Resilience as Hardiness

Hardiness, also known as "existential courage," refers to a personality style that influences the manner in which a person may interpret a critical incident, life stress, or traumatic event. Hardiness is thought to consist of three sets of cognitive styles or dimensions denoted by the terms *commitment*, *control*, and *challenge*. The dimension of *commitment* refers to the tendency to have meaningful engagement with people and events and to find meaning and purpose in potentially stressful events. *Control* is characterized as a sense of being in control with respect to ongoing struggles to maintain influence over the environment. *Challenge* means viewing each important environmental challenge as an opportunity for personal development (Kobasa, 1979; Maddi, 2004). Individuals with higher levels of hardiness are thought to be more resilient to the deleterious effects of stressors because they see meaning in their lives, feel in control of stressful events, and do not avoid challenging situations but see them as opportunities. Hardiness has been identified as a protective factor that may reduce the chances of developing PTSD and other forms of psychological distress (Andrew et al., 2008; Hoge, Austin & Pollack, 2007; King, King, Foy, Keane & Fairbank, 1999). A

widely used instrument developed to measure hardiness is the Dispositional Resilience Scale (DRS-15) developed by Bartone (2007). Using
this measure of hardiness, Bartone, Roland, Picano, and Williams
(2008) showed that hardiness is associated with completion of U.S.
Army Special Forces Training among training candidates (N = 1138).
Using the same measure of hardiness, Andrew and associates (2008)
demonstrated that higher levels hardiness are associated with lower levels of psychological distress among a sample of police officers from the
Buffalo New York Police Department (N = 105). These associations
were stronger in magnitude among police women than among men.

Resilience as Psychological Flexibility

An interesting addition to the literature on prevention of maladaptive consequences of life stress, occupational stress exposure, and exposure to potentially traumatic events comes from the literature on experiential avoidance. Experiential avoidance refers to internal behavior
directed at controlling thoughts and emotions that we consider to be
aversive (Biglan, Hayes & Pistorello, 2008). Attempts to avoid unwanted thoughts and feelings, denoted by the term private experiences, include a variety of strategies, many of which have been labeled as maladaptive coping. These can include any attempt to "escape, avoid or
modify" unwanted thoughts and emotions, including substance use,
avoiding situations that serve as reminders, and attempting to suppress
unwanted thoughts and emotions (Hayes, Strosahl & Wilson, 1999).
The opposite of experiential avoidance is acceptance or willingness to
have unpleasant thoughts and emotions while keeping a commitment
to valued action (Hayes et al., 1999). The therapeutic model known as
acceptance and commitment therapy (ACT) provides an empirically
tested theoretical foundation, grounded in behavior analysis, and clinical methods for helping individuals move from experiential avoidance
toward identification of values and commitment to taking valued action. Looking back at the section on hardiness we see an overlap in ter-
minology – commitment – that points to a similar meaning related to
committed occupational and social engagement. Since ACT targets experiential avoidance as a potentially maladaptive behavior and experiential avoidance is an important feature of PTSD, then it stands to reason that ACT may provide interventions for enhancing resilience to potentially traumatic events (Biglan et al., 2008; Lombardo & Gray, 2005;

Thompson, Arnkoff & Glass, 2011). ACT also has a strong mindfulness component related to strengthening the capacity to stay engaged with the present situation rather than struggling to avoid intrusive memories and emotions or anticipated future events (Hayes, Luoma, Bond, Masuda & Lillis, 2006). Mindfulness training has been shown to be associated with positive outcomes in individuals exposed to potentially traumatic events in various nonpolice populations (Thompson et al., 2011) and in police officers (Chopko & Schwartz, 2013). Mindfulness training is also being developed and applied in predeployment military training to protect against the effects of prolonged exposures to duty-related stressors (Jha, Stanley, Kiyonaga, Wong & Gelfand, 2010; Stanley, Schaldach, Kiyonaga & Jha, 2011). The ACT model, incorporating both mindfulness exercises and methods for reducing experiential avoidance, does not require the presence of a psychological disorder or symptoms in order to be applied in preventive interventions, making it a promising candidate for improving resilience (Biglan et al., 2008).

Resilience as Attachment

Insofar as social support is a factor in preventing the development of symptoms after exposure to a potentially traumatic event, then an individual's ability to connect with others and mobilize social support is an important factor in resilience. Secure attachment patterns in early childhood have been shown to help humans learn how to regulate affect, self-soothe, and cope with stress, and they also provide a template for other significant relationships in adulthood. Generally, if the child experiences the primary caretaker as responsive and nurturing, a secure attachment will form. If the child experiences the primary caretaker as unresponsive or inconsistently responsive, an insecure attachment may form, which can result in a variety of problems including attachment-related anxiety and attachment-related avoidance (Bowlby, 1997; Mikulincer & Shaver, 2012). Both attachment-related anxiety and avoidance interfere with individuals' ability to accurately appraise environmental threats and cope with them effectively, in addition to interfering with effective mobilization of social support (Caldwell & Shaver, 2012; Karreman & Vingerhoets, 2012; Shaver & Mikulincer, 2008). The ability to establish and utilize a social support system is critical to coping with stressors.

RESILIENCE IN CONTEXT:
THE IMPORTANCE OF SOCIAL SUPPORT

Support from family members, friends, and coworkers is thought to be important in the prevention and treatment of PTSD after exposure to a potentially traumatic event (Whealin, Ruzek & Southwick, 2008). This has been verified in studies involving various populations, including returning veterans, victims of violent crime, and victims of serious motor vehicle accidents (Andrews, Brewin & Rose, 2003; Barrett & Mizes, 1988; Pietrzak, Goldstein, Malley, Rivers & Southwick, 2010; Pietrzak, Johnson, Goldstein, Malley & Southwick, 2009; Robinaugh et al., 2011; Schumm, Briggs-Phillips & Hobfoll, 2006; Tsai, Harpaz-Rotem, Pietrzak & Southwick, 2012). Acute symptoms from exposure to potentially traumatic events can be disturbing to members of an individual's social group, potentially leaving them in relative social isolation. Negative reactions to acute or chronic trauma symptoms from family, friends, and coworkers can also reinforce the experiential avoidance that is characteristic of PTSD. Peer support groups who understand the nature of trauma symptoms can be helpful in providing social support and a feeling of being understood (Tsai et al., 2012).

RESILIENCE AS AN ADAPTIVE PROCESS

The most comprehensive definition of resilience to date is based on examining processes by which trajectories of resistance, adaptation, and maladaptation occur after potentially traumatic events (Bonanno, Mancini, et al., 2012; Bonanno et al., 2011; Norris et al., 2008; Norris et al., 2009). Resistance is generally defined as little or no increase in symptoms after exposure to a potentially traumatic event, whereas resilience points to a transient pattern of increase in symptoms followed by a complete return to normal experience and functioning (Norris et al., 2009). Other trajectories include the following: (a) recovery where there is a slower return to a higher baseline level of symptoms than before exposure, (b) chronic dysfunction, (c) delayed dysfunction with onset of more severe symptoms after some period of time with partially increased symptoms, and (d) relapse and remitting patterns characterized by increases and decreases of symptoms with permanent remission (Norris et al., 2009). These patterns have been observed in several longitudinal studies of populations exposed to military deployment and terrorist attacks (Bonanno, Kennedy, Galatzer-Levy, Lude & Elfstrom, 2012; Norris et al., 2009). As Bonanno and colleagues (2011) point out, the resilient trajectory is not uncommon. In fact, it is the most commonly observed pattern; other trajectories are less common. Because of this it does not make sense to think of resilience as something conditioned by unusual individual characteristics. Additionally, resilient trajectories can be influenced by external contextual factors as well as individual characteristics so that an individual may be more or less likely to have a resilient trajectory after exposure, depending on recent life history and availability of resources (Bonanno et al., 2011; Norris et al., 2008). One recent study showed that lower levels of negative emotion and higher levels of positive emotion were predictive of resilient trajectory in a longitudinal cohort of police officers (Galatzer-Levy et al., 2013). Beyond this result, there is little research on predictors of resilience as an adaptive process. This approach to defining and studying resilience requires longitudinal data, which are costly and take considerable time to develop. Recent publications using data of this nature are still working to define appropriate ways of representing trajectories and examining very limited demographic and behavioral correlates related to adaptive coping. Because of this, it is too soon to make recommendations, based on this definition of resilience, for interventions (Bonanno, Kennedy et al., 2012; Norris et al., 2009).

IMPLEMENTATIONS OF RESILIENCE TRAINING

One excellent example of an implementation of a resilience intervention is reported by Arnetz, Nevedal, Lumley, Backman and Lublin (2009). This intervention was based on combining structured relaxation methods and rehearsal of skills for dealing with known police work stressors with the goal of achieving "optimal focus, effective weapons management, and navigating novel environments during a critical incident" (Arnetz et al., 2009). This study is longitudinal in that the resilience intervention took place a year before the simulated critical incident. Compared to controls, the training group had lower levels of negative mood after the simulated critical incident and lower autonomic reactivity, as measured by increase from baseline heart rate, during the simulated critical incident. Objective observations of police performance during the incident were higher for the training group (Arnetz et al., 2009).

Policing is a high-stress occupation in which exposure to potentially traumatic events is common, and resistance, resilience, and recovery from exposure to potentially traumatic events are essential to maintaining the healthy and effectiveness of police officers. This chapter provides an overview of factors thought to be related to resilience and introduces the theory and practice of psychological flexibility as a potential new factor related to resilience. This topic is too large to be well-characterized in ten or twenty pages, so this overview is necessarily limited in details and depth that can be found in excellent references like the recently published edited book entitled *Resilience and Mental Health: Challenges Across the Lifespan* edited by Southwick and colleagues (2011).

Disclaimer: The findings and conclusions in this report are those of the authors and do not necessarily represent the views of the National Institute for Occupational Safety and Health.

REFERENCES

Andrew, M. E., McCanlies, E. C., Burchfiel, C. M., Charles, L. E., Hartley, T. A., Fekedulegn, D., & Violanti, J. M. (2008). Hardiness and psychological distress in a cohort of police officers. *International Journal of Emergency Mental Health, 10,* 137–147.

Andrews, B., Brewin, C. R., & Rose, S. (2003). Gender, social support, and PTSD in victims of violent crime. *Journal of Traumatic Stress, 16,* 421–427. doi: 10.1023/A: 1024478305142

Arnetz, B. B., Nevedal, D. C., Lumley, M. A., Backman, L., & Lublin, A. (2009). Trauma resilience training for police: Psychophysiological and performance effects. *Journal of Police and Criminal Psychology, 24,* 1–9.

Barrett, T. W., & Mizes, J. S. (1988). Combat level and social support in the development of posttraumatic stress disorder in Vietnam veterans. *Behavior Modification, 12,* 100–115. doi: 10.1177/01454455880121005

Bartone, P. T. (2007). Test-retest reliability of the dispositional resilience scale-15, a brief hardiness scale. Psychological Reports, 101(3), 943–944. doi: Doi 10.2466/Pro.101.3.943-944

Bartone, P. T., Roland, R. R., Picano, J. J., & Williams, T. (2008). Psychological hardiness predicts success in US Army Special Forces candidates. *International Journal of Selection and Assessment, 16,* 78–81. doi: 10.1111/j.1468-2389.2008.00412.x

Biglan, A., Hayes, S. C., & Pistorello, J. (2008). Acceptance and commitment: Implications for prevention science. *Prevention Science, 9,* 139–152. doi: 10.1007/s11121-008-0099-4

Bonanno, G. A. (2004). Loss, trauma, and human resilience – Have we underestimated the human capacity to thrive after extremely aversive events? *American Psychologist, 59*, 20–28. doi: 10.1037/0003-066x.59.1.20

Bonanno, G. A. (2012). Uses and abuses of the resilience construct: Loss, trauma, and health-related adversities. *Social Science & Medicine, 74*, 753–756. doi: 10.1016/j.socscimed.2011.11.022

Bonanno, G. A., Kennedy, P., Galatzer-Levy, I. R., Lude, P., & Elfstrom, M. L. (2012). Trajectories of Resilience, Depression, and Anxiety Following Spinal Cord Injury. *Rehabilitation Psychology, 57*, 236–247. doi: 10.1037/A0029256

Bonanno, G. A., Mancini, A. D., Horton, J. L., Powell, T. M., LeardMann, C. A., Boyko, E. J., . . . Team, M. C. S. (2012). Trajectories of trauma symptoms and resilience in deployed US military service members: Prospective cohort study. *British Journal of Psychiatry, 200*, 317–323. doi: 10.1192/bjp.bp.111.096552

Bonanno, G. A., Westphal, M., & Mancini, A. D. (2011). Resilience to loss and potential trauma. *Annual Review of Clinical Psychology, 7*, 511–535. doi: 10.1146/annurev-clinpsy-032210-104526

Bowlby, J. (1997). *Attachment* (vol. 1 of the *Attachment and Loss* trilogy). London: Pimlico.

Brewin, C. R., Andrews, B., & Valentine, J. D. (2000). Meta-analysis of risk factors for posttraumatic stress disorder in trauma-exposed adults. *Journal of Consulting and Clinical Psychology, 68*, 748–766. doi: 10.1037/0022-006x.68.5.748

Caldwell, J. G., & Shaver, P. R. (2012). Exploring the cognitive-emotional pathways between adult attachment and ego-resiliency. *Individual Differences Research, 10*, 141–152.

Chopko, B. A., & Schwartz, R. C. (2013). The relation between mindfulness and posttraumatic stress symptoms among police officers. *Journal of Loss & Trauma, 18*, 1–9. doi: 10.1080/15325024.2012.674442

Dobbs, D. (2012, December 24). A new focus on the "post" in post-traumatic stress. *New York Times*, p. D2.

Galatzer-Levy, I. R., Brown, A. D., Henn-Haase, C., Metzler, T. J., Neylan, T. C., & Marmar, C. R. (2013). Positive and negative emotion prospectively predict trajectories of resilience and distress among high-exposure police officers. Emotion, 13, 545–553. doi: 10.1037/a0031314

Hayes, S. C., Luoma, J. B., Bond, F. W., Masuda, A., & Lillis, J. (2006). Acceptance and commitment therapy: Model, processes and outcomes. *Behaviour Research and Therapy, 44*, 1–25. doi: 10.1016/j.brat.2005.06.006

Hayes, S. C., Strosahl, K. D., & Wilson, K. G. (1999). *Acceptance and Commitment Therapy*. New York: Guilford.

Hoge, E. A., Austin, E. D., & Pollack, M. H. (2007). Resilience: Research evidence and conceptual considerations for posttraumatic stress disorder. *Depression and Anxiety, 24*, 139–152. doi: 10.1002/Da.20175

Jha, A. P., Stanley, E. A., Kiyonaga, A., Wong, L., & Gelfand, L. (2010). Examining the protective effects of mindfulness training on working memory capacity and affective experience. *Emotion, 10*, 54–64. doi: 10.1037/A0018438

Karreman, A., & Vingerhoets, A. J. J. M. (2012). Attachment and well-being: The mediating role of emotion regulation and resilience. *Personality and Individual Differences, 53*, 821–826. doi: 10.1016/j.paid.2012.06.014

King, D. W., King, L. A., Foy, D. W., Keane, T. M., & Fairbank, J. A. (1999). Posttraumatic stress disorder in a national sample of female and male Vietnam veterans. Risk factors, war-zone stressors, and resilience-recovery variables. *Journal of Abnormal Psychology, 108*, 164–170. doi: 10.1037//0021-843x.108.1.164

Kobasa, S. C. (1979). Stressful life events, personality, and health: An inquiry into hardiness. *Journal of Personality and Social Psychology, 37*, 1–11.

Lombardo, T. W., & Gray, M. J. (2005). Beyond exposure for posttraumatic stress disorder (PTSD) symptoms – Broad-spectrum PTSD treatment strategies. *Behavior Modification, 29*, 3–9. doi: 10.1177/0145445504270853

Maddi, S. R. (2004). Hardiness: An operationalization of existential courage. *Journal of Humanistic Psychology, 44*, 279–298. doi: 10.1177/0022167804266101

Maddi, S. R. (2005). On hardiness and other pathways to resilience. *American Psychologist, 60*, 261–262. doi: 10.1037/0003-066X.60.3.261

Marmar, C. R., McCaslin, S. E., Metzler, T. J., Best, S., Weiss, D. S., Fagan, J., . . . Neylan, T. (2006). Predictors of posttraumatic stress in police and other first responders. *Annual NY Academy of Science, 1071*, 1–18. doi: 10.1196/annals.1364.001

Mikulincer, M., & Shaver, P. R. (2012). Adult attachment orientations and relationship processes. *Journal of Family Theory & Review, 4*, 259–274.

Norris, F. H., Stevens, S. P., Pfefferbaum, B., Wyche, K. F., & Pfefferbaum, R. L. (2008). Community resilience as a metaphor, theory, set of capacities, and strategy for disaster readiness. *American Journal of Community Psychology, 41*, 127–150. doi: 10.1007/s10464-007-9156-6

Norris, F. H., Tracy, M., & Galea, S. (2009). Looking for resilience: Understanding the longitudinal trajectories of responses to stress. *Social Science & Medicine, 68*, 2190–2198. doi: 10.1016/j.socscimed.2009.03.043

Ozer, E. J., Best, S. R., Lipsey, T. L., & Weiss, D. S. (2003). Predictors of posttraumatic stress disorder and symptoms in adults: A meta-analysis. *Psychological Bulletin, 129*, 52–73. doi: 10.1037//0033-2909.129.1.52

Pietrzak, R. H., Goldstein, M. B., Malley, J. C., Rivers, A. J., & Southwick, S. M. (2010). Structure of posttraumatic stress disorder symptoms and psychosocial functioning in veterans of Operations Enduring Freedom and Iraqi Freedom. *Psychiatry Research, 178*, 323.

Pietrzak, R. H., Johnson, D. C., Goldstein, M. B., Malley, J. C., & Southwick, S. M. (2009). Psychological resilience and postdeployment social support protect against traumatic stress and depressive symptoms in soldiers returning from Operations Enduring Freedom and Iraqi Freedom. *Depression and Anxiety, 26*, 745–751.

Robinaugh, D. J., Marques, L., Traeger, L. N., Marks, E. H., Sung, S. C., Beck, J. G., . . . Simon, N. M. (2011). Understanding the relationship of perceived social support to post-trauma cognitions and posttraumatic stress disorder. *Journal of Anxiety Disorders, 25*, 1072–1078. doi: 10.1016/j.janxdis.2011.07.004

Schumm, J. A., Briggs-Phillips, M., & Hobfoll, S. E. (2006). Cumulative interpersonal traumas and social support as risk and resiliency factors in predicting PTSD and depression among inner-city women. *Journal of Traumatic Stress, 19*, 825–836. doi: 10.1002/Jts.20159

Shaver, P. R., & Mikulincer, M. (2008). Adult attachment and cognitive and affective reactions to positive and negative events. *Social and Personality Psychology Compass, 2*, 1844–1865. doi: 10.1111/j.1751-9004.2008.00146.x

Southwick, S. M., Litz, B. T., Charney, D., Friedman, M. J. (2011). *Resilience and Mental Health: Challenges Across the Lifespan.* Cambridge: Cambridge University Press.

Stanley, E. A., Schaldach, J. M., Kiyonaga, A., & Jha, A. P. (2011). Mindfulness-based mind fitness training: A case study of a high-stress predeployment military cohort. *Cognitive and Behavioral Practice, 18*, 566–576. doi: 10.1016/j.cbpra.2010.08.002

Thompson, R. W., Arnkoff, D. B., & Glass, C. R. (2011). Conceptualizing mindfulness and acceptance as components of psychological resilience to trauma. *Trauma Violence Abuse, 12*, 220–235. doi: 10.1177/1524838011416375

Tsai, J., Harpaz-Rotem, I., Pietrzak, R. H., & Southwick, S. M. (2012). The role of coping, resilience, and social support in mediating the relation between PTSD and social functioning in veterans returning from Iraq and Afghanistan. *Psychiatry-Interpersonal and Biological Processes, 75*, 135–149.

Whealin, J. M., Ruzek, J. I., & Southwick, S. (2008). Cognitive-behavioral theory and preparation for professionals at risk for trauma exposure. *Trauma Violence & Abuse, 9*, 100–113. doi: 10.1177/1524838008315869

Wu, G., Feder, A., Cohen, H., Kim, J. J., Calderon, S., Charney, D. S., & Mathe, A. A. (2013). Understanding resilience. *Frontiers in Behavioral Neuroscience, 7*, 10. doi: 10.3389/fnbeh.2013.00010

Yuan, C. M., Wang, Z., Inslicht, S. S., McCaslin, S. E., Metzler, T. J., Henn-Haase, C., . . . Marmar, C. R. (2011). Protective factors for posttraumatic stress disorder symptoms in a prospective study of police officers. *Psychiatry Research, 188*, 45–50. doi: 10.1016/j.psychres.2010.10.034

Chapter 10

POSTTRAUMATIC STRESS DISORDER SYMPTOMS, PSYCHOBIOLOGY, AND COEXISTING DISORDERS IN POLICE OFFICERS

Erin McCanlies, Diane Miller, Michael Andrew, Oliver Wirth, Cecil M. Burchfiel, and John M. Violanti

Over the last 20 years, information describing PTSD has accumulated at an ever-increasing pace, as have scientific and anecdotal reports evaluating the efficacy of frequently used treatments. In-depth descriptions of this work can be found in a number of excellent books and research articles (Bisson & Andrew, 2009; Cloitre et al., 2012; Friedman, Resick, Bryant & Brewin, 2011; Ipser & Stein, 2012; Lanius, Bluhm & Frewen, 2011; Levine, 2010; Ogden, Pain & Fisher, 2006; Pitman et al., 2012; Porges, 2011; Schiraldi, 2000; Sharpless & Barber, 2011; Stein, Friedman & Blanco, 2011; van der Kolk, McFarlane & Weisaeth, 1996; Violanti, Paton & Dunning, 2000). This chapter will briefly review the current state of knowledge about PTSD and includes information on diagnosis, epidemiology, and neurobiology. We also discuss negative physical and mental health conditions that have been found to be associated with PTSD. Any review is necessarily eclectic, and it is impossible to include all research contributions. Therefore, the articles discussed in this chapter are representative, but not exhaustive, of the PTSD literature.

Dying for the Job

POSTTRAUMATIC STRESS DISORDER DIAGNOSIS

The World Health Organization (WHO) *International Classification of Diseases* (ICD-10) states that PTSD is "a response to a stressful event or situation of an exceptionally threatening or catastrophic nature, which is likely to cause pervasive distress in almost anyone (World Health Organization [WHO], 1992). Prior to 1980 when PTSD was established as a formal diagnostic entity, it was called by many different names, such as hysteria, shell-shock, soldier's heart, and delayed stress (Pitman et al., 2012; van der Kolk et al., 1996). As our knowledge and understanding of PTSD has changed, so too has the way we think about and diagnose PTSD (Friedman et al., 2011; van der Kolk et al., 1996). Historically, PTSD was thought to be a "normal response to an abnormal event." We now know that trauma initiates a complex psychological and biological process, and not all individuals exposed to the same traumatic event will develop PTSD (Keane, Marshall & Taft, 2006). Despite much research concerning PTSD, we have not been able to identify biomarkers, such as specific genes or blood markers that will help us to predict who will develop the disorder, or biomarkers that are specific to the disorder itself and do not overlap with other psychiatric disorders. Currently, a diagnosis of PTSD is given when an individual meets a certain set of criteria defined in the fourth, revised *Diagnostic and Statistical Manual of Mental Disorders* (DSM-IV-TR) (American Psychiatric Association [APA], 2007).

These criteria include seven main components: (1) experiencing, witnessing, or being confronted with an event or events that involved actual or threatened death or serious injury, or a threat to the physical integrity of self or others; (2) the response to the event involved intense fear, helplessness, or horror; (3) reexperiencing the traumatic event; (4) avoidance/numbing symptoms; (5) symptoms of hyperarousal; (6) symptoms must persist for a defined period of time; and (7) symptoms must result in significant distress or functional impairment (APA, 2007; Schnurr, Friedman & Bernardy, 2002; Spitzer et al., 2009; Yehuda, 2002).

Reexperiencing the event often comes in the form of intrusive memories, flashbacks, nightmares, or somatic sensations (APA, 2007; Schnurr et al., 2002; Spitzer et al., 2009; Yehuda, 2002). Even though the trauma occurred in the past, when triggered, individuals with PTSD feel as though they are reexperiencing the traumatic event and report feeling that they will have a foreshortened future. In an attempt to avoid being triggered, individuals with PTSD avoid people, places, conversations, or activities that remind them of the event. They may avoid thoughts and feelings about the event and may even be unable to remember important aspects of the event. Avoidance can also take the form of emotional numbing: feeling estranged and disconnected from self and others. Arousal may be experienced as difficulty falling or staying asleep, difficulty controlling emotions such as anger and irritability, difficulty concentrating, and a state of constant hypervigilance (APA, 2007). Along with these symptoms, to meet the DSM-IV-TR diagnostic criteria for PTSD, the duration of the symptoms must have lasted for more than 1 month and interfere with some important aspect of daily functioning, such as social or occupational. The definition of a traumatic event has broadened over time, however (Rosen & Lilienfeld, 2008). Previously, a traumatic event was defined as life threatening and causing intense fear and included events such as battle, car accidents, sexual assault, and so on. It is now recognized that events such as divorce, unemployment, and a diagnosis of diseases like cancer may result in symptoms of PTSD and that some individuals develop PTSD without having experienced "fear, helplessness, or horror" (APA, 2007; Calhoun et al., 2012; Friedman et al., 2011). These, and other changes in our understanding of PTSD symptomology will be reflected by modifications in the revised PTSD diagnostic criteria to be published as part of the APA's fifth version of the *Diagnostic and Statistical Manual of Mental Disorders* (DSM-5) (Friedman et al., 2011).

EPIDEMIOLOGY

Epidemiological research helps us to understand individual risk factors of PTSD; biological and neurological research helps us understand how trauma affects our bodies and our minds. Much of the existing research on PTSD has evaluated people who already have PTSD; this limits our ability to establish causation. Pretrauma prospective studies are needed to make progress in establishing causation and represent a crucial step in further developing effective treatments (Pitman et al., 2012). Even in light of current limitations, however, studies continue to help us better understand PTSD and how to treat it more effectively.

Research shows us that PTSD is more likely to occur in occupational groups that are frequently exposed to traumatic events (Berger et al., 2012). These special populations include military personnel and first responders, such as rescue workers, ambulance drivers, firefighters, and police officers (Marmar et al., 2006). Police officers are repeatedly exposed to traumatic situations, including motor vehicle accidents, armed conflicts, and witnessing violent death, across their working lives (Marmar et al., 2006). Approximately 7 percent to 19 percent of police officers qualify for a diagnosis of PTSD, and approximately 34 percent experience a number of PTSD symptoms but do not meet a full PTSD diagnosis (Carlier, Lamberts & Gersons, 1997; Gersons, 1989; Robinson, Sigman & Wilson, 1997). Following a traumatic incident, a number of different factors have been found to affect whether an individual will develop PTSD. These factors include, but are not limited to, having a prior history of trauma, coping styles, irregular work hours, rotating shifts, and lack of social support both inside and outside work (Carlier et al., 1997; Marmar et al., 2006). Differences by gender and ethnic group have also been observed, although this is not consistent across all studies (Bowler et al., 2010, 2012; Lilly, Pole, Best, Metzler & Marmar, 2009; Marmar et al., 2006). These studies indicate that developing PTSD is not a function of any one thing, but how an individual's brain processes and stores traumatic events.

TRAUMA AND MEMORY CONSOLIDATION

Memory research indicates that individuals without PTSD rarely recall sensory details of an event, such as smells, sensations, and movements of events; rather the brain reassembles and constructs stories around events, adding meaning and a narrative to create the "story" (Shapiro, 2002). In contrast, individuals with PTSD are able to report very specific yet fragmented sights, sounds, movements, and sensations that occurred during the traumatic event (van der Kolk et al., 1996). Specific neurohormones such as norepinephrine released at the time of the trauma may play a role in memory overconsolidation whereas vasopressin and endogenous opioids may result in amnesia for the traumatic event individuals with PTSD often display (van der Kolk et al., 1996). It has been suggested that due to these neurohormones, traumatized persons do not process the traumatic event into a meaningful narrative; therefore, trauma reminders result in the individual's reexperiencing the trauma as if it were occurring in the present rather than as an event of the past. This, in turn, triggers a physiological response, rereleasing the neurohormones, strengthening the memory neuropathways, and perpetuating symptomology.

PSYCHOBIOLOGY

Human beings are wired to manage, adapt, and learn from stressful events. The brain continually monitors the environment for danger (Levine, 2010; Siegel, 2010). In a process referred to as "neuroception," certain neural circuits involving the prefrontal, limbic, and brain stem areas determine which individuals and circumstances are safe or dangerous by detecting and evaluating body and facial movement as well as facial expression (Siegel, 2010). In the face of an actual or perceived threat, chemicals known as neurotransmitters (e.g., catecholamines) are released, resulting in the activation of either the sympathetic nervous system (SNS) or the parasympathetic nervous system (PSNS), the two branches of the autonomic nervous system (ANS) (Levine, 2010). Their activation produces automatic primitive neurobiological defense reactions, "fight-flight-freeze" responses (Levine, 2010). The fight or flight response is well-understood and controlled by the SNS, whereas the defense strategy of freezing or immobilization, thought to be a much older response from an evolutionary perspective, is less understood but is known to be controlled by the dorsal vagal branch of the PSNS (Porges, 2011). Its activation causes our blood pressure to drop and slows down our breathing and heart rate through its effects on nerve conduction and blood vessels (Porges, 2011; Siegel, 2010; Wilson & Keane, 2004).

Detection or perception of a threat or stressor also activates the hypothalamic-pituitary-adrenocortical (HPA) axis, resulting in the release of a species-specific glucocorticoid. For humans, it is cortisol that is released into the general circulation (O'Connor, O'Halloran & Shanahan, 2000; van der Kolk et al., 1996). Cortisol increases our metabolism so sufficient energy is available, enabling our muscles and nervous system to quickly and efficiently deal with the threat. Cortisol, acting in a classic negative feedback loop, shuts off the initiating steps of HPA activation by binding to glucocorticoid receptors in the brain, bringing the individual back to a state of homeostasis or "normal" function, ready to deal with the next threat. However, in individuals with PTSD, the brain and body systems dealing with danger or threat are overreactive or react in an abnormal way in comparison to individuals without PTSD (Kim et al., 2011).

The neurocircuitry of PTSD has received much attention and brain imaging studies, including various techniques that directly or indirectly image the function and structure of the brain, are helping us understand the neurological basis for some of the symptoms reported by individuals with PTSD (Hayes, Hayes & Mikedis, 2012; Lanius et al., 2011; Patel, Spreng, Shin & Girard, 2012; Pitman et al., 2012; Shin, Rauch & Pitman, 2006). Because it tracks brain metabolism, functional imaging allows the direct visualization of the centers of the brain involved in processing information. Many functional brain imaging studies show differential activation in some regions of the brain when individuals with PTSD are compared with individuals without PTSD (Hayes et al., 2012; Patel et al., 2012; Pitman et al., 2012). A meta-analysis of multiple functional imaging studies of those individuals diagnosed with PTSD found that the mid-anterior cingulate cortex, the dorsal anterior cingulate cortex (dACC), and the bilateral amygdala are the most hyperactivated regions. The most hypoactivated include the ventromedial prefrontal cortex (vmPFC), the inferior frontal gyrus, and the insula. These differences in activity of certain brain circuits lead to the hypothesis that PTSD is due to a failure of the vmPFC to inhibit the amygdala.

One job of the vmPFC is to help us predict the occurrence of threatening events based on our past experiences; this is referred to as fear conditioning. Eventually, however, if a threatening or painful event repeatedly does not occur following the fear conditioning stimulus, an extinction of the fear response occurs (Wessa & Flor, 2007). It has been suggested by behavioral psychologists that individuals with PTSD exhibit enhanced acquisition of the fear response, as well as a delay in its extinction. The initial traumatic event is the stimulus that triggers a fear response. Through additional conditioning, trauma-related reminders or cues appear to maintain the fear response and hinder fear extinction. Decreased activity in the vmPFC may play a role in maintaining the fear response and inhibiting fear extinction, possibly due to the inability of this brain area to reduce amygdala hyperactivity (Pitman et al., 2012).

Besides fear conditioning and extinction, the vmPFC is important in self-referential processing (Lanius et al., 2011). Lower activity in the vmPFC may result in disturbances in self-referential processing, which undermines an individual's sense of self and life purpose. It is associated with symptoms of shame, identity disturbance, and dissociation. It is also associated with an individual's ability to tune into and attend to the wants and desires of others (Lanius et al., 2011). Another job of the vmPFC is to communicate with the limbic system. Through this communication we are able to monitor and modify our own emotions. Therefore, reduced activity in this region of the brain may be one of the reasons why individuals with PTSD, once triggered, have difficulty identifying and controlling their emotional responses. Similarly, reduced activation of the insula has also been shown to be associated with the inability to label and identify emotions.

Other than the vmPFC, the insula is also associated with our ability to identify and label emotions. It is involved in interoceptive awareness of the body and the regulation of the sympathetic and parasympathetic systems, including the sensation of pain (Hayes et al., 2012; Lanius et al., 2011). Underactivation in this region of the brain may also be one of the reasons why individuals with PTSD become emotionally overwhelmed in the face of traumatic reminders.

Regions of the brain that appear to be more active in individuals with PTSD compared with those without PTSD are the dACC, the amygdala, and the hippocampus. The dACC plays a critical role in fear conditioning and extinction and is involved in pain perception, as well as appraisal and evaluation of the environment. Increased activity in this region of the brain may be the reason why individuals with PTSD are hypervigilant and report feelings of hyperarousal (Hayes et al., 2012).

A large number of functional imaging studies indicate individuals with PTSD have increased brain activity in the amygdala compared to individuals without PTSD (Hayes et al., 2012; Lanius et al., 2011; Pitman et al., 2012; van der Kolk et al., 1996). The amygdala is important in fear conditioning, modulation of memory consolidation, and emotional and social processing (Lanius et al., 2011). It is responsible for assigning emotional meaning to incoming stimuli that are further processed into a personal narrative in the neocortex via the hippocampus, hypothalamus, and basal forebrain (van der Kolk et al., 1996). Increased amygdala activity has been shown to have an inverse relationship with activity in the vmPFC (Hayes et al., 2012). It has been suggested that increased amygdala activation is associated with exposure to trauma in general and not PTSD specifically, because activity in this area did not differ when comparisons were made between those exposed to a trauma with and without PTSD (Patel et al., 2012). This finding also suggests it is important to include trauma-exposed and non–trauma-exposed controls in studies of PTSD.

The hippocampus lies next to the amygdala and plays a critical role in processing emotionally laden memories. It is important in short-term memory and is involved in the formation of autobiographical memories and interpreting environmental cues (Pitman et al., 2012; van der Kolk et al., 1996). Overactivation of this region along with the amygdala may contribute to intrusive thoughts frequently experienced by individuals with PTSD (Patel et al., 2012). Structural MRI studies initially indicated that the hippocampal volume was smaller in individuals with PTSD compared to those without, but the idea that a decrease in hippocampal size is linked to trauma exposure is controversial (Pitman et al., 2012). Subsequent research using identical twins found no difference in their hippocampal volume although the twin that experienced combat developed PTSD. Furthermore, the hippocampal size for both twins was smaller than twins discordant for combat where PTSD did not occur. These data suggest that hippocampal volume may be genetically determined and not specifically associated with trauma exposure (Pitman et al., 2012; van der Kolk et al., 1996). Further complicating the issue is the observation that hippocampal volume can be increased by pharmacological treatment (e.g., serotonin reuptake inhibitors), suggesting volume is malleable (Vermetten, Vythilingam, Southwick, Charney & Bremner, 2003). The size of other brain structures important in PTSD can be affected by exogenous treatments; for example, chronic corticosteroid therapy reduces amygdala as well as hippocampus volume (Brown et al., 2009). Finally, a recent meta-analysis found that trauma exposed individuals without PTSD have smaller hippocampal volumes when compared to individuals with no trauma exposure and no PTSD, suggesting trauma itself may cause a loss of volume (Woon, Sood & Hedges, 2010). Thus, there is still active debate as to the origins and role of hippocampal volume in PTSD and trauma exposure.

PHYSICAL AND PSYCHOLOGICAL CONSEQUENCES OF PTSD

Ongoing research has contributed to our understanding of the biological and neurological link between PTSD and coexisting physical and psychological disorders (Gupta, 2013; Hayes et al., 2012; Kim et al., 2011; Lanius et al., 2011; O'Connor et al., 2000; Pitman et al., 2012). Structural and functional neuroimaging studies indicate that, in individuals with PTSD, specific regions of the brain associated with memory consolidation, fear conditioning, and fear extinction, as well as emotion regulation, activate responses in the ANS (fight-flight-freeze response) and HPA axis (Hayes et al., 2012; Kim et al., 2011; Lanius et al., 2011; Pitman et al., 2012; Porges, 2011). Both the ANS, through the activation of catecholamines, and the HPA axis, through cortisol, act on multiple biological systems within the body (Gupta, 2013; Lukaschek et al., 2013). In addition, activation of the freeze response is mediated by the dorsal vagal complex, which carries nerve signals from the hypothalamus to the heart, digestive system, and lungs as well as receives nerve signals from these systems (Porges, 2011). Dysregulation of the ANS and HPA axis as seen in individuals with PTSD may be associated with coexisting psychological and biological disorders (Gupta, 2013; Lukaschek et al., 2013).

There are a number of studies that have focused on the general population and on police officers specifically, that indicate that individuals with PTSD are at an increased risk of CVD, coronary heart disease, hypertension, and possibly stroke (Coughlin, 2011; Sareen et al., 2007; Violanti, Andrew, et al., 2006; Violanti, Fekedulegn, et al., 2006). PTSD symptoms have also been found to be associated with metabolic syndrome and a reduction in brachial artery flow-mediated dilation (Violanti, Andrew, et al., 2006; Violanti, Fekedulegn, et al., 2006). In a cross-sectional study of 2,970 general population participants, those with PTSD were found to be three times more likely to have type 2 diabetes compared to individuals without a traumatic event (Lukaschek et al., 2013). Gupta (2013) conducted a review of the literature and found that PTSD has been shown to be associated with a wide range of chronic diseases other than CVD and diabetes (Gupta, 2013). These include diseases such as chronic fatigue syndrome, fibromyalgia, gastrointestinal disorders, autoimmune disorders, and chronic pain syndromes such as migraine headaches (Gupta, 2013). Although most of the studies included in the review were cross-sectional in nature, and therefore cause-effect relations could not be determined, and independent research studies are needed to confirm and expand many of these observed relationships, this review indicates that PTSD is associated with a large number of negative health outcome (Gupta, 2013; Sareen et al., 2007). Finally, it is important to note that the frequency of experienced traumatic events has been found to correlate with symptom severity (Suliman et al., 2009; Uddin et al., 2010). For this reason, officers who are exposed to multiple traumatic incidents may experience more severe symptoms compared to individuals who have had relatively few traumatic events.

Other than an increased risk of physical health conditions, individuals with PTSD are also more likely to experience a number of comorbid psychological conditions and suicidal ideation and to report reduced quality of life (Maia et al., 2007; Martin, Marchand & Boyer, 2009; Sareen et al., 2007). Sareen and colleagues (2007) found that PTSD was associated with major depression, mania, panic attacks, agoraphobia, social phobia, and substance abuse (Sareen et al., 2007). They also reported that PTSD was associated with high distress, high suicidal ideation, and poor psychological well-being (Sareen et al., 2007). In studies that have evaluated PTSD with indicators of poor health in officers, officers with PTSD were more likely to report more frequent medical appointments, more use of sick leave, and more hospital admissions compared to officers without PTSD (Maia et al., 2007; Martin et al., 2009). They were also more likely to report poorer health than individuals without PTSD (Maia et al., 2007; Martin et al., 2009).

SUMMARY

PTSD is frequently diagnosed following a single traumatic event. Epidemiological research, however, indicates that an individual's risk of PTSD increases with the number of traumatic experiences (Berger et al., 2012). In individuals with PTSD, repeated or chronic activation of the stress response systems (e.g., the SNS and HPA axis) may eventually result in their inefficient operation (Kim et al., 2011; O'Connor et al., 2000). This inefficient operation may result in the release of too much or too little of the physiologically active substances such as catecholamines and cortisol that play a role in dealing with threat (Kim et al., 2011; O'Connor et al., 2000). Abnormal levels of these substances are thought to be associated with the development of inflammatory, endocrine, cardiovascular, and psychiatric disorders in individuals with PTSD (Coughlin, 2011; Gupta, 2013; Lukaschek et al., 2013; Sareen et al., 2007). Because police officers are frequently exposed to traumatic incidents over their working lives, they are at an increased risk of PTSD. This in turn increases their risk of a number of other coexisting biological and psychological disorders such as CVD, diabetes, and depression (Gupta, 2013; Lukaschek et al., 2013; Marmar et al., 2006; Stearns, n.d.; Violanti, Andrew, et al., 2006; Violanti, Fekedulegn, et al., 2006). Because of the profound impact PTSD has on police officers, we should strive to prevent, diagnose, and treat this disorder in this population.

Disclaimer: The findings and conclusions in this report are those of the authors and do not necessarily represent the views of the National Institute for Occupational Safety and Health.

REFERENCES

American Psychiatric Association (APA). (2007). *Diagnostic and Statistical Manual of Mental Disorders* (IV-TR ed.). Arlington: American Psychiatric Association.

Berger, W., Coutinho, E. S., Figueira, I., Marques-Portella, C., Luz, M. P., Neylan, T. C., . . . Mendlowicz, M. V. (2012). Rescuers at risk: A systematic review and meta-regression analysis of the worldwide current prevalence and correlates of PTSD in rescue workers. *Social Psychiatry and Psychiatric Epidemiology, 47*, 1001–1011.

Bisson, J., & Andrew, M. (2009). Psychological treatment of post-traumatic stress disorder (PTSD). *Cochrane Database of Systematic Reviews, 1*, 99.

Bowler, R. M., Han, H., Gocheva, V., Nakagawa, S., Alper, H., DiGrande, L., & Cone, J. E. (2010). Gender differences in probable posttraumatic stress disorder among police responders to the 2001 World Trade Center terrorist attack. *American Journal of Industrial Medicine, 53*, 1186–1196.

Bowler, R. M., Harris, M., Li, J., Gocheva, V., Stellman, S. D., Wilson, K., . . . Cone, J. E. (2012). Longitudinal mental health impact among police responders to the 9/11 terrorist attack. *American Journal of Industrial Medicine, 55*, 297–312.

Brown, E. S. (2009). Effects of glucocorticoids on mood, memory, and the hippocampus treatment and preventive therapy. *Annals of New York Academy of Science, 1179*, 41–55. doi: 10.1111/j.1749-6632.2009.04981.x

Calhoun, P. S., Hertzberg, J. S., Kirby, A. C., Dennis, M. F., Hair, L. P., Dedert E. A., & Beckham, J. C. (2012). The effect of draft DSM-V criteria on posttraumatic stress disorder prevalence. *Depression and Anxiety, 29*, 1032–1042.

Carlier, I. V., Lamberts, R. D., & Gersons, B. P. (1997). Risk factors for posttraumatic stress symptomatology in police officers: A prospective analysis. *The Journal of Nervous and Mental Disease, 185*, 498–506.

Cloitre, M., Courtois, C. A., Ford, J. D., Green, B. L., Alexander, P., Briere, J., . . . Van der Hart, O. (2012). The ISTSS expert consensus treatment guidelines for complex PTSD in adults. Retrieved from http://www.istss.org/ISTSS_Complex_PTSD_Treatment_Guidelines/5205.htm

Coughlin, S. S. (2011). Post-traumatic stress disorder and cardiovascular disease. *The Open Cardiovascular Medicine Journal, 5*, 164–170.

Friedman, M. J., Resick, P. A., Bryant, R. A., & Brewin, C. R. (2011). Considering PTSD for DSM-5. *Depression and Anxiety, 28*, 750–769.

Gersons, B. P. (1989). Patterns of PTSD among police officers following shooting incidents: A two-dimensional model and treatment implications. *Journal of Traumatic Stress, 2*, 247–257.

Gupta, M. A. (2013). Review of somatic symptoms in post-traumatic stress disorder. *International Review of Psychiatry, 25*, 86–99.

Hayes, J. P., Hayes, S. M., & Mikedis, A. M. (2012). Quantitative meta-analysis of neural activity in posttraumatic stress disorder. *Biology of Mood and Anxiety Disorders, 2*, 9.

Ipser, J. C., & Stein, D. J. (2012). Evidence-based pharmacotherapy of post-traumatic stress disorder (PTSD). *The International Journal of Neuropsychopharmacology, 15*, 825–840.

Keane, T. M., Marshall, A. D., & Taft, C. T. (2006). Posttraumatic stress disorder: Etiology, epidemiology, and treatment outcome. *Annual Review of Clinical Psychology, 2*, 161–197.

Kim, M. J., Loucks, R. A., Palmer, A. L., Brown, A. C., Solomon, K. M., Marchante, A. N., & Whalen, P. J. (2011). The structural and functional connectivity of the amygdala: From normal emotion to pathological anxiety. *Behavioral Brain Research, 223*, 403–410.

Lanius, R. A., Bluhm, R. L., & Frewen, P. A. (2011). How understanding the neurobiology of complex post-traumatic stress disorder can inform clinical practice: A social cognitive and affective neuroscience approach. *Acta Psychiatrica Scandinavica, 124*, 331–348.

Levine, P. A. (2010). *In an Unspoken Voice: How the Body Releases Trauma and Restores Goodness*. Berkeley, CA: North Atlantic Books.

Lilly, M. M., Pole, N., Best, S. R., Metzler, T., & Marmar, C. R. (2009). Gender and PTSD: What can we learn from female police officers? *Journal of Anxiety Disorders, 23*, 767–774.

Lukaschek, K., Baumert, J., Kruse, J., Emeny, R. T., Lacruz, M. E., Huth, C., . . . KORA Investigators. (2013). Relationship between posttraumatic stress disorder and type 2 diabetes in a population-based cross-sectional study with 2,970 participants. *Journal of Psychosomatic Research, 74*, 340–345.

Maia, D. B., Marmar, C. R., Metzler, T., Nobrega, A., Berger, W., Mendlowicz, M. V., . . . Figueira, I. (2007). Post-traumatic stress symptoms in an elite unit of Brazilian police officers: Prevalence and impact on psychosocial functioning and on physical and mental health. *Journal of Affective Disorder, 97*, 241–245.

Marmar, C. R., McCaslin, S. E., Metzler, T. J., Best, S., Weiss, D. S., Fagan, J., . . . Neylan, T. (2006). Predictors of posttraumatic stress in police and other first responders. *Annals of the New York Academy of Science, 1071*, 1–18.

Martin, M., Marchand, A., & Boyer, R. (2009). Traumatic events in the workplace: Impact on psychopathology and healthcare use of police officers. *International Journal of Emergency Mental Health, 11*, 165–176.

O'Connor, T. M., O'Halloran, D. J., & Shanahan, F. (2000). The stress response and the hypothalamic-pituitary-adrenal axis: From molecule to melancholia. *Quarterly Journal of Medicine, 93*, 323–333.

Ogden, P., Pain, C., & Fisher, J. (2006). A sensorimotor approach to the treatment of trauma and dissociation. *Psychiatric Clinics of North America, 29*, 263–279.

Patel, R., Spreng, R. N., Shin, L. M., & Girard, T. A. (2012). Neurocircuitry models of posttraumatic stress disorder and beyond: A meta-analysis of functional neuroimaging studies. *Neuroscience & Biobehavioral Reviews, 36*, 2130–2142.

Pitman, R. K., Rasmusson, A. M., Koenen, K. C., Shin, L. M., Orr, S. P., Gilbertson, M. W., . . . Liberzon, I. (2012). Biological studies of post-traumatic stress disorder. *Nature Reviews Neuroscience, 13*, 769–787.

Porges, S. W. (2011). *The Polyvagal Theory: Neurophysiological Foundations of Emotions, Attachment, Communication, and Self-Regulation.* New York: Norton.

Robinson, H. M., Sigman, M. R., & Wilson, J. P. (1997). Duty-related stressors and PTSD symptoms in suburban police officers. *Psychological Reports, 81*, 835–845.

Rosen, G. M., & Lilienfeld, S. O. (2008). Posttraumatic stress disorder: An empirical evaluation of core assumptions. *Clinical Psychology Review, 28*, 837–868.

Sareen, J., Cox, B. J., Stein, M. B., Afifi, T. O., Fleet, C., & Asmundson, G. J. (2007). Physical and mental comorbidity, disability, and suicidal behavior associated with posttraumatic stress disorder in a large community sample. *Psychosomatic Medicine, 69*, 242–248.

Schiraldi, G. R. (2000). *The Post-Traumatic Stress Disorder Sourcebook: A Guide to Healing, Recovery, and Growth.* New York: Lowell House.

Schnurr, P. P., Friedman, M. J., & Bernardy, N. C. (2002). Research on posttraumatic stress disorder: Epidemiology, pathophysiology, and assessment. *Journal of Clinical Psychology, 58*, 877–889.

Shapiro, F. (2002). *EMDR as an Integrative Psychotherapy Approach: Experts of Diverse Orientations Explore the Paradigm Prism.* Washington, DC: American Psychological Association.

Sharpless, B. A., & Barber, J. P. (2011). A clinician's guide to PTSD treatments for returning veterans. *Professional Psychology Research and Practice, 42*, 8–15.

Shin, L. M., Rauch, S. L., & Pitman, R. K. (2006). Amygdala, medial prefrontal cortex, and hippocampal function in PTSD. *Annals of the New York Academy of Science, 1071*, 67–79.

Siegel, D. J. (2010). *The Mindful Therapist: A Clinician's Guide to Mindsight and Neural Integration.* New York: W. W. Norton.

Spitzer, C., Barnow, S., Volzke, H., Wallaschofski, H., John, U., Freyberger, H. J., . . . Grabe, H. J. (2009). Association of posttraumatic stress disorder with low-grade elevation of C-reactive protein: Evidence from the general population. *Journal of Psychiatric Research, 44*, 15–21.

Stearns, A. K. (n.d.). Trauma Aftermath-Who is really at risk? Retrieved May 4, 2013, from http://www.apa.org/index.aspx

Stein, D. J., Friedman, M., & Blanco, C. (Eds.). (2011). *Post-Traumatic Stress Disorder.* Hoboken, NJ: John Wiley & Sons, Ltd.

Suliman, S., Mkabile, S. G., Fincham, D. S., Ahmed, R., Stein, D. J., & Seedat, S. (2009). Cumulative effect of multiple trauma on symptoms of posttraumatic stress disorder, anxiety, and depression in adolescents. *Comprehensive Psychiatry, 50,* 121–127.

Uddin, M., Aiello, A. E., Wildman, D. E., Koenen, K. C., Pawelec, G., de Los Santos, R., . . . Galea, S. (2010). Epigenetic and immune function profiles associated with posttraumatic stress disorder. *Proceedings of the National Academy of Sciences U. S. A., 107,* 9470–9475.

van der Kolk, B., McFarlane, A. C., & Weisaeth, L. (Eds.). (1996). *Traumatic Stress. The Effects of Overwhelming Experience on Mind, Body, and Society.* New York: The Guilford Press.

Vermetten, E., Vythilingam, M., Southwick, S. M., Charney, D. S., & Bremner, J. D. (2003). Long-term treatment with paroxetine increases verbal declarative memory and hippocampal volume in posttraumatic stress disorder. *Biological Psychiatry, 54,* 693–702.

Violanti, J. M., Andrew, M. E., Burchfiel, C. M., Dorn, J., Hartley, T. A., & Miller, D. B. (2006). Posttraumatic stress syndrome symptoms and subclinical cardiovascular disease in police officers. *International Journal of Stress Management, 13,* 541–554.

Violanti, J. M., Andrew, M., Burchfiel, C. M., Hartley, T. A., Charles, L. E., & Miller, D. B. (2007). Post-traumatic stress symptoms and cortisol patterns among police officers. *Policing-An International Journal of Police Strategies & Management, 30,* 189–202.

Violanti, J. M., Fekedulegn, D., Hartley, T. A., Andrew, M. E., Charles, L. E., Mnatsakanova, A., & Burchfiel, C. M. (2006). Police trauma and cardiovascular disease: Association between PTSD symptoms and metabolic syndrome. *International Journal of Emergency Mental Health, 8,* 227–237.

Violanti, J. M., Paton, D., & Dunning, C. (2000). *Posttraumatic Stress Intervention: Challenges, Issues, and Perspectives.* Springfield, IL: Charles C Thomas.

Wessa, M., & Flor, H. (2007). Failure of extinction of fear responses in posttraumatic stress disorder: Evidence from second-order conditioning. *The American Journal of Psychiatry, 164,* 1684–1692.

Wilson, J. J. P., & Keane, T. M. (Eds.). (2004). *Assessing Psychological Trauma and PTSD* (2nd ed.). New York: Guilford Publications.

Woon, F. L., Sood, S., & Hedges, D. W. (2010). Hippocampal volume deficits associated with exposure to psychological trauma and posttraumatic stress disorder in adults: A meta-analysis. *Progress in Neuro-psychopharmacology & Biological Psychiatry, 34,* 1181–1188.

World Health Organization (WHO). (1992). ICD-10: *International Statistical Classification of Diseases and Related Health Problems* (10th rev. ed.). Geneva: WHO.

Yehuda, R. (2002). Post-traumatic stress disorder. *New England Journal of Medicine, 346,* 108–114.

Chapter 11

TREATING TRAUMA
IN LAW ENFORCEMENT

ERIN MCCANLIES, OLIVER WIRTH, MICHAEL E. ANDREW, DIANE MILLER,
CECIL M. BURCHFIEL, AND JOHN M. VIOLANTI

Due to the nature of police work, officers are repeatedly exposed to traumatic incidents that may include motor vehicle accidents, armed conflicts, and witnessing violent death, increasing their risk of PTSD (Marmar et al., 2006). In fact, between 7 percent and 19 percent of police officers qualify for a diagnosis of PTSD, and approximately 34 percent experience symptoms of PTSD but do not meet a full PTSD diagnosis (Carlier, Lamberts & Gersons, 1997; Gersons, 1989; Robinson, Sigman & Wilson, 1997). Individuals with PTSD are more likely to suffer from co-occurring psychological conditions such as depression, social phobia, panic attacks, and substance abuse (Gupta, 2013; Sareen et al., 2007) as well as several negative physical health outcomes such as cardiovascular disease (Coughlin, 2011; Violanti et al., 2006), diabetes (Lukaschek et al., 2013), and chronic pain (McWilliams, Cox & Enns, 2003; Sareen et al., 2007). It is a disorder that is both pervasive and invasive; therefore, it is important to effectively treat PTSD.

This chapter briefly reviews treatment modalities such as cognitive behavior therapy (CBT), pharmacotherapy, and eye movement desensitization and reprocessing that, in general, have been found to reduce PTSD symptoms in independent research studies (Bisson & Andrew, 2009; Cloitre, 2009). There is less evidence supporting the use of assistance animals, somatic psychotherapies, and yoga, but these treatments show promise and are also discussed (Ogden & Minton, 2000; Ogden,

Pain & Fisher, 2006; Streeter, Gerbarg, Saper, Ciraulo & Brown, 2012; Trauma Center, 2007).

TREATMENT OF PTSD

The brain is organized in a hierarchical fashion, with cortical structures composing the highest level. These are responsible for reasoning, abstract thought, language, and perception (MacLean, 1985; Ogden & Minton, 2000). The lower level, which is comprised of the more primitive ancient structures such as the limbic system and the reptilian complex (brain stem), is responsible for involuntary automatic reflexes in response to perceived danger (MacLean, 1985). Due to this hierarchical organization, when information is nonthreatening, higher-level processes can generally affect or override lower-level responses or behavior through intentional thought and reasoning. For example, one can ignore the signals indicating that one is hungry. Cognitive theory refers to this as top-down processing; it is initiated by the cortex and involves purposeful action and thought (Ogden & Minton, 2000). Higher-level functioning monitors and directs lower-level functions. Sensorimotor functios, instinct, and emotions, on the other hand, are referred to as bottom-up processing. The lower level is intimately linked to the higher level and vice versa; both influence the other. This has important implications for treating trauma. For example, pharmacotherapy relies on an understanding of the possible biology behind symptoms, so medication aimed at reducing symptoms is prescribed. Cognitive behavioral therapy and psychotherapy rely on top-down processing to manage bottom-up sensations and feelings through behavioral modification, cognitive distraction, and conscious regulation of thoughts and feelings (Freidman, 2001). Sensorimotor-based therapies, such as sensorimotor psychotherapy and Somatic Experiencing® rely on bottom-up processing to address physical and emotional arousal (Levine, 2010; Ogden & Minton, 2000). Research indicates that certain types of CBT may be less effective in the initial stages of trauma when the amygdala is highly activated (Bryant et al., 2005). Individuals also respond to trauma in different ways. Therefore, although one type of treatment may be effective with some, it may not work for all.

There are a number of psychological interventions currently being used to treat PTSD. It is impossible to include all potential interventions here; therefore, we have included brief descriptions of some of the most commonly used interventions that have been shown to reduce symptoms of PTSD in independent research trials. We have also included a brief description of somatic psychotherapy, somatic experiencing, and yoga; three treatments that show promise either alone or as adjuncts for treating PTSD. Regardless of the treatment type, most have three basic components that ameliorate symptoms of trauma: (1) helping the client achieve a sense of safety; (2) helping clients process and incorporate trauma memories through the development of a coherent narrative; and (3) helping clients reestablish social connections (Cloitre et al., 2012; Shapiro, 2002; van der Kolk, McFarlane & Weisaeth, 1996). Treatments are presented in alphabetical order.

Acupoint Stimulation

Acupoint stimulation has been referred to as emotional freedom techniques (EFT), thought field therapy (TFT), and energy psychology (Feinstein, 2012). During treatment a client is asked to think about the traumatic event while tapping specific points on the body. The theory behind EFT is that thinking about the trauma during acupoint stimulation reduces activation of the limbic system that is specifically tied to that memory (Feinstein, 2012). This, in effect, decouples the physiological response from the memory, allowing the memory to be recognized as having happened in the past. This theory is supported by brain imaging studies and studies that have measured the levels of cortisol, a stress hormone, released in times of extreme stress as well as in response to nonextreme conditions and stressors. Acupoint stimulation along with brain imaging studies have found that stimulation of specific points on the body using needles decreases activity in the amygdala, hippocampus, and other areas associated with the fear response (Feinstein, 2012). Tapping on these same areas in the body has been found to have a similar effect. Tapping has also been shown to reduce the levels of cortisol in individuals (Feinstein, 2012).

A recent review article that assessed the effectiveness of acupoint stimulation indicates that it is effective in treating PTSD (Feinstein, 2012). Three studies evaluated if EFT was effective in treating both adults and children who had been traumatized during the Rwandan genocide. All were determined to have PTSD. In all the groups, pre- and post-PTSD scores were significantly lower in the groups that received EFT/TFT compared to those that did not. Similar results have been obtained when a randomized controlled trial was conducted to determine if TFT would be effective in reducing symptoms of PTSD in veterans. In this case, fifty-nine veterans were randomly assigned either treatment or waitlist. Of the twenty-nine veterans who received six 1-hour EFT sessions, their PTSD scores dropped from 61.4 to 34.6, where 50 is the cutoff for PTSD. The control group's score remained virtually unchanged (66.6 to 65.3). The control group was then offered the treatment. Of the forty-nine veterans who ultimately received six 1-hour sessions, 86 percent no longer had scores high enough to warrant a diagnosis of PTSD (Church et al., 2013; Feinstein, 2012).

Studies that have compared EFT to other established treatments for PTSD found that EFT and eye movement desensitization and reprocessing (EMDR) were both very effective for treating PTSD. Similarly, EFT with CBT was found to be more effective than CBT alone for treating PTSD symptoms among individuals who had survived an earthquake in China (Feinstein, 2012; Zhang, Feng, Xie, Xu & Chen, 2011). Although more research needs to be done to confirm and extend these early studies, they do indicate that acupoint stimulation may effectively reduce PTSD symptoms.

Assistance Dogs

Assistance dogs may provide benefits to individuals with PTSD. These benefits come in several forms, such as specific work or tasks related to a disability or impairment, assistance to a professional therapist in the therapy process, direct emotional and physical comfort to the individual, and general companionship. Accordingly, individuals with PTSD might benefit from one or more different types of assistance animals, including a service dog, a therapy dog, a support dog, and a companion dog (Parenti, Foreman, Meade & Wirth, in press). A service dog, such as a Seeing Eye® dog or Hearing Ear dog, has been trained to provide work or tasks related to an individual's disability. The disability can be impairment in mobility, or physical or psychological function. The contribution of service dogs for psychiatric disorders, however, is a relatively new development that is being supported and promoted by organizations such as the Psychiatric Service Dog Society and the International Association of Assistance Dog Partners (International Association of Assistance Dog Partners [IAADP], 2012; Hart,

2010). An assistance dog is trained in basic or advanced skills to assist a health care or allied health care professional within the scope of a therapeutic treatment plan. For example, a psychologist or counselor might use dogs in a therapy session to create an opportunity to increase capacity for attachment by the release of oxytocin when the client pets the dog, as well as helping to establish an environment of trust and acceptance (Beetz, Uvnas-Moberg, Julius & Kotrschal, 2012; Kruger & Serpell, 2010; Mason & Hagan, 1999; Ross & Young, 2009; Stoesz, Hare & Snow, 2013). A support dog provides physical, psychiatric, or emotional support to individuals primarily in the home. Common labels used for support dogs include emotional support dogs, social therapy dog, skilled companions, and home-help dogs. Although pets may provide similar levels of support, there must be a connection between the owner's disability and the presence of the animal for it to be considered a support animal (Chumley, 2012).

Although well-designed research studies remain to be conducted, there is a considerable body of scientific evidence that supports, at least generally, the notion that interactions between humans and animals can positively affect health and well-being (Barker & Wolen, 2008; Beetz et al., 2012; Fine, 2010; Serpell, 2010). Several studies have evaluated the effects of human–animal interaction on specific behavioral, psychological, and physiological indices, many of which overlap with the criteria symptoms of PTSD. For example, a meta-analysis has found that assistance animals reduce symptoms of depression (Souter & Miller, 2007). Furthermore, dogs can be trained to provide tactile stimulation, which has been found to alleviate distractibility, anxiety, intrusive imagery, dissociation, and flashbacks (Ensminger, 2010). They also stay focused on the handler, which can prevent rumination and avoidance behavior. Dogs can be trained to turn on lights and safety check a room to minimize hypervigilance. They can also be trained to interrupt nightmares by waking up the individual, turning on lights to calm and reorient the individual, then turning off lights to help the individual resume sleep (Ensminger, 2010). These studies indicate that assistance dogs may positively affect individuals with PTSD; one way this may occur is by activation of the oxytocin system during human–animal interactions (Beetz et al., 2012; Ross & Young, 2009; Stoesz et al., 2013).

Cognitive Behavior Therapy

CBT is based on the premise that it is not the event but how a person processes and interprets the event that results in a particular emotional reaction. Along with this reaction is often a basic change in the individual's beliefs from the idea that the world is safe and they are competent, to the idea that the world is unsafe and they are incompetent (Freidman, 2001). The goal of CBT is to address the negative thinking and instill in the client a sense of safety, reduction of anxiety, and an ability to cope (Freidman, 2001). Prolonged exposure and stress inoculation training are two common forms of CBT that have been used to treat PTSD.

Eye Movement Desensitization and Reprocessing

EMDR is based on an adaptive information-processing model that posits that much of psychopathology associated with disturbing or adverse life events results from the maladaptive or incomplete processing of that event (Shapiro & Maxfield, 2002). Incomplete processing interferes with the individual's ability to integrate the experience in an adaptive manner. Through an eight-phase, three-pronged protocol that addresses past, present, and future clinical issues, the client is able to process and assimilate the traumatic memory (Shapiro, 2002; Silver, Rogers & Russell, 2008). EMDR processing uses a unique set of procedures in which dual focus of attention and alternating bilateral visual, auditory, and/or tactile stimulation are used to help the client process disturbing memories (Shapiro, 2001; Shapiro & Forrest, 2004). As the client processes the trauma over a number of visits, emotional and somatic distress related to the adverse event is decreased or eliminated, individuals often experience an improved view of themselves, and there is a resolution of current and future anticipated triggers (Shapiro, 2001; Shapiro & Forrest, 2004).

There is a large body of evidence showing that EMDR is effective for treating PTSD (Cloitre, 2009; Shapiro & Forrest, 2004; Sharpless & Barber, 2011). Meta-analyses found that in both military and civilian populations EMDR worked as well or was more effective than CBT and prolonged exposure (Cloitre, 2009; Sharpless & Barber, 2011). EMDR has also been shown to be superior to relaxation techniques, supportive counseling, and treatment as usual (Cloitre, 2009).

Pharmacotherapy

Drug therapy for PTSD is based on our understanding of the biological mechanisms behind the frequency and severity of intrusive/re-experiencing, numbing/avoidance, and hyperarousal symptoms (Stein, Ipser & McAnda, 2009; van der Kolk et al., 1996). A number of different types of medications have been evaluated for treating PTSD symptoms and include monoamine oxidase inhibitors, tricyclics, and selective serotonin reuptake inhibitors (SSRIs), beta-adrenergic blockers, and alpha$_2$-adrenergic agonists (Ipser & Stein, 2012; Stein, Isper & Seedat, 2009). Of these, SSRIs have been found to be most effective in treating PTSD symptoms (Ipser & Stein, 2012; Stein, et al., 2009). Initial findings also indicate that the noradrenergic reuptake inhibitor venlafaxine and the atypical antipsychotic risperidone may also be effective and warrant further study (Ipser & Stein, 2012; van der Kolk et al., 2007).

The length of time an individual takes the medication has also been shown to be important. Studies found that relapse of symptoms occurred in individuals who took medication for only a short time. For this reason, it is recommended that individuals with acute PTSD take the medication for 6 to 12 months and those with chronic PTSD take it for at least 12 months (Foa, Keane, Friedman & Cohen, 2009). Lastly, because most individuals who take medication are also undergoing psychotherapy, the contribution of psychotherapy cannot be overlooked. For example, in a study that compared the effectiveness of EMDR to the SSRI fluoxetine, after 8 weeks, 88 percent of the individuals treated with EMDR and 81 percent of the fluoxetine-treated group no longer met the criteria for a diagnosis of PTSD (van der Kolk et al., 2007). However, 6 months later, 57 percent of the individuals treated using EMDR were symptom free compared to none of the individuals treated with fluoxetine (van der Kolk et al., 2007). In general, these results indicate that the use of medication for treating PTSD symptoms can be helpful, but psychotherapy in which processing traumatic memories is a component, either alone or in combination with medication, may be the most effective in leading to symptom remission (Stein, Ipser & Seedat, 2009). Furthermore, because there is evidence that certain medication (e.g. benzodiazepines) may interfere with the effectiveness of some types of psychotherapy, the use of medication should be carefully considered (Stein, Ipser & Seedat, 2009).

Prolonged Exposure

Prolonged exposure incorporates imaginal exposure and systematic desensitization to treat PTSD. In imaginal exposure the client is asked to imagine and recount the details of the traumatic event. This occurs progressively over many sessions. The sessions are audiotaped and the client listens to the tapes at home. As clients continue exposure therapy, they report that their anxiety begins to subside and a coherent narrative is developed. Success of this procedure depends on emotional engagement, such as fear, but also the ability to regulate emotions so that the client does not feel panic or terror. For clients who have difficulty regulating their emotions, systematic desensitization is often effective (Allen, 2005). In this case, a client tries to maintain a greater state of relaxation while imagining the trauma (Allen, 2005). Numerous studies have shown the efficacy of prolonged exposure for treating PTSD in both military and civilian populations (Foa et al., 2009; Sharpless & Barber, 2011).

Sensorimotor Psychotherapy

Body or sensorimotor processing therapies include sensorimotor psychotherapy, hakomi, and Somatic Experiencing® (SE). Each is a method to help individuals recover from trauma by helping them integrate unassimilated sensorimotor reactions to the trauma (Ogden & Minton, 2000). The theory behind sensorimotor psychotherapy and hakomi is that trauma symptoms are the result of ineffective or interrupted defensive movements while fighting or fleeing a traumatic situation, or when escape is impossible, the result of disorganization and feeling overwhelmed within a persons' nervous system that triggers the freeze response (Ogden & Minton, 2000). Following a traumatic response, the unprocessed physical movement and disorganized nervous system interfere with an individual's ability to manage different states of arousal. If they stay within the optimal window of arousal they can contain their thoughts, feelings, and physical sensations. People who have unresolved trauma, however, are often outside this window in either the low arousal zone or the high arousal zone. Individuals in the low arousal zone report feeling emotionally or physically numb; they isolate and withdraw from social relations and report feeling like they are "not in their" bodies, a state referred to as dissociation. Individuals who are highly aroused on the other hand have difficulty sleeping, feel agitated, and are hypervigilant. Individuals with PTSD will often vacillate between these two states. Through the therapeutic relationship the counselor helps clients stay within the window of tolerance as they track and articulate body sensations while describing the traumatic experience or symptoms. As clients process the trauma they report being able to track and regulate disturbing thoughts and feelings more effectively, have an increased sense of safety, and reduction of PTSD symptoms such as nightmares and hyperarousal. Although there are a number of anecdotal reports from therapists and clients that sensorimotor psychotherapy is effective for treating symptoms of PTSD, independent research studies remain to be performed that will demonstrate how well it works.

SE is similar to somatic psychotherapy and hakomi because it also uses a bottom-up method to address trauma. The theory behind SE is that symptoms of PTSD are the result of our inability to have successfully released vast amounts of energy mobilized to confront the traumatic event specifically when the freeze response is engaged (Levine, 2010; Ogden & Minton, 2000). When, due to circumstances, fighting or fleeing are not viable options or in some cases may result in further risk of injury or death, then the freeze response is a powerful means of defense (Levine, 2010). The freeze response is a natural response that occurs when we are emotionally or physically overwhelmed. The theory behind SE is that the symptoms of PTSD, such as hyperarousal, avoidance, and difficulty sleeping, occur when the mobilized energy is not effectively discharged, preventing our system from returning to a state of equilibrium and internal balance. To help individuals safely access and release this energy, in effect bringing their body back into a state of equilibrium, SE uses a five-stage process that includes becoming aware of and integrating the sensations, images, behaviors, affect, and meaning of the traumatic event.

Two studies have shown that SE can be effective in treating PTSD (Leitch, 2007; Parker, Doctor & Selvam, 2008). Both studies evaluated how well an abbreviated SE treatment plan worked to alleviate PTSD symptoms in tsunami survivors. In the first study, early-intervention therapy, referred to as Trauma First Aide, was provided to survivors 1 month after a tsunami in Thailand in 2004 (Leitch, 2007). Fifty-three adults and children volunteered to be treated; all received one or two sessions. After treatment, 90 percent of the participants reported complete or partial relief from their symptoms, which included physical pain, sleep problems, anxiety/agitation, headaches, and flat affect. After 1 year, 90 percent of the twenty-two participants that could be found reported complete or partial relief from their symptoms (Leitch, 2007).

In the second study, a single 75-minute intervention was performed that consisted of four stages: (1) help the client focus on containing physiological arousal with instructions on how to use this resource on their own following the treatment, (2) build a coherent narrative around the client's experience of the tsunami along with noticing sensations in their bodies, (3) teach the client about stress and trauma and how it is stored in the body, and 4) guide the client as he or she tracked body experiences and changes to resolution (Parker et al., 2008). After weeks, 74.2 percent of the symptoms were somewhat better, a lot better, or completely resolved. After 8 months, 94.4 percent reported at least a 50 percent improvement in their symptoms (Parker et al., 2008). These early results suggest that SE is effective in reducing the symptoms of PTSD. Further research with larger populations will be important to confirm and extend these findings.

Stress Inoculation Training

Stress inoculation training was originally used to manage symptoms of anxiety but was adapted to treat PTSD symptoms in sexual assault victims (Cloitre, 2009; Foa et al., 2009). It is composed of a number of different techniques, including muscle relaxation, thought stopping, role play, guided self-dialogue, and graduated exposure techniques to address symptoms of PTSD (Cloitre, 2009). Stress inoculation training has been shown to be effective for treating female sexual assault victims, but research evaluating its effectiveness in treating PTSD symptoms in veterans is limited and inconsistent (Cloitre, 2009; Foa et al., 2009). Further research in larger veteran populations will be important to determine if this therapy is as effective in veterans and other populations, such as first responders, as it is in female sexual assault victims.

Yoga

Yoga is a client-centered practice that incorporates physical postures (asanas), regulated breathing (pranayamas), and meditation (Telles, Singh & Balkrishna, 2012). It has been suggested that yoga corrects underactivity of the gamma aminobutyric acid (GABA) system, thereby restoring homeostasis to the ANS, ameliorating symptoms of PTSD (Streeter et al., 2012). A recent review evaluated eleven studies that used yoga to manage trauma associated with combat, natural disasters, interpersonal violence, and being incarcerated (Telles et al., 2012). Among individuals who had experienced a natural disaster, yoga was seen to reduce symptoms of PTSD, anxiety, and feelings of sadness. Similar results were seen among children who had been exposed to combat, terrorism, and interpersonal violence. Among young adults who had been incarcerated, individuals who had participated in yoga postures and guided relaxation showed significantly reduced heart rate and breath rate, indicating lower physiological stress. Owing to the growing body of research indicating its efficacy in addressing symptoms of trauma, yoga is currently practiced in approximately 29 percent of Veteran's Administration PTSD treatment programs (Libby, Reddy, Pilver & Desai, 2012). However, examination of these treatment programs showed wide utilization of these therapies and wide variation in the nature and context in which they were offered, making it difficult to gauge their effectiveness. Some of the limitations include small participation rates, lack of information concerning the training level of the instructor, and lack of appropriate control groups. These studies and anecdotal reports suggest that yoga may be an effective adjunctive method for alleviating symptoms associated with trauma and PTSD; however, more research is needed to determine the true effectiveness of yoga for treating PTSD (Bussing, Michalsen, Khalsa, Telles & Sherman, 2012; Telles et al., 2012; Trauma Center, 2007).

TREATMENT OF PTSD IN POLICE OFFICERS

Police officers routinely have to deal with dangerous, difficult, and highly stressful events, which can lead to the development of PTSD (Marmar et al., 2006; Miller, 1995; Violanti, Paton & Dunning, 2000). Unfortunately, debriefing, a common practice used by police forces in an attempt to reduce the incidence of PTSD, may increase the risk of PTSD (Miller, 1995; Violanti et al., 2000). Research also indicates that although these populations would benefit the most from psychological services, they are the least likely to seek these services (Gilmartin, 2002; Hassell, 2006; Violanti, 2007; Wester, Arndt, Sedivy & Arndt, 2010).

A number of factors affect an officer's willingness to seek counseling. These include law enforcement identity, stigma with counseling, and fear of reprisal (Gilmartin, 2002; Nadler & Fisher, 1986; Pollack & Levant, 1998; Violanti, 2007; Vogel, Wade & Haake, 2006; Wester et al., 2010). Successful policing expects male and female officers to be detached, unemotional, in control, and investigative, so much so that instilling these attributes is often part of police training (Miller, 1995; Southworth, 1999). A conflict with this training arises when, after a traumatic event, in order to address trauma symptoms, officers need to open emotionally, relinquish control, and engage in the counseling process rather than remain detached (Good, Dell & Mintz, 1989; Pollack & Levant, 1998). Unfortunately, there is also often a stigma attached to seeking help, which is perpetuated by the negative image of both mental illness and obtaining psychological services in western cultures (Corrigan, 2004; Nadler & Fisher, 1986). Officers may be less likely to seek help because their peer group perceives seeking help as indicative of failure and weakness, or the sign of poor character (Corrigan, 2004; Miller, 1995; Nadler & Fisher, 1986). Because of this, police officers who seek help may be at risk of being labeled unfit for duty, and any diagnosis or having sought psychological services may end up on their permanent record. Both may affect their job status or ability to get promotions. For this reason, even if an officer recognizes the need for psychological services, the potential consequences deter her or him from seeking help (Brooks, 2001; Hassell, 2006). Both officers and counselors need to be aware of these potential obstacles to ensure that the officer obtains the most effective treatment with the least risk (Wester et al., 2010). Ideally, a shift in police culture that encourages officers to seek psychological services when necessary will provide them with an opportunity to increase their capacity to process traumatic events, develop resiliency, and ultimately become more effective officers.

SUMMARY

The lifetime prevalence of PTSD is approximately 7 percent to 12 percent (Keane, Marshall & Taft, 2006) and in populations frequently exposed to factors related to PTSD such as military personnel and police officers, rates of PTSD can be more than twice those observed in the civilian population (Carlier et al., 1997; Keane et al., 2006). PTSD affects multiple aspects of an individual's life including his or her sense of safety, sense of self, self-efficacy, and personal relationships (Allen, 2005; Sharpless & Barber, 2011; van der Kolk et al., 1996; Yehuda, 2002). It has been shown to be associated with a number of comorbid psychological and physical health conditions (Coughlin, 2011; Lukaschek et al., 2013; McWilliams et al., 2003; Sareen et al., 2007). Because PTSD is so devastating, treating it effectively is imperative. Herein, we have reviewed a number of treatments that have been found to reduce PTSD symptoms. Most treatments have three basic stages in common that have been found to increase treatment efficacy; these include (1) ensuring the client's sense of safety by increasing their capacity to manage and control physiological arousal, (2) helping clients process and assimilate the trauma memory, and (3) helping clients reengage in society and social relationships (Cloitre et al., 2012).

As our knowledge and understanding of how PTSD affects us at the cognitive, emotional and sensorimotor level increases, our knowledge and understanding of how best to treat PTSD will also continue to grow. Additionally, any effective treatment must ultimately be centered around a safe, stable environment with strong social support and a therapeutic relationship based on trust.

Disclaimer: The findings and conclusions in this report are those of the authors and do not necessarily represent the views of the National Institute for Occupational Safety and Health.

REFERENCES

Allen, J. G. (2005). *Coping with Trauma: Hope Through Understanding* (2nd ed.). Arlington, VA: American Psychiatric Publishing, Inc.

Barker, S. B., & Wolen, A. R. (2008). The benefits of human-companion animal interaction: A review. *Journal of Veterinary Medical Education, 35,* 487–495.

Beetz, A., Uvnas-Moberg, K., Julius, H., & Kotrschal, K. (2012). Psychosocial and psychophysiological effects of human-animal interactions: The possible role of oxytocin. *Frontiers in Psychology, 3,* 234.

Bisson, J., & Andrew, M. (2009). Psychological treatment of post-traumatic stress disorder (PTSD). *Cochrane Database of Systematic Reviews, 1,* 99.

Brooks, G. R. (2001). Counseling and psychotherapy with male military veterans. In G. R. Brooks & G. E. Good (Eds.), *The New Handbook of Psychotherapy and Counseling With Men: A Comprehensive Guide to Settings, Problems, and Treatment Approaches* (Vol. 1, pp. 206–226). San Francisco: Jossey-Bass.

Bryant, R. A., Felmingham, K. L., Kemp, A. H., Barton, M., Peduto, A. S., Rennie, C., . . . Williams, L. M. (2005). Neural networks of information processing in post-traumatic stress disorder: A functional magnetic resonance imaging study. *Biological Psychiatry, 58*, 111–118.

Bussing, A., Michalsen, A., Khalsa, S. B., Telles, S., & Sherman, K. J. (2012). Effects of yoga on mental and physical health: A short summary of reviews. *Evidence-Based Complementary and Alternative Medicine, 2012*, 165–410.

Carlier, I. V., Lamberts, R. D., & Gersons, B. P. (1997). Risk factors for posttraumatic stress symptomatology in police officers: A prospective analysis. *The Journal of Nervous and Mental Disease, 185*, 498–506.

Chumley, P. R. (2012). Historical perspectives of the human-animal bond within the Department of Defense. *US Army Medical Department Journal*, 18–20.

Church, D., Hawk, C., Brooks, A. J., Toukolehto, O., Wren, M., Dinter, I., & Stein, P. (2013). Psychological trauma symptom improvement in veterans using emotional freedom techniques: A randomized controlled trial. *The Journal of Nervous and Mental Disease, 201*, 153–160.

Cloitre, M. (2009). Effective psychotherapies for posttraumatic stress disorder: A review and critique. *CNS Spectrum, 14*(1 Suppl 1), 32–43.

Cloitre, M., Courtois, C. A., Ford, J. D., Green, B. L., Alexander, P., Briere, J., . . . Van der Hart, O. (2012). The ISTSS expert consensus treatment guidelines for complex PTSD in adults. Retrieved from http://www.istss.org/ISTSS_Complex_PTSD_Treatment_Guidelines/5205.htm

Corrigan, P. (2004). How stigma interferes with mental health care. *American Psychologist, 59*, 614–625.

Coughlin, S. S. (2011). Post-traumatic stress disorder and cardiovascular disease. *The Open Cardiovascular Medicine Journal, 5*, 164–170.

Ensminger, J. J. (2010). *Service and Therapy Dogs in American Society: Science, Law and the Evolution of Canine Caregivers*. Springfield, IL: Charles C Thomas.

Feinstein, D. (2012). Acupoint stimulation in treating psychological disorders: Evidence of efficacy. *Review of General Psychology, 16*, 364–380.

Fine, A. H. (Ed.). (2010). *Handbook on Animal-Assisted Therapy: Theoretical Foundations and Guidelines for Practice* (3rd ed.). San Diego: Elsevier Science.

Foa, E. B., Keane, T. M., Friedman, M. J., & Cohen, J. A. (Eds.). (2009). *Effective Treatments for PTSD: Practice Guidelines from the International Society for Traumatic Stress Studies*. New York: Guilford Publications, Inc.

Freidman, H. S. (Ed.). (2001). *The Disorders. Specialty Articles From the Encyclopedia of Mental Health*. San Diego: Academic Press.

Gersons, B. P. (1989). Patterns of PTSD among police officers following shooting incidents: A two-dimensional model and treatment implications. *Journal of Traumatic Stress, 2*, 247–257.

Gilmartin, K. M. (2002). *Emotional Survival for Law Enforcement: A Guide for Officers and Their Families*. San Diego: Praeger.

Good, G. E., Dell, D. M., & Mintz, L. B. (1989). Male role and gender role conflict: Relations to help-seeking in men. *Journal of Counseling Psychology, 36*, 295–300.

Gupta, M. A. (2013). Review of somatic symptoms in post-traumatic stress disorder. *International Review of Psychiatry, 25*, 86–99.

Hart, L. A. (2010). Positive effects of animals for psychosocially vulnerable people: A turning point for delivery. In A. H. Fine (Ed.), *Handbook on Animal-Assisted Therapy: Theoretical Foundations and Guidelines for Practice* (3rd ed., pp. 59–84). New York: Elsevier Science.

Hassell, K. (2006). *Police Organizational Cultures and Patrol Practices.* New York: LFB Scholarly Publishing LLC.

International Association of Assistance Dog Partners (IAADP). (2012). Service dog task for psychiatric disabilities. Retrieved from http://www.iaadp.org/psd_tasks.html

Ipser, J. C., & Stein, D. J. (2012). Evidence-based pharmacotherapy of post-traumatic stress disorder (PTSD). *The International Journal of Neuropsychopharmacology, 15,* 825–840.

Keane, T. M., Marshall, A. D., & Taft, C. T. (2006). Posttraumatic stress disorder: Etiology, epidemiology, and treatment outcome. *Annual Review of Clinical Psychology, 2,* 161–197.

Kruger, K. A., & Serpell, J. A. (2010). Animal assisted interventions in mental health: Definitions and theoretical foundations. In J. A. Serpell (Ed.), *Handbook on Animal Assisted Therapy* (3rd ed., pp. 33–48). New York: Elsevier.

Leitch, M. L. (2007). Somatic experiencing treatment with tsunami survivors in Thailand: Broadening the scope of early intervention. *Traumatology, 13,* 11–20.

Levine, P. A. (2010). *In an Unspoken Voice: How the Body Releases Trauma and Restores Goodness.* Berkeley, CA: North Atlantic Books.

Libby, D. J., Reddy, F., Pilver, C. E., & Desai, R. A. (2012). The use of yoga in specialized VA PTSD treatment programs. *International Journal of Yoga Therapy, 2012,* 79–87.

Lukaschek, K., Baumert, J., Kruse, J., Emeny, R. T., Lacruz, M. E., Huth, C., . . . KORA Investigators. (2013). Relationship between posttraumatic stress disorder and type 2 diabetes in a population-based cross-sectional study with 2970 participants. *Journal of Psychosomatic Research, 74,* 340–345.

MacLean, P. D. (1985). Brain evolution relating to family, play, and the separation call. *Archives of General Psychiatry, 42,* 405–417.

Marmar, C. R., McCaslin, S. E., Metzler, T. J., Best, S., Weiss, D. S., Fagan, J., . . . Neylan, T. (2006). Predictors of posttraumatic stress in police and other first responders. *Annals of the New York Academy of Science, 1071,* 1–18.

Mason, M. S., & Hagan, C. B. (1999). Pet-assisted psychotherapy. *Psychological Reports, 84,* 1235–1245.

McWilliams, L. A., Cox, B. J., & Enns, M. W. (2003). Mood and anxiety disorders associated with chronic pain: An examination in a nationally representative sample. *Pain, 106,* 127–133.

Miller, L. (1995). Tough guys: Psychotherapeutic strategies with law enforcement and emergency services personnel. *Psychotherapy, 32,* 592–600.

Nadler, A., & Fisher, J. D. (1986). The role of threat to self-esteem and perceived control in recipient reaction to help: Theory development and empirical validation. In L. Berkowitz (Ed.), *Advances in Experimental Social Psychology* (Vol. 19, pp. 81–122). San Diego: Academic Press.

Ogden, P., & Minton, K. (2000). Sensorimotor psychotherapy: One method for processing traumatic memory. *Traumatology, 6*, 149–173.

Ogden, P., Pain, C., & Fisher, J. (2006). A sensorimotor approach to the treatment of trauma and dissociation. *Psychiatric Clinics of North America, 29*, 263–279.

Parenti, L., Foreman, A., Meade, B. J., & Wirth, O. (in press). A revised taxonomy of assistance animals. *Journal of Rehabilitation Research and Development.*

Parker, C., Doctor, R. M., & Selvam, R. (2008). Somatic therapy treatment effects with tsunami survivors. *Traumatology, 14*, 103–109.

Pollack, W. S., & Levant, R. F. (Eds.). (1998). *New Psychotherapy for Men.* New York: Wiley and Sons.

Robinson, H. M., Sigman, M. R., & Wilson, J. P. (1997). Duty-related stressors and PTSD symptoms in suburban police officers. *Psychological Reports, 81*, 835–845.

Ross, H. E., & Young, L. J. (2009). Oxytocin and the neural mechanisms regulating social cognition and affiliative behavior. *Frontiers in Neuroendocrinology, 30*, 534–547.

Sareen, J., Cox, B. J., Stein, M. B., Afifi, T. O., Fleet, C., & Asmundson, G. J. (2007). Physical and mental comorbidity, disability, and suicidal behavior associated with posttraumatic stress disorder in a large community sample. *Psychosomomatic Medicine, 69*, 242–248.

Serpell, J. A. (2010). Animal-assisted interventions in historical perspective. In A. H. Fine (Ed.), *Handbook on Animal-Assisted Therapy: Theoretical Foundations and Guidlines for Practice* (3rd ed., pp. 17–32). New York: Elsevier.

Shapiro, F. (2001). *Eye Movement Desensitization and Reprocessing* (2nd ed.). New York: The Guilford Press.

Shapiro, F. (2002). *EMDR as an Integrative Psychotherapy Approach: Experts of Diverse Orientations Explore the Paradigm Prism.* Washington, DC: American Psychological Association.

Shapiro, F., & Forrest, M. S. (2004). *EMDR: The Breakthrough Therapy for Anxiety, Stress and Trauma.* New York: BasicBooks.

Shapiro, F., & Maxfield, L. (2002). Eye movement desensitization and reprocessing (EMDR): Information processing in the treatment of trauma. *Psychotherapy in Practice, 58*, 933–946.

Sharpless, B. A., & Barber, J. P. (2011). A clinician's guide to PTSD treatments for returning veterans. *Professional Psychology Research and Practice, 42*, 8–15.

Silver, S. M., Rogers, S., & Russell, M. (2008). Eye movement desensitization and reprocessing (EMDR) in the treatment of war veterans. *Journal of Clinical Psychology, 64*, 947–957.

Souter, M. A., & Miller, M. D. (2007). Do animal-assisted activities effectively treat depression? A meta-analysis. *Anthrozoos, 20*, 167–180.

Southworth, R. N. (1999). Taking the job home. In L. Territo & J. D. Sewell (Eds.), *Stress Management in Law Enforcement.* Durham, NC: Carolina Academic Press.

Stein, D. J., Ipser, J., & McAnda, N. (2009). Pharmacotherapy of posttraumatic stress disorder: A review of meta-analyses and treatment guidelines. *CNS Spectrums, 14*, 25–31.

Stein, D. J., Isper, J. C., & Seedat, S. (2009). Pharmacotherapy for post traumatic stress disorder (PTSD). *Cochrane Database of Systematic Reviews* (1).

Stoesz, B. M., Hare, J. F., & Snow, W. M. (2013). Neurophysiological mechanisms underlying affiliative social behavior: Insights from comparative research. *Neuroscience & Biobehavioral Reviews, 37*, 123–132.

Streeter, C. C., Gerbarg, P. L., Saper, R. B., Ciraulo, D. A., & Brown, R. P. (2012). Effects of yoga on the autonomic nervous system, gamma-aminobutyric-acid, and allostasis in epilepsy, depression, and post-traumatic stress disorder. *Medical Hypotheses, 78*, 571–579.

Telles, S., Singh, N., & Balkrishna, A. (2012). Managing mental health disorders resulting from trauma through yoga: A review. *Depression Research and Treatment, 2012*, 401–513.

Trauma Center. (2007). Yoga as a complimentary treatment for PTSD. Retrieved from http://www.traumacenter.org/products/publications.php

van der Kolk, B.A., McFarlane, A. C., & Weisaeth, L. (Eds.). (1996). *Traumatic Stress. The Effects of Overwhelming Experience on Mind, Body, and Society.* New York: The Guilford Press.

van der Kolk, B. A., Spinazzola, J., Blaustein, M. E., Hopper, J. W., Hopper, E. K., Korn, D. L., & Simpson, W. B. (2007). A randomized clinical trial of eye movement desensitization and reprocessing (EMDR), fluoxetine, and pill placebo in the treatment of posttraumatic stress disorder: Treatment effects and long-term maintenance. *Journal of Clinical Psychiatry, 68*, 37–46.

Violanti, J. M. (2007). *Police Suicide: Epidemic in Blue.* New York: Charles C Thomas.

Violanti, J. M., Paton, D., & Dunning, C. (2000). *Posttraumatic Stress Intervention: Challenges, Issues, and Perspectives.* Springfield, IL: Charles C Thomas.

Violanti, J. M., Andrew, M. E., Burchfiel, C. M., Dorn, J., Hartley, T. A., & Miller, D. B. (2006). Posttraumatic stress syndrome symptoms and subclinical cardiovascular disease in police officers. *International Journal of Stress Management, 13*, 541–554.

Vogel, D. L., Wade, N. G., & Haake, S. (2006). Measuring the self-stigma associated with seeking psychological help. *Journal of Counseling Psychology, 53*, 325–337.

Wester, S. R., Arndt, D., Sedivy, S. K., & Arndt, L. (2010). Male police officers and stigma associated with counseling: The role of anticipated risks, anticipated benefits and gender role conflict. *Psychology of Men & Masculinity, 11*, 286–302.

Yehuda, R. (2002). Post-traumatic stress disorder. *New England Journal of Medicine, 346*, 108–114.

Zhang, Y., Feng, B., Xie, J. P., Xu, F. Z., & Chen, J. (2011). Clinical study on treatment of the earthquake-caused post-traumatic stress disorder by cognitive-behavior therapy and acupoint stimulation. *Journal of Traditional Chinese Medicine, 31*, 60–63.

INDEX

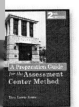